Home-based Childcare

For childminders & nannies

LEVEL
3
UNIT
CYPOP 5

Sheila Riddall-Leech

www.pearsonschoolsandfe.co.uk

✓ Free online support
✓ Useful weblinks
✓ 24 hour online ordering

0845 630 44 44

Heinemann

Part of Pearson

Heinemann is an imprint of Pearson Education Limited, Edinburgh Gate, Harlow, Essex, CM20 2JE.

www.pearsonschoolsandfecolleges.co.uk

Heinemann is a registered trademark of Pearson Education Limited.

Text © Sheila Riddall-Leech, 2010

First published 2010

14 13 12 11 10
10 9 8 7 6 5 4 3 2 1

British Library Cataloguing in Publication Data
A catalogue record for this book is available from the British Library.

ISBN 978 0 435045 90 6

Edited by Maria Anson
Designed by Pearson Education Limited
Typeset by Phoenix Photosetting, Chatham, Kent
Original illustrations © Ben Kirchner/Heart, 2010
Cover design by Pearson Education Limited
Picture research by Susie Prescott
Cover illustration © Jess Mikhail/United Artists
Cover photo © Waterlilly/Shutterstock
Printed in Italy by Rotolito Lombarda

Hotlinks
There are links to relevant websites in this book. In order to ensure that the links are up to date, that the links work, and that the sites are not inadvertently linked to sites that could be considered offensive, we have made the links available on the following website: www.pearsonhotlinks.co.uk. When you visit this website, type in the title of this book or the ISBN to access the page containing the links for this book.

Websites
The websites included in the useful resources section of this book were correct and up to date at the time of publication. Pearson Education Limited is not responsible for the content of any external internet sites.

Every effort has been made to contact copyright holders of material reproduced in this book. Any omissions will be rectified in subsequent printings if notice is given to the publisher.

Contents

Acknowledgements

Author acknowledgements

I would like to thank the editorial team at Heinemann and everyone at the NCMA for their support and helpful suggestions during the writing of this book. Thanks must go to all the registered childminders and nannies who have trained with me and provided material for the case studies and anecdotes. Special thanks to Peter for his continued love and support and remembering my late parents, especially my father who encouraged my thirst for learning.

Acknowledgements

The publisher and author would like to thank the following individuals and organisations for permission to reproduce material:

p. 26 Reproduction of Ofsted self-evaluation form contains public sector information licensed under the Open Government Licence v1.0.

p. 50 Early Years Foundation Stage material licensed under the Open Government Licence v1.0. / Birth to Five Service

p. 51 Early Years Foundation Stage material licensed under the Open Government Licence v1.0. / Birth to Five Service

p. 53 Early Years Foundation Stage material licensed under the Open Government Licence v1.0. / Birth to Five Service

p. 69 BSI Group

p. 69 The British Toy & Hobby Association

p. 86 http://www.rospa.com/homesafety/adviceandinformation/childsafety/accidents-to-children.aspx

p. 145 Crown Copyright Click use licence C2008002221. Department for Children, Schools and Families

Photo credits

The publisher and author would like to thank the following individuals and organisations for permission to reproduce photographs:

(Key: b-bottom; c-centre; l-left; r-right; t-top)

Alamy Images: Barry Mason 66, Peter Titmuss 64, Picture Partners 71, Spencer Grant 167.
Imagestate Media: Bananastock 8.
Pearson Education Ltd: Gareth Boden 106, 125, Jules Selmes 88, 114br, 115tl, 119, StillVision 7, 14, 17, 24, 25, 30, 32, 37, 41, 44, 49, 52, 57, 58, 61, 80, 95, 99, 101, 109, 127, 133, 141, 153, 161, 173, 184, Studio 8 154, Tudor Photography 114tl.
Science Photo Library Ltd: Mark Thomas 92.
Shutterstock.com: 42, Alena Ozerova 56, d.dz 93tr, David Davis 93, mu che 122.
Thinkstock: Comstock 137, Comstock / Jupiter images / Getty Images 144, Hemera 115br, 150, 170, 175.

All other images © Pearson Education

Every effort has been made to trace the copyright holders of material reproduced in this book and we apologise in advance for any unintentional omissions. We would be pleased to insert the appropriate acknowledgement in any subsequent edition of this publication.

About the author

Sheila Riddall-Leech began her professional career as a primary school teacher and has worked in many settings within various parts of the UK and abroad, eventually becoming a deputy head of a large primary school with a thriving nursery unit. Sheila was also a childminder for a number of years and a pre-school supervisor. She moved into further and higher education in the mid-1990s, teaching on a wide range of early years courses, degree programmes and awards. Sheila became an Ofsted inspector in 1998 and is an assessor for the NCMA Children Come First childminding networks.

Sheila has been a key note speaker at several regional NCMA conferences. She works closely with CACHE on several awards, is a member of CACHE Expert Panel and is an external examiner for Staffordshire University Early Years Foundation Degree.

As well as running her own training company, delivering CACHE awards and professional development events, Sheila writes for numerous professional journals and publishing companies. This is her sixth book for Heinemann and her 14th book in total.

Sheila is married to Peter and lives in rural Shropshire. She has two grown-up daughters. In her spare time, Sheila enjoys gardening and walking her two dogs. There is also a menagerie of ducks, hens, geese, cows and pigs to care for, not to mention a large greenhouse and the upkeep of the 300-year-old cottage where she lives.

Foreword

The Children's Workforce Development Council (CWDC) has launched a new Diploma for the Children's Workforce. The intention of the Level 3 Diploma for the Children and Young People's Workforce is to provide a broad knowledge of all the subject areas within the childcare sector. This would not only allow more fluid progression between children's service professionals but would also simplify the qualifications programme by having one single qualification instead of a patchwork of many different ones.

This book is designed to give you everything you will need to support the option unit of the Level 3 qualification: Understand how to set up a home-based childcare service. The unit will provide registered childminders and nannies with the knowledge they will need to deliver a high-quality home-based childcare experience for the children in their care. The National Childminding Association (NCMA) has worked in partnership with the CWDC on the syllabus requirements. The intention was to tailor the unit to the practical needs of registered childminders and nannies. This book will provide a really practical resource to support home studying for the unit.

Using Sheila Riddall-Leech's considerable experience and practical support, this book should provide everything you need to complete the Home-based unit, including support on assessment.

This book is invaluable for many different audiences. Less experienced registered childminders or nannies will find the direct conversational style user friendly, while trainers can use it to lift out examples to show practitioners how they can use the guide to influence practice. The format is varied and helps to keep the reader's interest. There are clear headings for content, boxed sections with points to consider and practical examples.

There are also tips every step of the way and the book will be essential reading for any newly registering childminder or nanny. There are great practical examples as well as tips on completing assessment tasks. I hope this will help you to complete the Home-based unit of the Diploma with ease and that it will serve as a point of reference in your day-to-day childminding practice.

Susanna Dawson

Registered Childminder and Chair of the National Childminding Association

Introduction

For several years, people caring for children in their own homes or the child's home have been able to study the CACHE Level 3 Diploma in Home-based Childcare or an NVQ Level 3 in Children's Care, Learning and Development. These qualifications have significantly raised the profile of home-based childcarers, (childminders and nannies) and have enabled many to continue their professional development beyond Level 3. The introduction of the Early Years Foundation Stage (EYFS) in England – Foundation Phase in Wales – in September 2008, was highly significant for home-based childcarers as it put them on the same footing as all other settings. The childcare profession is dynamic and vibrant, and it is only right that qualifications for this sector reflect this.

In September 2010 the Children's Workforce Development Council (CWDC) introduced a single Level 3 qualification for the children and young people's workforce in England. This qualification is called the Level 3 Diploma for the Children and Young People's Workforce. (In Wales, new qualifications in Children's Care, Learning and Development are being introduced from January 2011 at Levels 2 and 3.)

The Diploma has three pathways:
1. Early Years and Childcare – all practitioners working in settings required to deliver the Early Years Foundation Stage (EYFS), including all home-based workers (childminders) working with children aged 0–5 years (registered childminders in Wales 0–8)
2. Learning Development and Support Services (LDSS) – learning mentors
3. Children's Social Care – foster carers, including private foster carers and children's social care workers.

These pathways allow great flexibility for people working with children and young people; for example, if a childminder decides to become a foster carer they can study optional units relating to the third pathway.

The Diploma is made up of units that are a combination of knowledge and skills. Some units are mandatory, some are core units, while others are optional and relate to a chosen pathway. Each of the units is given credits, with 65 credits making up the full Diploma. This book is designed to support the optional unit 'Understand how to set up a home-based childcare service' (CYPOP 5). This optional unit carries four credits.

Who is this book for?

Home-based childcare is a career choice that people can take at different stages of their life. Some childminders are new to the idea of home-based childcare, starting on this career path when their own children are small. Such people may not be new to the concept of study, but their knowledge and skills are often not related to childcare and children in general. Some people starting in home-based childcare may not have children of their own and so this book will be an invaluable source of information. It is hoped that this book will support all home-based childcarers – those who are just starting, those who have experience but have not had this knowledge formally accredited with a qualification and those who want to continue their professional development.

The unit should also be regarded as a stepping stone in that you can go on to complete more optional units and the core and mandatory units, and eventually achieve the full Level 3 Diploma.

People who provide home-based childcare offer a very valuable service to a great many children and their parents. It requires not only a love of children, but also a good understanding of children and a professional approach to the work. Studying this unit will help you to raise your professional profile and improve the quality of service you are able to offer to families.

About this book

This book is designed to support the optional unit 'Understand how to set up a home-based childcare service' and will follow closely all the learning outcomes of the unit. It provides both the information that you will need to complete the unit and practical help in completing the assessment requirements. However, the book also includes a great deal of additional information beyond the learning outcomes and assessment criteria of the unit, and explores the broader context in which you are working. Extra sections in the book cover the wider childcare market, Early

Years frameworks and policies, support systems and the Common Core of Skills and Knowledge for the Children's Workforce.

The book is divided into ten chapters. These are:

1. The home-based childcarer – what is it all about?
2. How to set up a home-based childcare service
3. The Early Years Foundation Stage and other frameworks
4. Establishing a safe and healthy home-based environment
5. Working in partnership with parents
6. Child development
7. Establishing routines
8. Providing play and activities to support equality and inclusion
9. Safeguarding children
10. Promoting positive behaviour.

In all sections links have been made to the 'shared core' units for the Level 3 Diploma where appropriate (those units that are shared with Skills for Care and Development and the wider Children's Workforce). There are four shared core units:

- Promote communication in children and young people's settings
- Promote equality and inclusion in children and young people's settings
- Engage in personal development in children and young people's settings
- Principles for implementing duty of care in children and young people's settings.

In addition the ten chapters above are linked to the National Occupational Standards (NOS) as shown in the table below.

How to use this book

Throughout the book there are a number of learning features designed to enhance your understanding of key aspects.

There are **Case studies** with questions to encourage reflective practice and link theory to practice. These case studies are based on real situations and people; some will reflect good practice while others are designed to make you question and reflect on the situations. It is not intended to portray either nannies or childminders in a negative light in the less than ideal case studies, merely to encourage reflective practice in the reader. These are supplemented with some quotes from home-based childcarers; all of these have been gathered through interviews and discussions. In all case studies and quotes, names have been changed to maintain confidentiality of all concerned.

In addition to the case studies are **Find it out** features providing opportunities for you to investigate further, or develop and extend your understanding and learning. Important **Key terms** are highlighted and explained wherever they first occur, and a complete list of their definitions is included in a **Glossary** section at the end of the book.

There are also **Think about it** features in each chapter, which provide tips and hints that will be of general interest or are designed to encourage reflective practice. **Links to assessment** tasks give practical advice on how to approach your assignments and they show clearly which Assessment criteria you will be working towards. **Keys to good practice** features provide a checklist of recommendations for best practice and are a handy way of remembering the key learning points.

NOS number	NOS description	Chapter
CCLD 302	Develop and maintain a healthy, safe and secure environment for children	Chapters 1, 4 and 7
CCLD 303	Promote children's development	Chapters 3, 6, 7 and 8
CCLD 305	Protect and promote children's rights	Chapters 2, 9 and 10
CCLD 316	Maintain and develop a registered childminding business	Chapters 2, 4 and 5

Table 1: Links to the National Occupational Standards.

The book's unique **ncma says...** features contain useful professional advice and help reinforce key learning points. They have been written by the National Childminding Association (NCMA), so you can be sure that you are up to date with current guidelines and best practice.

Hotlinks — there are links to relevant websites in this book. In order to ensure that the links are up to date, that the links work, and that the sites are not inadvertently linked to sites that could be considered offensive, we have made the links available on the following website: www.pearsonhotlinks.co.uk. When you visit the website, type in the title of this book or the ISBN to access the page containing the links for this book.

At the end of the book are suggestions for further reading and useful information sources such as addresses, websites and contact details for organisations relating to children and young people.

The term 'home-based childcarer' is used throughout the book to refer to registered childminders, those registered on the voluntary register (in Wales registered to care for children 0–8), and approved nannies.

How to prepare for assessment

This unit has seven learning outcomes which have been cross-referenced to the relevant chapters in this book (see Table 2 on the following pages), so you can see at a glance where to find all the information you need. A learning outcome is the specific knowledge that you are expected to acquire. Each learning outcome has several assessment criteria (AC), which are more specific ways of assessing or measuring your knowledge and understanding. Each criterion has a number which links to the learning outcome. For example, AC 2.5, Explain how to store and administer medicines, is part of Learning Outcome 2, Understand how to establish a safe and healthy home-based environment for children.

You will need to produce evidence for each assessment criterion to show that it has been met; however, one piece of evidence can be used to support more than one criterion.

Building your portfolio

As you work through each learning outcome and so complete the unit, you will start to build a portfolio of items, such as policies, activity plans, routines or records of professional discussions. This portfolio will be a major part of the assessment for the unit. Each piece of evidence may be needed by the awarding organisation for this unit for confirmation of the standards by an external assessor. Evidence can be scanned and it is recommended that each piece of work is produced using A4 paper.

Assessment requirements may vary depending on your awarding organisation, but all assessment must be carried out in line with the Skills for Care and Development assessment strategy. Your awarding organisation and your assessor will provide further guidance.

A range of assessment methods can be used to give the opportunity for different learning styles and allow the individual needs of each learner to be taken into account. These may take the form of work products, a professional discussion between you and your assessor, written records, and even recognition of prior learning.

Some awarding organisations may also provide assessment tasks for you to complete, so the book also contains tips and suggestions on ways that you could present information and activities you could do to practise for possible tasks. These have been developed based on the knowledge assessment tasks published by CACHE; but if you are registered with a different awarding organisation you may find that the information can still be used. Check with your assessor before embarking on any of the activities suggested in the Link to assessment features in the book.

The following table shows where you can find information that links directly to the learning outcomes and tasks set by the awarding body CACHE.

Learning Outcomes and Assessment Criteria	CACHE Assessment Task	Chapter and page
1 Understand how to set up a home-based childcare service		**Chapter 2**
1.1 Outline the current legislation covering home-based childcare and the role of regulatory bodies.	Task 1	21, 27
1.2 Develop policies and procedures and explain how these will be implemented.	Task 2	34
1.3 Explain the importance of confidentiality and data protection.	Task 3	38
1.4 Develop a marketing plan for own home-based childcare service.	Task 4	48
1.5 Demonstrate financial planning for own home-based service.	Task 4	48
1.6 Identify sources of support and information for the setting up and running of your home-based childcare business.	Task 4	48
2 Understand how to establish a safe and healthy home-based childcare environment for children		**Chapter 4**
2.1 Explain the key components of a healthy and safe home-based environment.	Task 5	82, 91
2.2 Explain the principles of safe supervision of children in the home-based setting and off site.	Task 5	67
2.3 Identify ways of ensuring that equipment is suitable for children and meets safety requirements.	Task 5	75
2.4 Know where to obtain current guidance on health and safety risk assessment of the home-based work setting.	Task 5	72
2.5 Explain how to store and administer medicines.	Task 5	94
3 Understand the importance of partnerships with parents for all aspects of the home-based childcare service		**Chapter 5**
3.1 Explain the importance of partnership with parents for all aspects of the childcare service.	Task 6	98, 108
3.2 Describe how partnerships with parents are set up and maintained.	Task 6	105
4 Understand the principles of development of routines for home-based childcare		**Chapter 7**
4.1 Explain how routines are based on meeting children's needs, agreements with parents and participation of children.	Task 6	140
4.2 Explain how they would adapt routines to meet the needs of children at different ages and stages of development.	Task 6	140

Continued

Continued

Learning Outcomes and Assessment Criteria	CACHE Assessment Task	Chapter and page
4.3 Explain how they ensure that each child is welcomed and valued in the home-based work setting.	Task 6	140
5 Understand how to provide play and other activities for children in home-based settings that will support equality and inclusion		**Chapter 8**
5.1 Explain the importance of play to children's learning and development and the need for an inclusive approach.	Task 7	147
5.2 Plan a challenging and enjoyable learning environment in the home that includes using everyday domestic and household items.	Task 7	154
5.3 Explain what can be learned about children by observing them at play.	Task 7	159
5.4 Indentify how and why it is important that children receive equal treatment and access, based on their individual needs and acknowledging their rights.	Task 7	143, 146
5.5 Compare how other resources available for children support their play.	Task 7	160
6 Understand how home-based childcarers can support the safeguarding of children in their care		**Chapter 9**
6.1 Explain the concept of safeguarding and the duty of care that applies to all practitioners.	Task 8	168
6.2 Outline the possible signs, symptoms, indicators and behaviours that may cause concern in the context of safeguarding.	Task 8	167
6.3 Outline regulatory requirements for safeguarding children that affect home-based childcare.	Task 8	168
6.4 Explain procedures that need to be followed by lone workers in home-based settings when harm or abuse is suspected or alleged either against them or third parties.	Task 8	172
7 Understand the principles of supporting positive behaviour in home-based childcare settings		**Chapter 10**
7.1 Describe typical behaviours exhibited by children linked to their stage of development and key events in their lives.	Task 9	179
7.2 Explain how ground rules for behaviour and expectations are developed and implemented.	Task 9	185

Table 2: Links between the Assessment Criteria for each Learning Outcome and the CACHE Assessment Tasks.

1. THE HOME-BASED CHILDCARER – WHAT IS IT ALL ABOUT?

A home-based childcarer is an individual who works in a home setting, and can be a registered childminder, an approved nanny or an approved over-7 childminder. A home-based childcarer can be either self-employed or, in the case of a nanny, employed by a family. In most cases the general information introduced in this chapter will be developed in later chapters.

This chapter covers:

- why people become home-based childcarers
- things to consider before you begin, from both a personal and business perspective
- skills, knowledge and qualities needed
- the importance of a contract.

Why people become home-based childcarers

People become home-based childcarers for a variety of reasons. Many childminders enjoy the freedom and flexibility of working for themselves, in their own homes; nannies also can benefit from the same sense of freedom and flexibility. Childminders and nannies get pleasure from working with people, especially children. They give a very valuable service to a great many children and their parents. Childcaring can be a very demanding job, but at the same time very rewarding. It is a skilled job that requires not only a love of children, but also a good understanding of children. It is very important that home-based childcarers, like any other professionals, access training and develop their skills and knowledge; in other words they should undertake **continuing professional development (CPD)**.

Do you enjoy being with children?

Key term

Continuing professional development (CPD) – ongoing training and updating of relevant skills and knowledge.

You must enjoy being with children and caring for them, otherwise you would not have thought about becoming a registered home-based childcarer. These are probably the most important reasons for choosing this job. When you become a registered home-based childcarer you take full responsibility, in every way, for the children you care for. That responsibility is for all the time that the children are with you. You do not get a coffee or tea break, or time off for lunch. You will need eyes in the back of your head and a sixth sense! You will also need lots and lots of patience and a good sense of humour.

For many years there was a rather negative perception of home-based childcarers, particularly childminders. It was seen as the 'Cinderella role' of the childcare profession and it was not uncommon for some people to say to childminders, 'When are you going to get a proper job?, or 'It must be good to stay at home all day playing with children.' However, this perception is slowly changing.

Many home-based childcarers employ an assistant to work alongside them. This can be highly beneficial for both the childminder and the assistant as workloads can be shared and there is always the social aspect of working with another person. If the assistant is registered independently this means that the business and the service offered to families can be expanded.

Things to consider before you begin, from both a personal and business perspective

Personal issues

Changing your career, or embarking on a new one, can present major issues in your personal life. Becoming a home-based childcarer will affect your family and your home in many different ways and there are many issues that you need to consider.

Case study: Faye's professional profile

Faye had a demanding job and when she became pregnant she took her full entitlement of maternity leave. However, when the time came for her to return to work she found the separation from her baby very difficult and so decided to give up her job and retrain as a childminder. She became registered and built a successful business; she took childcare qualifications and thoroughly enjoyed the change of career. But Faye was very saddened to find that when talking to her peers about her work, she was frequently met with negative views of her job, and many did not understand its demands and complexities. Comments such as 'Will you go back to work when Josh starts school?' or 'You can run the school fete as you're at home all day' were only too frequent and Faye began to feel as though she was not valued.

Faye is very professional and was delighted when she got 'outstanding' in her recent **Ofsted** inspection. Furthermore the local newspaper ran an article about her, which helped to raise her profile with her peers. Faye firmly believes that it is up to childminders themselves to raise their professional profile by becoming qualified and keeping up to date with new developments and initiatives. She said, 'I really do believe that we owe it to the children to be the best we possibly can, and if that means giving up an evening or a Saturday to do training then I will do it.'

- What would you do and say to someone who was negative about your job?
- What do you think are good ways to raise the professional profile of home-based childcarers?

Commitment

Caring for other people's children is a big commitment, whether this is in the child's home or in your home. Parents need to have reliable childcare arrangements that can provide continuity for their child.

So ask yourself, 'Am I able to commit to providing a professional and dependable service for children and their families?'

Can you think of anything that might stop you committing to this profession?

Living away from home

If you plan to be an approved nanny, have you thought about the implications of living and working in someone else's home? It might be in a rural area that is quite different from where you have lived before and you may need to drive children to activities and school. You may not have friends in the area and may have to build a new social circle.

So ask yourself, 'How do I feel about making new friends and establishing a new social life?'

Key term

Ofsted – the Office for Standards in Education (England), the government department responsible for the inspection of childcare settings, schools and local education authorities.

Effects on your home

Think carefully about the impact that caring for children will have on your home. Unless you can offer a separate part of your house, completely cut off from your family space, your business will affect your home life. There will inevitably be wear and tear on any home with children, but it will be greater with more children. This applies not just inside the house but also in your garden. Safety is paramount so you may have to fence off ponds or greenhouses, and this may not be acceptable to other family members.

So ask yourself, 'How will my family cope with the inevitable changes that will have to take place in order to ensure the safety of other children in my care?'

Working hours and family life

Have you thought about the hours you will work and the impact this could have on your family? If you have children of your own they may have commitments such as after-school clubs and activities that may clash with your responsibilities relating to other people's children. What about your own children's toys and personal possessions? Will you keep them away from minded children, and if so, where and how? What about your children's demands on your time? How might your 8-year-old feel if you cannot listen to them read when they come in from school, or cannot help with homework when the child asks? How might they feel about 'sharing' you?

So ask your own children, 'How do you feel about having more children around?'

Are you able to commit to providing a professional and dependable service for children and their families?

Different age groups

What about the age group that you plan to work with? Some people cope very well with a mixed age range from babies to older school children; others prefer under-5s, others want children that are similar in age to their own. It is a matter of personal choice. Before you make a firm decision you need to think about where your strengths lie and which age group you prefer. It makes good sense that, if you are having fun, the children will too.

So ask yourself, 'What are my strengths, what things do I really like doing with children?'

Working patterns

Are you going to work full- or part-time, term time only, or flexible hours to meet shift work patterns? Working in school holidays will bring different challenges as you may have a mixed age group and this will also impact on your own children. If you only work term time it will impact on your income.

So ask yourself, 'How much income do I ideally need to have to make this business financially worthwhile?'

Being a home-based childcarer, in many ways, can be a lonely, isolated job (especially if you have changed career from one where you previously had frequent contact with other adults). Yes, you are your own boss and can be flexible, but the contact that you have with other adults can be limited. You have to be quite proactive and seek out other childminders or join 'drop-in' groups. You may decide that you will work with someone else; a childminder can take on an assistant or a student helper, or work with another registered childminder. Some childminders work with their partners or older children, such as mother and daughter; these arrangements can be very successful but you do have to be careful that any disagreements in your working life do not spill over into your personal life. A nanny might be employed in a family that has other staff.

So ask yourself, 'What are the implications of working on my own?'

Case study: Lindy's new assistant

Lindy has been a registered childminder for several years, with a very good reputation in her locality. A few years ago she was asked to take on a student, Alex, who was studying a childcare course at a local college, for two days each week. Lindy agreed and this proved to be a very rewarding experience for them both. The time that Alex completed her studies coincided with Lindy's decision to expand her business. Lindy had been turning families away as she was always up to her registered numbers.

In the beginning Lindy employed Alex for a probationary period before taking on any more children, just to make sure that they could work together. It became very clear that Lindy and Alex had a good working relationship and so the business expanded.

- Do you want to work on your own or with someone else?
- Are you quite social and proactive about seeking out like-minded people?

Business issues

A registered childminder needs to have good business skills. You need to be organised about:

- keeping accounts and staying within a budget
- keeping up-to-date records about the children, planning and requirements from Ofsted (in England), the Care and Social Services Inspectorate Wales (CSSIW) or other regulatory bodies, depending on where you live.

Getting started in home-based childcare will involve some financial outlay, such as registration fees, insurance and equipment, before you begin getting any money back so you must be certain that you can afford it. In some areas start-up grants are available, but you need to check with your own local authority.

Ask yourself, *'How good are my business skills, such as keeping accounts, and should I get some help?'*

Any business that is starting up needs to have some form of market research to make sure that there is actually a need for the service. It might be a good idea for you to work from home, but if there are other childcare settings in the area you need to be certain that your business will be viable. So ask yourself the following questions.

- What type of childcare do parents need/require?
- How will parents get to me? Is my home on a good bus route? Have I got adequate safe parking for cars?
- Am I within walking distance of a railway station?
- Am I near a school? (If so, you can offer before and after-school care as well as drop-offs, pick-ups, school holiday care and care during school in-service days.)
- Are there other registered childminders in my area?
- Are they full or do they have vacancies? Ask them if they have had many enquiries and also ask about their rates for childcare.

Remember – undercutting another childminder's rates of care might seem a good idea at the time, but is it realistic? Can you run a professional, quality service in this way?

Are there other childcare settings in your area, such as private day care nurseries or children's centres? These offer different childcare from a home-based practitioner and it is often down to parental choice where their child is cared for. However, get in touch with these settings; ask about their fees (if any) and whether they are full or have vacancies. Be informed about your competition.

So ask yourself, *'What can I offer that is different from other settings in my area?'*

See below for more about your unique selling point (USP).

New developments in your area, such as housing, business parks or new companies setting up, could all be advantageous to a new home-based childcarer or nanny.

So ask yourself, 'Should I contact the Human Resources department of the business near me to advertise my childcare business?'

Find it out

Contact your local authority. They should be able to tell you whether there is a need for childminding services in your area. Most local authorities in England and Wales have a department which deals with disseminating information about childcare to parents and carers. This department is called the Family Information Service (FIS) and you can register your details with them, such as name, location, contact phone number, any vacancies and unique features of your business.

Skills, knowledge and qualities needed

All the skills, areas of knowledge and qualities discussed in this section relate to the Children and Young People's core units of the full Level 3 Diploma.

You need to have good communication skills, not just with children but also with parents and other professionals. How you develop your relationships with parents could impact on your business both positively and negatively. You need to understand how to keep the relationship businesslike and professional. It is important that you understand how to develop a partnership with the parents, so that the well-being of the child is your first consideration. There is a fine line between having a professional relationship with parents and one that is almost too friendly.

ncma says...

It is a good idea to take advantage of Skills for Life training that is available and improve your skills as appropriate.

Communicating with children can take many forms, both verbal and non-verbal, for example speech, gestures, touch, facial expressions and so on. How you communicate with children will help them settle in your home-based childcaring service and come to terms with being cared for by a different person. It will also affect your relationships with the children and their development.

Think about it

Have you got a unique selling point (USP) that will make your service different and better than another? For example, can you offer:
- a setting that is environmentally aware, for example, home-produced vegetables or free-range eggs
- pick-ups from different schools
- hours to suit shift patterns, including weekends

- awareness and experience of a specific medical condition, such as diabetes, asthma or epilepsy
- proficiency in Makaton?

You can find more information about these factors in Chapter 2.

Case study: Keeping relationships professional

Ceri felt that her relationships with the parents of the children in her care were friendly but professional. One parent invited Ceri and her family to a weekend barbecue to celebrate a 'big' birthday. Ceri was pleased to be invited but felt very uncomfortable when the parent began to talk about other parents and almost 'quiz' her. She made her excuses and left early with her partner and children. Ceri said, 'It was really difficult, I thought we were friends, but now I realise that it is not easy to be professional and be friends as well. In future I shall keep my business life separate from my social life.'

- Can you understand Ceri's dilemma?
- Think about the difference between a friend and a professional.
- How can you get the balance right? You want a good relationship with effective communication but you need to remain professional.

So to answer the question 'Who is the home-based childcarer' is not as straightforward as it may first appear. Every home-based childcarer is different because we are all individuals and do things in our own unique ways, while meeting the requirements of registration. Home-based childcare is a very rewarding profession; it is also challenging and does need quite specific skills, knowledge, attitudes and attributes. You need to be reflective and honest about what you can do and what you cannot.

Think about it

Listed in Table 1.1 are some of the skills, areas of knowledge and qualities that a home-based childcarer should have. Think about each one and then tick the appropriate box.

Skill, knowledge or quality	I can do this confidently	I need to develop this more
Have good communication skills with children and adults		
Am well organised		
Can keep confidences		
Can be professional		
Understand how children develop and learn		
Understand how to meet all children's needs		
Understand how to keep children safe		
Understand how to keep children healthy		
Have a sense of humour		
Can keep calm		
Have a flexible approach		
Am patient		
Am caring		
Am respectful of all people		

Table 1.1: Checklist of skills, knowledge and qualities needed.

How well can you communicate with children?

ncma
says...

It is good practice always to be thinking of ways you can increase your knowledge and keep up to date – this is known as continuing professional development (CPD).

It does not matter how many boxes you ticked in each column; what is important is that you have thought about and reflected on this aspect of your work. As you progress through this chapter, you should find that some of the boxes you have ticked to show that you need to develop this area will be met. These will be clearly highlighted in the following chapters. You may develop some of the skills as your home-based childcare business progresses and you become more experienced. For example, you may become more organised and flexible as you gain in confidence; you may become more assertive as you deal with parents.

Remember – the true mark of any professional is that they do not rest on their laurels, but are open-minded, willing to learn more and develop their knowledge and skills.

The importance of a contract

A **contract** is an agreement between two parties, in this case between you and the parents. It is a legal document. A contract should make your responsibilities and those of the parents very clear. There should be no ambiguities, or words that could be misinterpreted. The agreement between you and the family is about the care and well-being of the child – the most important reason for having the contract.

> ## Key term
>
> **Contract** – a written agreement setting out the specific terms and conditions, for example, about the care of a child.

You should **never** take on a child, under any circumstances, without having a signed contract. Not only is it unprofessional, it will invalidate your insurance and you could be committing an offence.

> ## ncma
> says...
>
> We advise using NCMA contracts, which have been tested in a court of law and meet regulatory requirements.

All registered childminders must have written, or computer-produced, contracts for each family that they are involved with. The National Childminding Association (NCMA) produces comprehensive contracts with clear guidance notes on how to complete them. The NCMA contract has three copies – one for your files, one for the parents and one for any agencies involved.

Contracts should be signed by both parties and dated. Contracts should be reviewed regularly, and especially when circumstances change. For example, you might have agreed a contract to care for a child three days a week, then the mother increases her hours of work and asks you to care for the child five days a week. In this case you will need a new contract to reflect the new circumstances. Contracts must be agreed, signed and dated regardless of the number of days or hours you will be caring for a child and regardless of the period of time, whether it is only one day, one week or for the foreseeable future.

Why you and parents need a contract

- Having a written contract with parents is a professional and businesslike way of conducting your childcare affairs. It should give parents a good impression of your professionalism and of how you run your business.
- It makes it clear exactly what you are willing to do, what you expect from the parents and so prevents misunderstandings.
- Each contract is personal to each family, taking into account the individual needs of that family and the child. However, at the same time the contract can have standard clauses, such as details of fees, pick-up and drop-off times, and holiday dates, that apply to all families.
- Contracts that are signed and dated by both parties are legally binding. This could be very important if you have problems later on.

You must make time to discuss the contract with the parents before you agree to take on the child. Explain, if needed, each part of the contract and make sure that the parents are in full agreement with all aspects of it. Do not be pressurised into agreeing to something that will have an adverse effect on either you or the other children that you care for. Be firm and use your communication skills to explain to the parents why you have written the contract in the way that you have. Make sure that both you and the parents are very clear about what will happen if any part of the contract is broken.

Case study: Breach of contract

Mike is a registered childminder and cares for two children, Liam and Kerry, as well as his own baby. The contract that Mike has with both sets of parents clearly states that payment will be made weekly on the last day of care. In Liam's case this is Thursday morning. For the first six weeks Liam's father gave Mike either cash or a cheque. In the seventh week the cheque was returned by the bank and Mike had to give it back to the father, who was very apologetic and gave Mike the cash the next week. The following week, Liam's father said that he had forgotten his cheque book; the next week Liam was dropped off by his grandmother, who said that the parents were busy and that the payments were nothing to do with her.

Mike felt that he was being put in a difficult position, especially as his own partner thought the parents were taking advantage of Mike's goodwill, and that his childminding was a business and not a charity. Mike recognised that he had to do something as Liam's family had broken their contract. Mike decided to telephone the father and ask him to come a few minutes earlier as he wanted to discuss things with him. The father did not keep this appointment. Mike felt he had no option but to write to the parents giving them a week's notice that he would not be able to care for Liam unless they paid him the outstanding fees. The result of this was that Liam's grandmother gave Mike cash for the outstanding fees and said that her son had decided that he would care for Liam himself. Although Mike was sorry that his relationship with this family had not been very good, he did acknowledge that he could not afford to offer a free childminding service. Also, taking positive action meant that he had less worry and stress.

- In your view, did Mike do the right thing?
- Was there anything else that Mike could have done? If so, what?

Planning permission

Some local authorities in Wales require prospective childminders to have confirmation that they do not need to have permission from the planning department of the local authority. This is often to assess the impact of your business on the immediate area, your neighbourhood, and will look at issues such as parking, access and possible increased traffic. Your local authority will give you guidance on planning issues and whether you need to have their permission before you commence work. In England it is a good idea to check out the situation in your local authority area.

Becoming a home-based childcarer is a professional undertaking with demanding responsibilities. It is not a nine-to-five job that you can walk away from; it will require commitment. But it is very rewarding and satisfying, so do not be put off. Get yourself qualified and trained to the best of your abilities and work with our most precious possessions – children.

2. HOW TO SET UP A HOME-BASED CHILDCARE SERVICE

It is important to start your childcaring career as you mean to continue, and that you take a professional approach from the first day. Part of being professional is about how you market your business and your approach to financial planning and confidentiality. You need to keep up to date with legislation and professional development issues. You also need to understand how to develop policies and procedures and where to go for support and help.

This chapter covers:

- current and relevant legislation
- the role of regulatory bodies
- policies and procedures
- the importance of confidentiality and data protection
- marketing
- financial planning
- sources of support.

- This chapter links to Learning Outcome 1: Understand how to set up a home-based childcare service.
- All assessment criteria (1.1 to 1.6) for this learning outcome are covered, and guidance is given for CACHE assessment tasks 1–4.
- It also has links to the Children and Young People's Core units of the Level 3 Diploma for the Children and Young People's Workforce.

is the Children Act (2004), which arose from the Green Paper 'Every Child Matters'. It identifies five outcomes for children:

- be healthy
- stay safe
- enjoy and achieve
- make a positive contribution
- achieve economic well-being.

These outcomes form the basis of inspections and should underpin your practice. Other relevant **legislation** is summarised in Table 2.1.

Current and relevant legislation

There are numerous laws relating to children and young people in the UK. The most influential of these

Key term

Legislation – laws, rules and regulations passed by Acts of Parliament.

Legislation	Focus of legislation
Sex Discrimination Act (1975)	Supported by the Equal Opportunities Commission to ensure that individuals are not discriminated against on the grounds of their sex
Race Relations Act (1976) Amended in 2000	Equality of opportunity must be promoted and settings should develop a policy which is monitored and assessed
Education Act (1981)	First official recognition of: • parents' rights regarding children's education • special educational needs
Public Health (Control of Disease) Act (1984)	Covers the notification and exclusion periods for certain infectious diseases
Education Reform Act (1988)	National Curriculum introduced into schools
Children Act (1989)	First acknowledgement in UK law of children's rights, encapsulated by the phrase: 'the needs of the child are paramount'
Education Act (1993)	Secretary of State required to publish a code of practice for children with special educational needs Parents of children under 2 years have the right to ask for the child to be formally assessed
Code of Practice for the Identification and Assessment of Children with Special Educational Needs (1994, revised in 2001)	Guidance on the responsibilities of local education authorities and governing bodies of schools towards children with special educational needs
Reporting of Injuries, Diseases and Dangerous Occurrences Regulations (RIDDOR) (1995)	Specify certain accidents and incidents that must be by law be reported

Continued

Continued

Food Safety (General Food Hygiene) Regulations 1995	Set out basic hygiene requirements (not yet applicable to registered childminders, but a Basic Food Hygiene Certificate is considered good practice); this is part of the registration process
Family Law Act (1996)	Sets out guidance relating to safeguarding children
Disability Discrimination Act (1995)	Aims to ensure that rights of disabled individuals are met in England, Scotland, Wales and Northern Ireland
Education Act (1997)	Incorporated all Acts since 1944 into one Set a time frame on the legal process for identifying and assessing a child's needs as set out in the Code of Practice
Code of Practice for First Aid (1997)	Gives guidance on the provision of trained first aiders and first aid provision
Human Rights Act (1998)	Became legal in 2000, the result of requirements laid down by the European Convention on Human Rights
Protection of Children Act (1998)	Requires a list to be kept of people considered to be unsuitable to work with children
Data Protection Act (1998)	Prevents confidential and personal information being passed on without a person's consent; in the case of children the consent must be given by the parents
Special Educational Needs and Disability Act (2001)	Protects children from discrimination on the basis of disability, and settings must make reasonable adjustments to their provision to meet the needs and rights of the child
Care of Substances Hazardous to Health (COSHH) Regulations (2002)	Deal with the identification, storage and use of potentially harmful substances, such as cleaning fluids
Health Protection Agency Act (2004)	Established the Health Protection Agency, a UK-wide public body dedicated to protecting people's health
Children Act (2004)	Arose from the Green Paper 'Every Child Matters' and identifies five outcomes for all children: • be healthy • stay safe • enjoy and achieve • make a positive contribution • achieve economic well-being
Childcare Act (2006)	Introduced the Early Years Foundation Stage (EYFS) in England

Table 2.1: Key current relevant legislation.

Think about it

The United Nations Convention on the Rights of the Child (UNCRC) was drawn up in 1989; the UK is a signatory and the Convention was approved in 1991. Although it is not legislation, the ethos of the UNCRC underpins many recent pieces of legislation, such as the Children Act (2004). It gives children and young people under the age of 18 their own rights. These rights are discussed in greater detail in Chapter 8.

All children are covered by the 54 articles contained within the UNCRC, which essentially state that all children must be shown respect and that their interests are paramount. Of the 54 articles, seven primarily affecting childcare practitioners, are shown in Table 2.2. Note that Article 7 is taken from the earlier Declaration of the Rights of the Child (1959). These articles are relevant and important for home-based childcarers because they should make us think about the way we relate to children. They should reinforce that all children are special and that each one is unique and entitled to be treated with dignity and respect.

- How do we listen to children?
- How do we recognise and respond to their comments and views?

Article no.	Key aspect
2	Children have a right to be protected from all forms of discrimination
3	The best interests of the child must be the primary consideration in all activities and actions concerning children
7	The child shall have 'full opportunity for play and recreation, which should be directed to the same purposes as education; society and the public authorities shall endeavour to promote the enjoyment of this right'
12	A child has a right to express his or her views freely and that view is to be given appropriate weight in accordance with the child's age or maturity
13	Guarantees a child's right to freedom of expression and exchange of information regardless of frontiers
16	Children have a right to privacy
28	A child has a right to education with a view to achieving this right progressively on the basis of equal opportunities

Table 2.2: Seven key articles on children's rights.

The role of regulatory bodies

Getting registered

Home-based childcarers must be registered with the regulatory body for their country before they can care for other people's children in their own home. All the regulatory bodies publish requirements, or standards and procedures that childminders have to meet in order to be registered. It is a fineable offence to work as a home-based childcarer and not be registered.

Regulatory bodies in the UK

- In England the regulatory body is Ofsted.
- In Wales it is the Care and Social Services Inspectorate Wales (CSSIW) Standards.
- In Scotland it is the Scottish Commission for the Regulation of Care.
- In Northern Ireland it is the local Health and Social Services Trust.

Arrangements for registration and regulation differ little between the four countries. The registration system exists so that Ofsted (or other regulatory body) can make sure that you:

- meet the welfare requirements and learning and development requirements as set out in the Early Years framework for your home country. For England, these are in the **Statutory** *Framework for the Early Years Foundation Stage*
- are a suitable person to provide care for children
- can promote an environment where children are well cared for, are safe and their learning and development is catered for.

Key term

Statutory – something that is legal, has been made law.

The regulatory bodies have processes and systems to control home-based childcare in the following ways.

- **Registration** – This covers checks on you, other adults who live with you and the premises where you plan to carry out your business.
- **Inspection** – This is when inspectors carry out checks on the service you offer and on you, once you are registered. They produce a report, which is then available on the websites of the regulatory bodies and must be offered to parents.
- **Investigation** – Following a complaint or concern, an inspector may carry out an investigation into your childcare service to make sure that you are meeting and complying with the welfare requirements. This is in addition to an inspection.
- **Enforcement** – If you do not meet the welfare requirements or standards of your country, the regulatory body can take action against you.

You may find that you will be invited to a briefing meeting by your local authority, which will give you more details of the requirements of registration and will assist with the completion of forms and other paperwork.

You will have to:

- complete an application form
- apply to the Criminal Records Bureau (CRB) for an **enhanced disclosure** for yourself. You will also need an enhanced disclosure for every member of your family over the age of 16
- organise a health check with your doctor
- pay a registration fee (not in Wales).

In some cases (always in Wales) you may need a social services check and/or to provide a reference; however, your local authority will be able to give you more information on this at the briefing session. You will need to carry out training in home-based childcare within six months of your registration; in Wales the training must take place before you can be registered. In both England and Wales you must complete first aid training before registration. The first aid training must be a course that has been designed especially for people who work with young children. Your local authority will be able to give you details of training and first aid courses in your area.

ncma says…

It is good practice to do training **before** registering so that you are fully prepared.

> *I found the childminder briefing sessions really useful. Not only did I get lots of information, I also met other new people who were in the same position as myself. The sessions really helped me through registration and gave me lots of useful advice.*
>
> *Sue, registered childminder*

What happens next?

If you are working in England, an Ofsted inspector will visit your home, at a prearranged time, to discuss how you meet the welfare requirements (or if you are in another home country, you will discuss the standards of your country). In England there are five general welfare requirements:

- **safeguarding** and promoting children's welfare
- suitable people
- suitable premises, environment and equipment
- organisation
- documentation.

Key terms

Enhanced disclosure – a written document issued by the Criminal Records Bureau (CRB) which proves that the named person has no criminal convictions that would mean they were unsuitable to work with and care for children.

Safeguarding – protecting, looking after and maintaining the well-being of children.

Each of the welfare requirements are set out in three sections:

1. overarching general legal requirements
2. specific legal requirements
3. statutory guidance.

More detailed information on the welfare requirements can be found in the booklet *Statutory Framework for the Early Years Foundation Stage* in the Early Years Foundation Stage Pack. You may be given a pack at the briefing meeting or you can contact the Department for Education (DfE) – details are in the useful addresses section at the back of the book) – or access it from the Hotlinks section – see page 3.

Enhanced
Page 1 of 2

Applicant Personal Details

Surname: SMITH

Forename(s):   JANE ALISON

Other names: n/a

Date of Birth: 25 OCTOBER 1955

Place of Birth: BARNET HERTFORDSHIRE

Gender: FEMALE

ISA Reg No.:

Number: 000000000

Date of Issue: 05 May 2010

Employment Details

Position applied for:
CHILDMINDER

Name of Employer:
ANY COUNTY COUNCIL

Countersignatory Details

Registered Person/Body:
ABC COMPANY

Countersignatory:
CHRISTINE JONES

Police Records of Convictions, Cautions, Reprimands and Warnings
NONE RECORDED

Information from the list held under Section 142 of the Education Act 2002
NONE RECORDED

ISA Children's Barred List Information
NONE RECORDED

ISA Vulnerable Adults' Barred List Information
NOT REQUESTED

Other relevant information disclosed at the Chief Police Officer's discretion
NONE RECORDED

This document is an Enhanced Criminal Records Certificate within the meaning of sections 113B and 116 of the Police Act 1997.

Continued on page 2

An example of an enhanced disclosure form. Have you completed one of these for every member of your family who is aged over 16?

An Ofsted inspector will visit your home. Are you familiar with the welfare requirements they will be checking you meet?

Keys to good practice

Welfare requirements

- Read through welfare requirements, or the standards for your country, very carefully and make sure that you understand what each one involves before the inspector visits you. If you do not understand something, contact your local authority or the National Childminding Association (NCMA).

- Display your registration certificate in a prominent place in your setting so that all parents can see it.

During the visit to your home the inspector will interview you to assess whether you are a suitable person to be registered and whether you are ready to begin working as a home-based childcarer. You will probably be given oral feedback before the inspector leaves your setting; this will be followed by a written report which will set out very clearly any actions you need to carry out or conditions that might be imposed on you. For example, anything that is considered to be a hazard — such as a pond or greenhouse — may need to be securely fenced off from children before they can use your garden.

Remember to ask the inspector to explain any actions or conditions you are not sure about. You will be given an Ofsted number (in England), which you will need to quote on all business correspondence, and a certificate of registration containing your name, address and any conditions that may have been imposed with regard to your registration.

At the present time nannies do not have to be registered with a regulatory body unless they work for three or more families, in which case they should be registered with Ofsted (in England) or the regulatory body of their home nation. However, there is a voluntary approval scheme for nannies. Although it does not determine whether a nanny is suitable for any particular family, nannies who join the approval scheme are inspected by Ofsted and therefore have a recognised form of quality assurance. A nanny cannot join the approval scheme unless they can provide evidence that they:

- have relevant qualifications or have attended an approved induction course in childcare
- have a valid first aid certificate appropriate to the care of babies and children
- have an enhanced CRB disclosure
- are over 18 years old.

In addition if you are planning to care only for children over the age of 7 you can apply to become registered on the Voluntary register.

After registration

Periodically the inspectors will inspect your setting to make sure that you are meeting the welfare requirements or standards. You will be given short notice, but will not know the exact time or day. The inspector will produce a report, which will be sent to you and also made available on the websites of the regulatory bodies. In Wales, inspections happen twice a year and every year childminders have to produce a Quality of Care review, which has to be submitted to the CSSIW (Care and Social Services Inspectorate Wales).

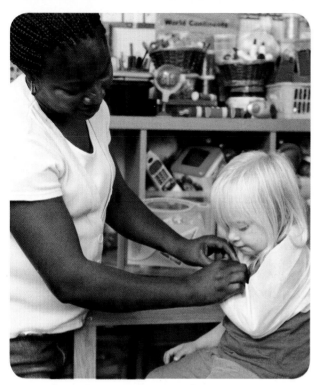

Do you know how to administer first aid?

Self-evaluation form

Ofsted issues a self-evaluation form (SEF), see overleaf, to all home-based childcarers prior to the inspection. The form can be accessed via a secure link to the website – see the Hotlinks section on page 3. It can be completed and submitted online, or you can print it off and handwrite the information. The form has questions for you to answer and you are able to grade yourself, using the grading system shown below.

You are asked to provide information about:

- your setting
- the views of those who use your setting
- the quality of your provision
- the outcomes for children, including the extent to which they:
  - achieve and enjoy their learning
  - feel safe
  - adopt healthy lifestyles
  - make a positive contribution
  - develop skills for the future
- outcomes for children in the EYFS
- leadership and management
- how effective you are in promoting equality and diversity

- the effectiveness of safeguarding children
- the effectiveness of your self-evaluation and how you plan to improve your practice
- the effectiveness of partnerships
- the statutory requirements.

ncma says...

Completing an SEF is a skill that you will not have until you have been a childminder for a while. Check what support is available locally for this. There is an SEF tool from the NCMA, available online.

Keys to good practice

The self-evaluation form

- Tackle the SEF in stages; do not try to complete it in one go.

- Do not skimp on the information you provide, but keep it relevant, concise and factual. The more information you give the inspector before the visit, the better prepared both of you will be.

- Do not be frightened of 'singing your own praises'; if you do something well, say so.

- Review and revise your information at regular intervals.

The inspection report produced by Ofsted covers the following areas:

- description of your setting
- overall effectiveness of the Early Years provision
- what steps need to be taken to improve provision further
- the leadership and management of the Early Years provision
- the quality and standards of the Early Years provision.

Apart from the description of your setting, each of the other areas will be graded on a four-level scale:

- Grade 1 – Outstanding
- Grade 2 – Good
- Grade 3 – Satisfactory
- Grade 4 – Inadequate.

raising standards
improving lives

Early years self-evaluation form

For settings delivering the Early Years Foundation Stage

Age group: Birth to 31 August following a child's fifth birthday

Published: September 2009

Reference no: 080104

Please leave blank for Ofsted use

EY Self-evaluation form

An example of a self-evaluation form (front page). Have you seen one of these before?

The inspector will give you one overall grade at the end of the inspection. The regulatory body can request that you make changes if necessary or, if you do not conform to the welfare requirements or standards, end your registration.

Link to assessment AC 1.1

Task 1, Part 2: On the information sheet you created for Part 1, outline the role of regulatory bodies.

- This information sheet is a continuation of the one you created for Task 1, Part 1. Decide who it is for. Is it for parents, other home-based childcarers, or other professionals? This will determine the type of language you use.
- How are you going to produce this sheet?
  - On a computer
  - Handwritten – make sure your handwriting is legible and clear
  - Make sure you use A4-sized paper
- Read the sections about the regulatory bodies carefully and decide which key information you need to include on your information sheet.
- Remember to include information about the regulatory body of your country.
- Decide how the key information can be presented clearly and effectively.

If you are not following the CACHE task you could provide evidence for this assessment criterion. Use the Internet to get details of the requirements of the relevant regulatory body to where you work and then show your assessor that you can meet them. You could discuss how you will be inspected, what requirements you will have to meet and what evidence you will need for the inspector.

Find it out

The regulatory bodies for the four countries of the United Kingdom are broadly similar; however, see if you can find out the differences between them.

Policies and procedures

A **policy** is a course of action that you intend to take, or guidelines for good practice. Policies are not written in stone, but should be constantly updated and reviewed in line with statutory changes, new developments and changes in your service. A policy is a working document, not just a piece of paper to be filed away and brought out to show parents or an inspector. A policy needs **procedures** that you follow in your work. You need to understand why you have such procedures or guidelines and how they can help you develop and reflect on your practice.

Key terms

Policy – a written statement setting out a particular course of action in given situations, or a set of guidelines.
Procedure – the method or course of action required to carry out a policy.

Keys to good practice

A good policy should reflect:

- the aims, philosophy and ethos of your childminding service
- The Every Child Matters outcomes for children (or equivalent in your country)
- EYFS welfare requirements (or equivalent in your country)
- relevant legislation
- the practice in your setting.

A good procedure describes:

- step-by-step detailed written information about how the policy will be put into practice
- step-by-step written information that clearly describes what actions you and other adults should take
- what you will do in different situations which may arise.

Think about it

In writing a step-by-step procedure it might be helpful for you to think of it as telling a story.
- The policy is the title page of the story.
- The aspects of the procedure are the chapters of the story.
- The procedures are the actual story.

The welfare requirements for documentation state that you must maintain policies and procedures for the safe and efficient management of your setting and to meet the needs of children. Your policies should be available for parents to read and sign before you begin to care for their child. There are many policies that you may have, but they do not have to be complicated. It is better to have short, straightforward policies that use clear language, and are easy to read and well laid out. Your complaints policy should be in writing and shared with parents.

ncma says...

It is good practice to make sure all your policies are **written** to avoid misunderstandings.

Some local authorities will have a list of policies that all registered childminders should have, so you need to check what is required. If you decide later on in your practice that you want to join a childminding network (further details later in this chapter), you will be asked to write more policies. However, while there is no set number of policies that you will need, the following should be regarded as a minimum (in Wales you are required to have all these):

- complaints
- health and safety to include **accidents**, **incidents**, **illness** and **emergencies**
- **behaviour**
- safeguarding
- equal opportunities.

Key terms

Accident – an unforeseen, unplanned mishap, calamity or mistake that may cause distress or injury to another individual.
Incident – something that happens, an occurrence (minor or more serious).
Illness – a medical condition of sickness, poor health.
Emergency – a crisis or situation that requires immediate action.
Behaviour – the way an individual acts or the actions that they carry out.

These policies are specifically mentioned in Assessment criterion 1.2 and form part of Task 2. Other policies that you may wish to develop are:

- confidentiality
- admissions (could be included in your equal opportunities policy)
- special needs and inclusion (could be included in your equal opportunities policy)

- outings and trips (could be included in your health and safety policy)
- administering medicines, sun lotion protection (could be included in your health and safety policy)
- bullying (could be included in your behaviour policy)
- partnership with parents
- learning and play
- lost children (in Wales this is a requirement).

Find it out

If you are struggling to begin writing your policies, the NCMA website has sample policies that you can download and adapt for your personal circumstances. You can access the website from the Hotlinks section (see page 3). Alternatively, ask another registered childminder if you can have a look at their policies. You can find details of the NCMA and other useful organisations on pages 187–193.

ncma says...

Your local authority may have a buddy scheme – this is useful and will enable you to see what other childminder policies are like.

How to write a policy

How you write your policies is very much a matter of personal preference; there is no set way, but there are important things that you should consider.

- What is the policy about?
- Does it have a clear opening statement? For example, for a safeguarding policy, 'As a registered childminder I have a duty to protect all the children in my care at all times.'
- Does your policy go on to say **what** you will do, **how** you will do it and **when**?
- If appropriate, does your policy also say under what circumstances you will implement your policy actions and when you will review it?

Sharing policies with parents and others

As mentioned earlier, a policy is a working document; therefore it should be shared, discussed, monitored and reviewed by all concerned, including children. It is good practice for older children to develop policies, for example, concerning behaviour management, safety, risk and challenging play, and independence when outside.

You cannot assume that because you give parents a file of your policies or procedures, they will read them. We are all guilty of this in some ways. For example, have you really read the instruction book for your washing machine from page one to the end, and can you remember what you read? Parents can provide you with valuable feedback on your service because children may tell them about what they have been doing. This feedback can influence and inform your practice and feed into your policies.

In the same way children can tell you important information about your service. If you take time to listen to them they may tell you about things they like and things they dislike. This will provide opportunities to talk about issues where a child might think you have not been fair – for example, when managing behaviour. Discussing all children's individual needs will help older children become more aware of needs, differences, feelings and their rights.

You may be asked to share your policies, procedures and/or guidelines with other professionals. If you join a childminding network your coordinator will ask to see your policies. Ofsted or your regulatory body may ask to see some (CSSIW **will** need to see these before registration), especially those on behaviour management and safeguarding children's welfare. If you are caring for a child with specific needs or difficulties, it may be appropriate for other health or education professionals to share your policies. Also it might be helpful to share some policies with other settings, such as schools, especially if you have a behaviour management strategy for a child that is effective in promoting **positive behaviour**.

Positive behaviour – ways an individual acts that are considered socially and morally acceptable.

One of the Common Core of Skills and Knowledge for the Children's Workforce is 'Sharing Information'. This is about understanding how and when to share information, your responsibilities and the impact of legislation on sharing and holding information. Your policies must be shared, otherwise you would not be able to monitor, evaluate and review them.

Monitoring, evaluating and reviewing your policies

The NCMA recommends that all policies and procedures be reviewed and evaluated at least once a year. Many home-based childcarers will monitor and evalute their policies more frequently – for example, when legislation changes or a new child starts, if they change their working hours and obviously if it becomes clear that something is not working well.

How do you gather information about your service? For example, do you have regular meetings with everyone involved? What else could you do?

Keys to good practice

Monitoring, evaluating and reviewing your policies
This is much more than just reading them through or printing out another copy and putting a different date at the bottom! It involves:

- gathering information, both informally and formally (such as questionnaires and interviews), about your service

- listening to the views of everyone involved with your service, including children, parents, your development worker and the feedback from your inspector

- taking into account new developments and changes to legislation

- being realistic and reflective about your service and being able to take positive criticism as well as praise.

Health and safety policy and procedures

As outlined earlier, your health and safety policy and procedures need to include provision for accidents, incidents, illness and emergencies.

An accident is something that happens, which is not expected or planned, and is not caused deliberately. Accidents can be prevented, or at least their effects can be limited. As a registered childminder your responsibility is to try to prevent accidents from happening but, if they do happen, then you must know what to do; this is where your policy is critical. You may decide to put accidents and emergencies into one policy, which is quite acceptable.

An emergency, like an accident, is unexpected. It can involve only you or several people. Emergencies are often the result of accidents. Even though you cannot predict accidents and emergencies, you can be prepared. The best way to cope is to have a personal emergency plan or policy, so that you are prepared for the worst. Such a policy will help you remain calm and more able to cope.

Case study: May's behaviour policy

May works as a registered childminder and has one child of 8 months, a 3-year-old, a 4-year-old and two over-7s. She developed a behaviour management policy when she started childminding two years ago. However, she has not reconsidered the policy since and some circumstances have changed; for example, the two older children are now at school full-time.

- Why does May need to review this policy?
- Who should be involved?

Personal emergency plans

A personal emergency plan is exactly that – it is personal to you and it must work for you. It is good practice to write out your personal emergency plan so that other people can follow it if something were to happen to you. This is effectively your policy. You should also look at your policy regularly and change it if necessary. This is especially important for keeping up-to-date records of the children. The NCMA has produced a form that you and the parents can complete with details of addresses, telephone numbers, emergency contacts, medical details and other useful information. You could also make up your own forms, but ensure you include all details about the children that you need to know in order to keep them safe.

Think about it

When carrying out your risk assessments, don't forget to check window and door locks and stairgates, as these can lead to places where children could fall. For more information on accidents, see pages 86–87.

It is good practice to mentally 'rehearse' an emergency. This will help you plan what you need to do first and will help you feel more confident and more able to reassure the children in a real emergency. You also need to practise your emergency evacuation procedure regularly.

Keys to good practice

Personal emergency plan

- Do not panic, keep calm, take a few deep breaths.

- Deal with the emergency following the 4Bs (see page 89 for further information).

- In the case of a fire emergency, get all the children and yourself out of the building as quickly as possible.

- Check the safety of all the children and, if possible, remove them from the immediate area; never leave them unattended.

- If necessary make telephone calls to the emergency services or doctor. Make sure you are talking to the correct person; identify yourself and explain clearly why you are calling.

- Contact the parents of the child or children. If you leave a message, make sure that it is brief, but gives all the necessary information without causing the parents to panic. Remember to leave a contact number for the parents to get in touch with you.

You should also include in your accident, illness and emergency policy information about:

- caring for sick children
- administering medicines
- safe storage of medicine and other medical equipment, such as inhalers.

Do you have an up-to-date list of contact numbers for each child so you know who to contact if there is an incident?

Behaviour

Most parents accept the need for children to have boundaries for behaviour, but your views and those of the parents may not be the same. This is one very good reason why you need a policy. Your behaviour policy should replicate your views on behaviour and what is or is not acceptable in your home. You must discuss your policy with parents and get their agreement. It is also important to remember that your behaviour policy should still apply to the minded children whether a parent is in your setting or not. Your policy should focus on promoting positive behaviour, not necessarily the sanctions you could deploy if a child's behaviour was deemed to be 'unacceptable' or causing concern.

More information about promoting positive behaviour can be found in Chapter 10.

Overleaf is an example of a behaviour management policy from a working registered childminder.

Annie Jones, Registered Childminder – Ofsted no: 000000

Behaviour Management Policy

I have very few 'rules' in my childcare setting, but I do expect all children that I care for in my home to learn to accept them, and their parents to support me in implementing my policy.

1. I will discuss the boundaries for behaviour with all the children. If the children know and understand why we have boundaries they will be more secure.
2. When setting boundaries I will be firm and fair and will take into account the age and stage of development and the needs of each individual child.
3. I will praise the children when they behave well and encourage them.
4. I will be a positive role model for them at all times.
5. I will never use any form of physical punishment.
6. I will never humiliate, restrain or isolate a child.

The boundaries are:

- We will all care for each other.
- We will not do anything that might hurt another person, or is dangerous or offensive.

I will record all incidences of unwanted behaviour that cause concern and will discuss these concerns with you and if I have any concerns about your child if appropriate.

I will review this policy when a new child comes into my care and/or if asked to do so by parents or in response to new legislation.

If you would like to talk to me about this behaviour management policy please speak to me when you bring or collect your child, or telephone me in the evening on 01234 567890.

October 2010

An example of a behaviour management policy. What would you include in your own policy?

Think about it

Read the above policy.
- Do you think it is clear and uses straightforward language?
- Would you change or add anything?

Safeguarding

You will obviously do everything possible to keep the children in your care safe from harm at all times. There may be times, however, when, despite all your good practices, children may need protecting from harm and ill-treatment. It is therefore essential that you have a clear safeguarding policy. You will probably find that your local authority will arrange safeguarding courses and training for you to attend, either before you become registered or just after. The welfare requirements set out very clearly what necessary steps you must take to safeguard and promote the welfare of children. You will find this information on pages 22–24 of the *Statutory Framework for the Early Years Foundation Stage*. It will help you to draw up your policy and procedures.

You can find more information about safeguarding children in Chapter 9. Safeguarding and promoting the welfare of the child is one of the Common Core of Skills and Knowledge for the Children's Workforce and more information can also be found in Chapter 3 page 59.

When developing your policy you need to think about how you will meet the individual needs of all the children. This can be challenging at times and you may have to make adjustments to your setting so that all children can be included, supported and valued. For example, you may need to have a range of resources which reflect different family backgrounds, or make other reasonable adjustments to enable a child to experience all that is available within the setting.

Keys to good practice

Your policy and procedures
These must comply with the requirements of your Local Safeguarding Children Board (LSCB) and should make reference to:

- significant changes in a child's behaviour
- any deterioration in their well-being
- unexplained bruising and marks
- neglect
- comments and disclosures that children make which give you cause for concern.

Equal opportunities

This is about treating children and their families as individuals – it is not about treating everyone the same. This is impossible to do as all children are different and should be valued and respected for their different personalities, needs, interests and abilities. An inclusive setting is one where children (and their families) feel valued and welcomed, trusted and respected, and where all children have equal access to an appropriate range of facilities and activities. (You can find more information about equality and **inclusion** in Chapters 7 and 8.)

Key term

Inclusion – the process of recognising, understanding and overcoming obstructions or barriers to participation.

Find it out

On page 25 of the *Statutory Framework for the Early Years Foundation Stage* you will find information about the statutory guidance which should be included in your policy. Read it through and make sure you understand what you need to cover.

Link to assessment **AC 1.2**

Develop policies and procedures for the following and explain how these will be implemented:

- accidents, illness and emergencies
- behaviour
- safeguarding
- equal opportunities.

CACHE Task 2
Write a policy for each of the following and a procedure to explain how each of the policies will be implemented; four policies and four procedures are required:

- accidents, illness and emergencies
- behaviour
- safeguarding
- equal opportunities.

This CACHE task can be used regardless of whether you are registered with CACHE or with another awarding body.

Remember, a policy is a statement of **what** you will do under certain circumstances in your setting.

A procedure is **how** you will carry out your policy.

Look again at the section on how to write a policy. Neither the policy nor the procedure has to be complicated; the more complex it is the more confusing it can be and misunderstandings could arise. Straightforward language is always best to avoid misunderstandings.

The policy and the procedure will be individual to you. It must work for you and be something meaningful and useful, not just something that is filed away. Because policies and procedures are individual to each setting there will inevitably be differences between yours and those of other registered childminders. This does not matter. How you implement your policy is what is important.

You will need to produce policies and procedures as outlined above whether or not you are working with CACHE.

Key term

Confidentiality – privacy, discretion, keeping information secret.

You must regard all information that you have on a child as confidential and it should only be shared between yourself, the child's parents and the child. There may be times when some children need support and help from other professionals, such as speech therapists. You must seek written parental permission before you disclose information about a child. The only exception to this may be in the case of safeguarding, when telling the parents might jeopardise the safety of the child.

> " *I was given an excellent tip from a very experienced childminder when I had just started. She told me to have a 'never talk about' list and to think about how I would feel if things about me or my family became common knowledge.* "
>
> *Gwyn, registered childminder*

The importance of confidentiality and data protection

Home-based childcarers acquire a lot of information about the children and families with whom they work. Some of it may be told directly to them by the parents or other professionals such as teachers (with the parents' permission); some of it may be picked up indirectly, perhaps from the children. The crucial characteristic of **confidentiality** is not sharing with other people or passing on personal information about the families with whom you are working.

The importance of handling data about children and families in a confidential way

Children and their families have a legal right to privacy. The Data Protection Act (1998) is designed to prevent confidential and personal information being passed on without a person's consent. It now includes not just information stored on computers but also on paper and screen, including photographs.

It is important to remember that written information should not be removed from the setting or home, so medical cards, for example, should remain in the child's home if at all possible. **Observations** and a child's personal details should remain in the home of the registered childminder. Photographs of children should only be taken with the written consent of the parent and, if appropriate, the agreement of the child. Many registered childminders have a cupboard or filing cabinet, which can be securely locked where they keep confidential information; a shoebox under the bed is not secure or professional.

Key term

Observation – watching, studying, examining or scrutinising the actions of others.

You should password-protect your computer files. This ensures that information can be kept confidential and is not accessible to other adults or children.

ncma
says…

Good practice is to have a lockable separate business filing system that cannot be accessed by the rest of your family or other visitors to your setting.

While you may be very careful with written or digitally stored information, it is all too easy to breach confidentiality in general conversations with other home-based childcarers and practitioners. For example, when talking about your work, planned activities or behaviour concerns at perhaps a toddler group, you could inadvertently breach confidentiality and give away enough information for the child and their family to be identified by another person. Always think very carefully before you start to discuss professional issues with other people.

Why and how confidentiality must be maintained and circumstances in which it can be breached

The information that you need to share with parents is confidential, and so is the information that they share with you. This can include:

Keys to good practice

Confidentiality

- Never discuss one set of parents with another.

- Take care when having casual conversations with your own friends and family.

- When preparing assignments and course work, make sure that you do not identify any child and their family. Do not refer to them by their real names – use initials or a pseudonym.

- Discuss with parents what to say when dealing with other professionals, and get their written agreement and permission to share information about the child (unless it is an issue or cause for concern about safeguarding the child).

- Password-protect your computer.

- Have a secure, locked cupboard or cabinet where you can keep personal information about the children in your care.

- contract details, such as fees, hours, addresses and contact details
- information about yourself, your qualifications, experience and training
- information from when a new child starts your setting, such as how the child asks for the toilet, whether they have special words with specific meanings
- what you will do in an emergency
- routine events, such as nappy changing, toileting, and ways to meet parents' and children's needs
- medical issues
- education records
- parents' employment details, and any family details such as custody arrangements
- religious beliefs
- children's likes and dislikes
- how and when you exchange daily information.

Think about it

Consider situations where you might find yourself likely to pass on information when you should not.

- Ask yourself, 'Is this gossip?'
- Are there people or certain circumstances that put pressure on you to share information in ways that you know you should not?
- What can you say to people when they are trying to get you to breach confidentiality?
- How do you respond if another childcare practitioner shares confidential information with you in an inappropriate way?

Most parents want the best for their children and that would include the support and help of other professionals so that the needs of their children can be met. This may mean that certain information will have to be shared. The only exception to this is a safeguarding issue, when sharing information may put the child at greater risk.

There are only two sets of circumstances in which confidentiality can be breached:

- if parents have given permission for you to pass on information
- if it is essential to do so in the best interests of a child, for example, safeguarding or medical emergency.

Are you careful not to discuss sensitive information at all times?

There may be times when another professional may wish to discuss or share information about a child. For example, if you collect children from school, or another Early Years setting, the teacher may need to discuss the child's progress with you; or if you have taken a child for a regular health check, the health visitor may want to talk to you about the child. If you do not

Case study: Confidentiality with permission

Karly is an approved nanny for Roisin, who is having speech therapy. Roisin's parents both travel extensively and have given written permission to the speech therapist for Karly to attend appointments and consultations on their behalf and discuss Roisin's therapy.

- How can Karly make sure that information about Roisin is shared with the parents?

Sadia is a registered childminder and has noticed bruises on the arms and legs of one of the children in her care. She is concerned that the child may be in need of protection and so contacted the Local Safeguarding Children Board (LSCB) to report her concern. Sadia did not tell the parents that she had done this.

- Why did Sadia not talk to the parents?

have written parental permission to discuss or share information with these professionals, you will need to explain that to do so would breach confidentiality and be unprofessional. Discuss these incidents with parents and reach agreement on what you should do.

ncma
says...

It is important that you get permission to share a child's learning journey with other professionals.

We have seen earlier in this chapter that one of the Common Core of Skills and Knowledge for the Children's Workforce is 'Sharing Information'. It is important that you understand and respect issues and legislation surrounding the control and confidentiality of information. (You can find more information about the Common Core of Skills in Chapter 3.)

Marketing

All businesses need to market their services continually. Even if you are fully employed and have no vacancies, it pays to make sure that your business and childcare services get the best publicity they can. So start as you mean to carry on.

Working with local information and other services

It is very important that you register your details with your local Family Information Service (FIS). Make sure that you complete any forms they send you and try to answer every question. If your details change — for example, a vacancy arises or you gain an additional qualification — let the FIS know as as soon as possible. Under the Data Protection Act (1998) any information that you give your FIS will be held by them and supplied to the public and on the Internet only if you given your consent to do so, usually by a signature on the contact and vacancy details form. If you do not give such permission the information will only be used for statistical purposes, but the other disadvantage is that you will not receive any free publicity.

Registered childminders should consider joining a quality-assured childminding network where available. Not only will you have support of the network coordinator when you have vacancies to fill, you may also get the chance to become quality assured or **accredited** and offer Early Years education — another positive marketing point.

Link to assessment

AC 1.3

Explain the importance of confidentiality and data protection.

CACHE Task 3
Write an explanation of the importance of confidentiality **and** data protection. An explanation means that you give reasons why something is important, that you can make it clear, with appropriate detail and evidence.
For this assessment criterion you must write about **both** confidentiality and data protection. Think about the following:
- Do you understand what confidentiality means?

- Do you understand the implications of data protection for a home-based childcarer?
- Why is each essential for best practice?
- How do they underpin your policies and procedures and why are they central to your practice?

Instead of the CACHE task you could have a professional discussion with your assessor, during which you could show that you understand the importance of confidentiality and data protection. Your assessor could also observe you in practice, where inference of knowledge is evident in what you do.

All home-based childcarers should make every effort to get involved with their local **Children's Centre**. It should be noted that services offered vary. Nevertheless this may well provide opportunities to extend your services in different directions, such as offering respite, wraparound care, out-of-hours or holiday care.

> ## Key terms
>
> **Accredited** – having produced a portfolio of evidence to show that you have met the NCMA's Quality Standards for Children Come First (CCF) Networks.
>
> **Children's Centre** – a one-stop establishment for children and parents where professionals from different agencies can offer support, for example, health visitors, Basic Skills tuition, Early Years education.

Marketing materials and advertising

All business have their unique benefits and selling points. It is good practice to put together a list of your key selling points. Registered childminders might want to think about the following areas.

The home

- Is it safe and secure as shown by your Ofsted report?
- Is it part of a local community and near local amenities?
- Are you sure it will be a non-smoking environment?
- Has it been checked by local fire safety officers?
- Does it have good transport links?
- Do you have lots of parking space?
- How close is it to schools (the ones you pick up from and drop off at)?
- Can you offer weekend care and overnight stays? (You will need Ofsted agreement to offer overnight care.)
- Have you got a dedicated play area and a safe garden?
- What food will you offer?
- Are you able to care for children with special or additional needs?
- Can you drive and so take children to different after-school activities? Do you have a clean driving licence?
- Are you a member of a local childminding group?

What do you think your key selling points are?

Skills, qualifications and experience

All home-based childcarers can use their own skills, qualifications and experience as selling points. Think about:

- your first-aid qualification
- your initial training, pre-registration or approval
- membership of a professional organisation such as the NCMA
- other qualifications or training you have or are working towards, such as the Level 3 Diploma for the Children's Workforce; awards in baby massage, British Sign Language, Makaton, communication, caring for a new-born baby, working with children who have a specific medical condition such as diabetes or cystic fibrosis, inclusion training rather than specific medical model training
- belonging to a childminding network and being quality assured
- speaking more than one language, including sign language
- your personal health checks
- enhanced CRB disclosure
- experience with particular forms of childcare, such as a disabled child, triplets, premature babies
- previous childcare experience, such as working in a day nursery, after-school club or holiday play scheme, which may give you a useful knowledge base
- whether you can provide evidence that you offer a wide range of stimulating, creative and enjoyable experiences and opportunities for development and learning
- working towards a quality improvement scheme
- continuing professional development (CPD).

Areas you may want to highlight to parents

There are other selling points that you may want to think about.

- Are you eligible for tax credit claims?
- As a nanny, do you have public liability insurance? (All registered childminders must have this.)
- Do you have a vehicle that is insured for business use?
- Does your house insurance cover damage?
- Are you prepared to be flexible to match parents' shift patterns, for example, working at weekends?
- Do other members of your family have CRB disclosures?

The above lists are suggested points only and are by no means complete. They are intended to help you recognise your unique selling points and no doubt you can think of plenty more.

Advertising your service

Now you have a list of your selling points, what next? How do you advertise yourself? If you are happy about your name and contact telephone number being published, you could consider advertising in the following media:

- FIS
- free ads newspapers
- local evening or weekly papers
- parish newsletters, school fair programmes, newsletters of other organisations; you must be clear that these groups are not endorsing your business
- on the Internet, by setting up your own website or joining a group of like-minded people and setting one up together

Case study: Specialised care

Belle and her partner are vegans and grow all their own food, following organic practices. Both are registered childminders and charge a higher rate per hour than other childminders in the area. They justify this by offering an 'organic and vegan' childminding service.

Ameera has become qualified to give massage and therapy to children with cystic fibrosis. As a nanny she specialises in caring for children with this condition and her income reflects her specific capabilities.

- What could you offer that is different from other home-based childcarers and could have a direct impact on your rates and income?

- your local radio station
- extended schools — speak to your local authority about what this means.

Think about it

Look at a search engine that matches parents with local childcare providers. You can advertise your service for free and receive enquiries from parents in your area who are looking for childcare. Find out more by accessing the website from the Hotlinks section (see page 3).

Keys to good practice

Contact details

It is not a good idea to put your address on advertising material. You could get unwanted and nuisance callers or put children, yourself and your family at risk. It is better just to put a phone number.

ncma says...

You could consider using a separate mobile number for business use only.

Business cards and leaflets

You can also organise some business cards and/or leaflets either by doing them yourself on a computer or using a local print shop. Some websites will print free advertising material for you and you pay only for the postage. Give these out to:

- parents you already know
- your home-based childcare group coordinator or members
- Children's Centres
- friends
- neighbours
- midwives
- health visitors
- social workers
- staff at schools and pre-school groups
- creche managers
- staff running parenting classes, such as Surestart
- staff running exercise classes for pregnant women and new mothers.

How and where will you advertise your home-based childcare service?

Registered childminder

Sandy Jones

Telephone: 12345 678 900
Email: S.Jones@childminder.com

What information should you include on your business card?

Other ways to advertise

Other things that you can do include:

- putting a sign in your garden or window if you are a registered childminder
- joining an agency; there are many highly reputable nanny agencies
- putting a poster in your car
- putting a business card or leaflet in local shops, libraries, colleges, schools, leisure and health centres
- putting your CV/details on an Internet job site and searching relevant sites for vacancies.
- having advertising on T-shirts and so on, and other items to give out, for example, key rings (freebies).

How much marketing you do is obviously up to individual choice, but it is important to remember that you need to present a professional image at all times.

Some registered childminders find that they rarely have to advertise, and actually have waiting lists. This is an extremely fortunate position to be in and comes about after quite some time of providing a professional, reputable service. It is a great compliment for a childminder to get a personal recommendation from a family, and something for you to strive for.

Think about it

Mike is a registered childminder. He has a vacancy for a child over 2 years old for five mornings a week (maximum of four hours). Mike's childminding business closes on bank holidays and for three weeks in August. He charges £12 per morning, including a mid-morning snack and a light lunch. His telephone number is 01230 567890, and there is an answer machine.
Using the above information, design a small advertisement, about the size of a postcard, that could be put on the notice board of the local health centre.

Case study: Candice's ineffective advert

Candice is a registered childminder with several vacancies that she does not seem to be able to fill. She wrote out brief details of her service on the back of an envelope and paid 50p for a week's advertising in her local newsagent. She had one enquiry from parents who wanted a drop-off and pick-up from school each day, plus holiday care, but were only prepared to pay £2 per hour, when the going rate in the area was £3.50. Candice's support worker suggested that the advert did not give the best impression; it was a bit rough and ready. Candice's elder son produced an attractive flier on his computer, which she used to replace the envelope in the newsagent. She also put it in the health centre and on the parents' notice board at the local school, and contacted the local FIS.

Candice had several enquiries following this advertising and, although she did not fill all her vacancies, she was able to provide a service for several families.

Think about how you advertise.

- Is it effective, does it work?
- Can you advertise better with higher-quality materials?
- Does your local FIS have your details?

Financial planning

As a registered childminder you are self-employed and therefore need to understand how to keep accounts for a small business. It is important that you are organised and approach financial issues in a professional way. There is no set way to run your finances. It is very much a matter of personal preference. However, if you do not approach this aspect of your work in a well-organised manner you may start making costly mistakes. Many of the high street banks and financial institutions will give free advice on setting up your business, so it is worth calling in and asking them.

Financial issues and problems are some of the most common troubles that registered childminders have. It is very important that you start as you mean to carry on and that you have discussed these issues before you sign a contract. (You can find more information on starting out in Chapter 1). Many registered childminders are moving to Internet banking and have set up direct debit arrangements for parents. This avoids the need to bank money every week and means that cheques or large sums of cash are not left in your house.

Your responsibilities

As a self-employed person you have responsibility for:

- registering with HM Revenue and Customs (HMRC) (formerly the Inland Revenue) as self-employed
- keeping accurate and up-to-date financial records that show your income and expenditure
- having legal and public liability insurance
- ensuring you have insurance to cover yourself, your home and contents, and your car
- paying income tax and national insurance contributions.

The importance of adequate public liability insurance

It is important that every home-based childcarer is fully insured. Public liability insurance will protect against unforeseen comeback and is part of the welfare requirements. Public liability will not stop or prevent accidents but insurance will provide you with legal liability cover against:

Keys to good practice

Financial planning

- Set up a separate bank account for your childminding business.

- Keep on top of your accounts, preferably doing them weekly, or at the very least every month.

- Keep all receipts safe. It is a good idea to number each receipt and then put this number next to the item in your accounts. Some people staple all receipts for one week or month together and file them.

- accidental injury or death to any person, including the children that you are caring for, caused by your negligence or activities
- any damage that may be caused to other people's property by the children that you are caring for.

Many companies will arrange public liability insurance, and costs do vary considerably. The NCMA has arranged public liability insurance for home-based childcarers with a leading insurance company, so it is well worth getting in touch with them and becoming a member so that you can access these benefits.

ncma says...

Check out the NCMA website to find out about various other member benefits.

It is important to consider your house, contents and car insurance policies. Many insurance companies do not cover childminder households. Again the NCMA offers specialist house and contents insurance. Car insurance is slightly different as many insurance companies will insure you provided you let them know that the vehicle is to be used for business; the nature of the business does not seem to matter. However, it is good practice to let your insurance company know, in writing, that you offer home-based childcare to avoid any comeback.

How to maintain accurate financial records, including deductible costs, to meet statutory requirements

The NCMA produces a cashbook and attendance register, which is a good way of recording income and expenditure on a weekly basis. Some practitioners prefer to keep their accounts on a computer, using a program such as Excel. However, the NCMA has agreed with HMRC that the format of the cashbook is an adequate record of trading. The NCMA has also agreed with HMRC some expenses specific to home-based childcare. Table 2.3 shows the agreed figures relating to registered childminders working at least 40 hours per week. Table 2.4 shows other general allowable expenses and some specific to home-based childcare.

These lists are not exhaustive, but HMRC may still refuse an allowance if the cost is not 'wholly exclusive and necessary' for the purpose of the business. Larger items such as buggies, car seats and high chairs will be treated as assets of the business and subject to capital allowance; that is, the costs of the assets would be spread over a number of years as an allowable expense. (It is interesting to note that home-based childcarers who are not members of the NCMA may find that HMRC may not accept those allowances which have been agreed with NCMA.)

For several years registered childminders may have been contacted by HMRC asking for help to confirm the childcare they provide for families claiming the

Other allowable expenses similar to any other business	Additional items you can claim for
Stationery and printing	Additional food (if providing breakfast/lunch/dinner/snacks)
Telephone	Toys and books
Vehicle expenses	Outings
Insurance	Safety equipment
Professional fees	Cleaning/hygiene
Subscriptions	Nappies

Table 2.4: Other general and specific allowable expenses for childcarers.

childcare element of the Working Tax Credit. This help will now extend to other approved childcarers.

When claiming income-related benefits, such as housing benefit, council tax benefit or income support, registered childminders have a special concession that

Expense	Amount allowed
Heating and lighting	33.3% of costs
Water rates	10% of costs
Council tax	10% of costs
Wear and tear	10% of gross income
Rent	10% of costs
Free milk	You can claim one-third of a pint of milk per child per day under the age of 5 years

Table 2.3: Agreed expenses for registered childminders working 40+ hours per week.

Are you aware of all the items you can claim for? How do you keep track of your expenses?

is not available to other people. It is called the 'two-thirds disregard'. This means that two-thirds of your total income from childminding is disregarded when your entitlement to these benefits is calculated. Your business expenses, such as food, stationery, heating and lighting costs, are not taken into account. For other benefits and tax credits the amount you receive will be based on your net income — your total (or gross) income less your actual business expenses.

Income support is usually only available to people who work for fewer than 16 hours each week. However a special rule allows some registered childminders to claim it even if they are working full-time.

The Department for Work and Pensions (DWP) has more information on benefits and tax credits. You can find more information by accessing the website from the Hotlinks section (see page 3). NCMA members can find more information in the fact sheets online.

> *Keeping on top of the financial side of my business is very important. I'm a member of the NCMA and I find that they have very useful publications that help me work out what my taxable income actually is. Also my local HMRC enquiry centre is very helpful.*
>
> *Tricia, registered childminder*

Some banks and other financial institutions offer free advice for small businesses, so it may be worth asking at your local branch. Check to make sure that this service is free and not one where you will incur costs, if not at the beginning, at some later date.

Keys to good practice

Benefits and tax credits
To check whether you are eligible for tax allowances, tax credits and other benefits it is a good idea to have a comprehensive benefits check. This can be done by an Into Work Adviser or Lone Parent Adviser. Both can be contacted at:

- your local JobCentre or JobCentre Plus
- the Citizens Advice Bureau
- the Welfare Rights Service.

You must register with your local tax office as a self-employed person within three months of beginning to earn money as a registered childminder and this will affect your National Insurance contributions. You may be liable for a fine if you do not. There are different charges for National Insurance and, depending on what rate you decide to pay, your entitlement to certain benefits — such as sick pay or maternity pay — will be affected. You should contact your local tax office for advice and help.

Sources of support

All practitioners, regardless of how professional they are, will find that at some point they need support and information. Childcare is a very demanding job and being self-employed can be quite isolating, especially as far as adult company is concerned. However, you must remember that anything to do with a child or the family is confidential, and you should not discuss such information with another person.

Local childminder groups

Many childminders set up local groups so they can enhance the quality of their practice by providing social interaction opportunities for their children. Sometimes they can meet in each other's homes, depending on the numbers, or in local amenities, such as a sports centre. These groups can be great fun and good sources of support. Sometimes people of your own profession are the only people who can really understand some of the issues involved in childcare. The local groups also provide the opportunity to share information and ideas, and to generate new ideas for activities. In many areas nannies set up groups for support and social activities for themselves and the children.

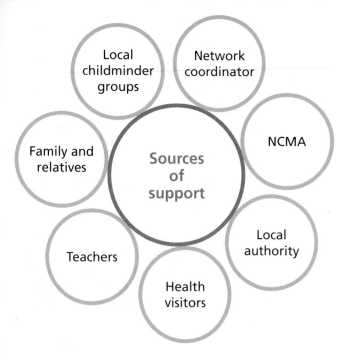

There are many sources of support available to you. Do you know how to find each one?

Network coordinator

Childminding networks are growing all over the country and these can also be valuable sources of information and support. Each network should have a coordinator who will be able to tell you what training and courses are available in your area.

The NCMA

The National Childminding Association (NCMA) is the only organisation in England and Wales specifically for childminders and other home-based childcarers. It is committed to promoting quality of childminding and improving the status and conditions for home-based childcarers, children and their parents. The NCMA has a national network of development workers and support staff. It is also very effective in liaising with government departments on issues concerning childcare, and home-based childcare in particular.

Practitioners who join the NCMA are provided with a wealth of information, including:

- a bi-monthly magazine *Who Minds?*
- free legal advice

- special offers for insurance
- training opportunities
- the chance to purchase useful publications and stationery, such as account books.

There is also a 'My NCMA' area on the website, where members can find a range of things to make childminding life easier.

Local authority

All local authorities have set up Children and Young People's Workforce Development teams. Many of these teams employ development officers with special responsibilities for home-based childcarers. These people can put you in touch with other home-based childcarers and also provide information about courses that are being run in your area. Your development officer can be a very useful source of support and help. They can often put you in touch with other local authority personnel and social services staff, such as child protection officers.

Health visitors

Health visitors, either your own or those of the children that you mind, can be a valuable source of support and help. Health visitors have a good understanding of children's growth and development, which they gain through carrying out child health surveillance and developmental checks. They can also put you and parents in touch with other professionals, particularly in the medical world, if you think there may be a problem.

Qualified teachers

More and more registered childminders who are part of an approved network are getting accredited and so are able to accept nursery education funding. This means they must offer activities to 3–5-year-olds that are part of the EYFS in England (or Foundation Phase in Wales). Teachers can be an invaluable source of support and advice for childminders offering this service, and many good professional relationships can be developed along with an exchange of ideas and activities. Teachers can also be supportive with children's learning difficulties and emotional and behavioural problems. It is likely that a child who has such problems at the practitioner's home, or their own home, will also have them at school. You should work with the teacher to support the child and hopefully deal effectively with the difficulty or problem.

Family and relatives

Before you started your business you should have discussed it with your family, partner, children and anyone else who could be affected, such as elderly relatives. Hopefully they will have supported you in your new venture, otherwise you could have problems.

Anyone who works full-time and has family responsibilities and commitments can find, at times, that it is difficult to meet all the demands placed on them. It can be difficult to balance the needs of your family against the needs of your professional life. This may be more difficult for childminders as they

are working in their own homes. Many self-employed people work from home, but often have a separate work area, so that their business life does not encroach on their family life. This is not the case for most childminders. There will be other children and partners in their home. There will be changes in the family routine and your working hours may mean that you have less time to spend with your own family. These issues should have been thought out and discussed with your family before you started your business.

If your family understand the demands of your business, then it should not be unreasonable to expect them to support you. This might mean taking a greater share in the running of the family home, such as doing the weekly family shop or doing the running repairs and DIY around the house that will be incurred with having more children around.

Case study: Ameera's supportive family

Ameera has decided to become a registered childminder. She stopped working a year ago, following the birth of her son, and she has another child who is at school. Ameera and her husband live with his parents. The house has a large back garden that is accessible through a conservatory. Ameera plans to use the conservatory as a playroom for her business and will use the big kitchen to serve the children's meals. There is a downstairs bathroom with separate toilet.

At first her in-laws think that the house will be full of other people's children, that it will be noisy and they will lose their privacy. Ameera tries to reassure them that this will not be the case and agrees that the children will not have access to the family sitting room or any of the rooms upstairs. Her in-laws agree to see how things go for six months.

Ameera meets an experienced childminder at the pre-registration meeting. She explains

her concern to the childminder, who suggests that Ameera bring her in-laws to see how she runs her business, which hopefully might allay their concerns. Ameera and her in-laws visit the childminder's house and they see for themselves that it is possible to run this kind of business and at the same time keep areas of the house private.

A few weeks after Ameera was registered, she noticed that her father-in-law would often be about as the children were leaving, making a special point of using their names when he said goodbye. Her mother-in-law began cooking a few extra sweetmeats 'for Ameera to share with the children'. Ameera now felt confident that she had the support of all of her family, thanks in part to the help of an experienced childminder.

- What can you learn from this case study?
- How could you make sure that all your family are supportive of your business?

Link to assessment

Develop a marketing plan for a home-based childcare service.

Demonstrate financial planning for your own home-based childcare service.

Identify sources of support and information for the setting up and running of your home-based childcare business.

CACHE Task 4

Develop a business plan which includes information on:
- marketing
- financial planning
- sources of support and information for the setting up and running of your home-based childcare business.

Your business plan will be unique to you. It should clearly outline the following.
- What steps you plan to take to market and advertise your service. It is a good idea to include a copy of the business card that you plan to use or a flier or advertisement. Make a list of the places where you will advertise and market.

- Your start-up costs. These should be listed with an indication of where the money will come from.
- What practical banking arrangements you have made. For example, have you set up a separate account, do you have Internet and/or telephone banking?
- Your charges. Are these hourly, sessional (such as morning and afternoon), before and after school, or daily?
- How you will be paid. Will you invoice parents weekly or monthly? Will you set up direct debit payments direct to your bank account? Will parents pay in advance or in arrears?
- Where you will find support from a personal and business perspective, and how you will access these services.

Your marketing plan can be used regardless of whether you are registered for this unit with CACHE. Evidence of your financial planning can be shown by how you manage your accounts and banking arrangements. You could make a list of sources of support and information that are available to help set up your business.

3. THE EARLY YEARS FOUNDATION STAGE AND OTHER FRAMEWORKS

Registered childminders can, and often do, work with children across a wide age range. Because of this it is good practice to have a sound understanding of the curricula and frameworks that affect the children in your care.

This chapter covers:

- the Early Years Foundation Stage (England)
- the Pre-school Expansion Programme (Northern Ireland)
- Birth to Three – Supporting Our Youngest Children/ A Curriculum Framework for Children 3 to 5 (Scotland)
- the Foundation Phase (Wales)
- the National Curriculum
- working with mixed aged groups
- the Common Core of Skills and Knowledge for the Children's Workforce.

As you work through this chapter you will be covering aspects of the Shared Core Units relating to communication, equality, diversity and inclusion and personal development of the full Level 3 Diploma for the Children and Young People's Workforce.

The Early Years Foundation Stage (England)

It is important that you have a good, detailed working knowledge of the framework for your country; it underpins your inspection and the activities and routines that you plan, to meet the needs of the children in your care.

Since 2008 all childcare practitioners (in England) who care for children aged from birth to 5 years have followed the Early Years Foundation Stage (EYFS). This was a significant move for registered childminders as it put them, for the first time, on an equal footing with all other settings. Wales has developed the Foundation Phase as part of the Learning Country programme, and similar initiatives are happening in Northern Ireland and Scotland. The National Curriculum is delivered in state-registered schools for children from 5 to 16 years of age.

Find it out

You can find and download copies of the EYFS and National Curriculum documents, and the equivalent documents for Wales, Northern Ireland and Scotland by accessing the relevant websites from the Hotlinks section (see page 3).

Every Child Matters

The EYFS is a central part of the ten-year strategy, 'Choice for parents, the best start for children', and also of the Childcare Act (2006). It was introduced in all settings in England in September 2008. The overarching aim of the EYFS is to help young children achieve the five Every Child Matters outcomes, which are:

- stay safe
- be healthy
- enjoy and achieve
- make a positive contribution
- achieve economic well-being.

The EYFS sets the standards for learning, development and care that young children should encounter while they are in settings outside the family home. It provides for equality of opportunity and makes sure that every child is included and not disadvantaged for any reason. The EYFS creates a framework for a partnership between parents and professionals in all the settings a child attends. The welfare requirements of the EYFS set standards that apply to all settings, aiming to improve quality and consistency of care. Therefore you need to be very familiar with the welfare requirements. Finally, the EYFS sets out a foundation for future learning through learning and development that is planned around the individual interests and needs of the child, informed by ongoing observation.

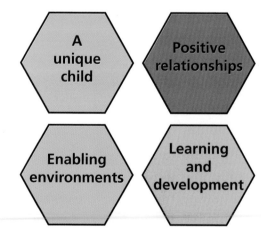

The four themes of the EYFS.

The EYFS pack contains:

1. the Statutory Framework booklet where you will find the welfare requirements
2. Practice Guidance booklet where you will find details of the six areas of learning and development
3. 'Principles into Practice' cards, which are colour coded to match the EYFS **themes** and explain how you can use the cards in your day-to-day work
4. a wall poster which shows the themes and **commitments**
5. a CD-ROM containing a wealth of information, links to websites to develop your knowledge and understanding as well as copies of all the printed documents mentioned above.

Your local authority may provide you with an EYFS pack and with training. It is very important that you attend the training.

Key terms

Themes – the four guiding subjects or topics of the EYFS.
Commitments – describe in detail how the principles and themes of the EYFS can be put into practice.

Themes and commitments

There are four complementary themes that should guide your work. These describe how you can support the development and learning of young children. The themes are as follows.

1. A unique child – this recognises that every child is a competent learner from birth.
2. Positive relationships – recognises that strong, loving and secure relationships are fundamental.
3. Enabling environments – tells you that the environment plays a vital role in extending a young child's development and learning.
4. Learning and development – acknowledges that children learn in different ways and at different rates and that all areas of learning and development are interrelated and interconnected.

Each of the themes has four commitments and is colour coded: blue, purple, green and orange. The colours are used through the booklets, practice cards and CD-ROM to make it easy for you to follow. The colour-coded themes and commitments are outlined in Table 3.1.

Theme	Commitments			
1. A unique child	1.1 Child development	1.2 Inclusive practice	1.3 Keeping safe	1.4 Health and well-being
2. Positive relationships	2.1 Respecting each other	2.2 Parents as partners	2.3 Supporting learning	2.4 Key person
3. Enabling environments	3.1 Observation, assessment and planning	3.2 Supporting every child	3.3 The learning environment	2.4 The wider context
4. Learning and development	4.1 Play and exploration	4.2 Active learning	4.3 Creativity and critical thinking	4.4 Areas of learning and development

Table 3.1: Colour-coded EYFS themes and commitments.

How could you make your environment even more effective at helping a young child's learning and development?

Key term

Holistic – the co-dependency of one area of development on another.

The Statutory Framework

This booklet is divided into four sections.

1. Introduction – this describes the four themes that support best practice. These are the themes that will underpin everything that you do. For example, you will plan activities and experiences that you know will interest the children you care for, which means that you are taking into consideration individual interests and needs.

2. Learning and development requirements – this section gives you an outline of how you must support children's learning and development in a really **holistic** way. You must remember that every child is unique and will develop and learn at different rates, so you should not compare one child with another.

3. Welfare requirements – this section is set out into key areas:
   - safeguarding and promoting children's welfare
   - suitable people
   - suitable premises, environment and equipment
   - organisation
   - documentation.

   The aim is that by having five key areas you will find it easier to plan and deliver activities and experiences that meet the welfare requirements.

4. Other information – this section focuses on equal opportunities and special needs. You will find this helpful in making sure that you develop effective working relationships with your local authority and other agencies that can support you.

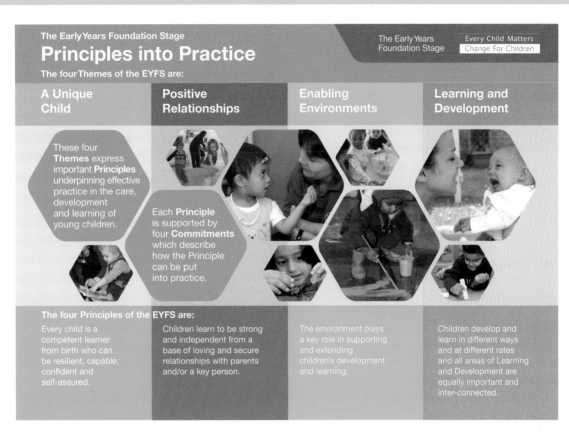

The Early Years Foundation Stage

Principles into Practice

The Early Years Foundation Stage

Every Child Matters
Change For Children

The four Themes of the EYFS are:

A Unique Child	Positive Relationships	Enabling Environments	Learning and Development

These four **Themes** express important **Principles** underpinning effective practice in the care, development and learning of young children.

Each **Principle** is supported by four **Commitments** which describe how the Principle can be put into practice.

The four Principles of the EYFS are:

Every child is a competent learner from birth who can be resilient, capable, confident and self-assured.	Children learn to be strong and independent from a base of loving and secure relationships with parents and/or a key person.	The environment plays a key role in supporting and extending children's development and learning.	Children develop and learn in different ways and at different rates and all areas of Learning and Development are equally important and inter-connected.

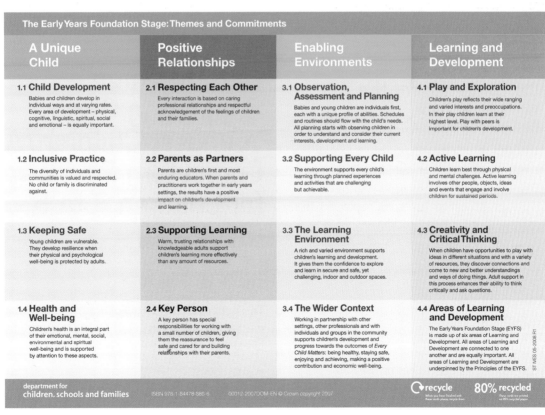

The Early Years Foundation Stage: Themes and Commitments

A Unique Child	Positive Relationships	Enabling Environments	Learning and Development
1.1 Child Development Babies and children develop in individual ways and at varying rates. Every area of development – physical, cognitive, linguistic, spiritual, social and emotional – is equally important.	**2.1 Respecting Each Other** Every interaction is based on caring professional relationships and respectful acknowledgement of the feelings of children and their families.	**3.1 Observation, Assessment and Planning** Babies and young children are individuals first, each with a unique profile of abilities. Schedules and routines should flow with the child's needs. All planning starts with observing children in order to understand and consider their current interests, development and learning.	**4.1 Play and Exploration** Children's play reflects their wide ranging and varied interests and preoccupations. In their play children learn at their highest level. Play with peers is important for children's development.
1.2 Inclusive Practice The diversity of individuals and communities is valued and respected. No child or family is discriminated against.	**2.2 Parents as Partners** Parents are children's first and most enduring educators. When parents and practitioners work together in early years settings, the results have a positive impact on children's development and learning.	**3.2 Supporting Every Child** The environment supports every child's learning through planned experiences and activities that are challenging but achievable.	**4.2 Active Learning** Children learn best through physical and mental challenges. Active learning involves other people, objects, ideas and events that engage and involve children for sustained periods.
1.3 Keeping Safe Young children are vulnerable. They develop resilience when their physical and psychological well-being is protected by adults.	**2.3 Supporting Learning** Warm, trusting relationships with knowledgeable adults support children's learning more effectively than any amount of resources.	**3.3 The Learning Environment** A rich and varied environment supports children's learning and development. It gives them the confidence to explore and learn in secure and safe, yet challenging, indoor and outdoor spaces.	**4.3 Creativity and Critical Thinking** When children have opportunities to play with ideas in different situations and with a variety of resources, they discover connections and come to new and better understandings and ways of doing things. Adult support in this process enhances their ability to think critically and ask questions.
1.4 Health and Well-being Children's health is an integral part of their emotional, mental, social, environmental and spiritual well-being and is supported by attention to these aspects.	**2.4 Key Person** A key person has special responsibilities for working with a small number of children, giving them the reassurance to feel safe and cared for and building relationships with their parents.	**3.4 The Wider Context** Working in partnership with other settings, other professionals and with individuals and groups in the community supports children's development and progress towards the outcomes of Every Child Matters: being healthy, staying safe, enjoying and achieving, making a positive contribution and economic well-being.	**4.4 Areas of Learning and Development** The Early Years Foundation Stage (EYFS) is made up of six areas of Learning and Development. All areas of Learning and Development are connected to one another and are equally important. All areas of Learning and Development are underpinned by the Principles of the EYFS.

department for children, schools and families

ISBN 978-1-84478-886-6   00012-2007DOM-EN © Crown copyright 2007

recycle   80% recycled

EYFS Principles into Practice cards. Do you use these cards when talking to parents?

The CD-ROM

The CD-ROM reproduces all the information in the EYFS pack. For example, drop-down boxes appear beneath important titles to explain key features further and signpost where you can find more information. There are video clips to illustrate key points and notes to accompany them. It is easy to navigate your way around by clicking on a subject that particularly interests you. You will find the CD-ROM an invaluable resource as you continue your studies and professional development.

Principles into Practice cards

All the cards follow a similar format and are designed to be a starting point for further reading and research. As mentioned earlier, they are colour coded to match the four themes and well illustrated. You should take time to read the cards and become familiar with them. You can share them with parents to help explain aspects of a child's development or learning, and they can also help with planning and assessment.

The poster included in the pack reproduces some of the information from the cards and will help both you and parents become more confident with the EYFS.

Practice Guidance for the EYFS

This booklet gives detailed guidance on how all the different sections of the EYFS fit together. It also has information about phases of development and how children acquire knowledge and skills in each of the six areas of learning and development. (You can find more information about these areas in Chapter 6.) This information is designed to help practitioners develop and assess children's progress, and is split into four areas:

* development matters
* look, listen and note
* effective practice
* planning and resourcing.

The development pages should not be used as checklists, but rather as a guide to help you observe and assess each child. You should read across all four sections; this way you will get a better idea of things that you can do to meet each child's needs.

The Pre-school Expansion Programme (Northern Ireland)

A review of the effectiveness of pre-school education in Northern Ireland was instigated in 2004 with the aim of providing a full year of pre-school education for every child whose parents wish it.

The Pre-school Expansion Programme is part of the government's wider policy to provide an integrated and consistent range of care and education services to meet the needs of the youngest children and their parents. The research carried out for the 2004 review resulted in a curriculum for pre-school children that takes into consideration the characteristics and needs of the pre-school child and provides opportunities, through play, to develop learning that is associated with:

* the arts
* language development
* early mathematical experiences
* personal, social and emotional development
* physical development and movement
* the world around us.

Birth to Three – Supporting Our Youngest Children/A Curriculum Framework for Children 3 to 5 (Scotland)

Birth to Three

This approach looks above all at the role of the practitioner and is organised around three key features of practice which should be established:

* relationships
* responsive care
* respect.

Table 3.2 shows the key considerations of this approach.

Key feature	Key considerations
Establishing effective relationships	• Providing opportunities for the child to establish warm and affectionate bonds with significant people • Providing opportunities for the child to interact with others, both adults and children • Maintaining respectful and inclusive partnerships between all those involved with the child • Developing environments that promote security and consistency • Developing environments that promote trust and understanding
Establishing responsive care	• Building a knowledge of the individual child • Building an understanding of the needs and dispositions of each child • Ensuring adults are interested, appreciative and affectionate • Using flexible, relaxed and personalised approaches • Working to enhance respect and sensitivity
Establishing **respect**	• Valuing diversity, in terms of each child's language, faith and family circumstance and ethnic background • Respecting children's different experiences • Being sensitive to and understanding differences, to ensure fairness, equality and opportunity

Table 3.2: Key features of Birth to Three in Scotland.

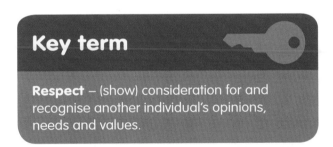

Key term

Respect – (show) consideration for and recognise another individual's opinions, needs and values.

A Curriculum Framework for Children 3 to 5

The current Scottish curriculum is based on five areas of learning:

- emotional, personal and social development
- communication and language
- knowledge and understanding of the world
- expressive and aesthetic development
- physical development and movement.

It is intended that each setting has its own approach to delivering the curriculum, including the experiences that children are offered and the ways in which parents are involved. Settings should build on children's prior learning experiences before they commence pre-school education. The Scottish Consultative Council on the Curriculum is constantly reviewing pre-school provision. The Curriculum Framework is based on the fundamental principle of equality of opportunity, with effective learning and teaching taking place in an atmosphere of mutual trust, respect and security.

The Foundation Phase (Wales)

Desirable Learning Outcomes for Children's Learning before Compulsory School Age

In 2000 the Qualifications, Curriculum and Assessment Authority for Wales (ACCAC) published Desirable Outcomes for Children's Learning before Compulsory School Age. The Welsh Assembly has a ten-year strategy called 'The Learning Country' and has reviewed Early Years education. As a result of the review the Foundation Phase for children from 3 to 7 years has been implemented.

The Desirable Learning Outcomes form part of the Foundation Phase for children from 3 to 7 years. Early Years education is usually provided on a part-time basis for children aged 3–4 and full-time for those between 4 and 5 years. The Desirable Learning Outcomes are divided into seven areas:

- Personal and Social Development, Well-Being and Cultural Diversity
- Knowledge and Understanding of the World
- Mathematical Development
- Language, Literacy and Communication Skills
- Welsh Language Development
- Physical Development
- Creative Development.

More information can be obtained from the video *Play Learn Grow: Working in Early Years, Childcare and Play*, published by the Department for Children, Education, Lifelong Learning and Skills or by accessing the website from the Hotlinks section (see page 3).

Think about it

There are many similarities between the curricula offered in England, Northern Ireland, Scotland and Wales. One key feature is the emphasis on positive relationships and the use of observations and assessments in day-to-day practice to help practitioners plan and develop appropriate experiences and activities for children in their care.

The National Curriculum

Home-based childcarers are often employed to care for children before and after school and during school holidays. Quite often these will be children that you cared for before they started full-time schooling and you will know them well. So that you can support the development, growth and learning of school-age children it is important that you have some understanding of what they will be doing at school.

Children between the ages of 5 and 11 attending state primary schools all study the same nine subjects

— referred to in England and Wales as the National Curriculum. Scotland and Northern Ireland have their own, similar versions. The National Curriculum also covers subjects studied by children in state secondary schools, but they do not all study the same nine subjects. The nine subjects for children aged 5–11 are:

- English
- Mathematics
- Science
- Physical Education
- Technology
- History
- Geography
- Art
- Music.

The National Curriculum is divided into four Key Stages (KS):

- Key Stage 1 for children from 5 to 7 years
- Key Stage 2 for children from 7 to 11 years
- Key Stage 3 for children from 11 to 14 years
- Key Stage 4 for children from 14 to 16 years.

Creative development is as vital as development in other areas. What creative activities do you do with the children you care for?

The National Curriculum was first introduced into schools in 1988 to ensure that all schools provided a consistent standard of education. Each subject is divided into attainment targets, or levels, so that children can be assessed against the targets. All state schools must offer all nine subjects (plus Welsh in Wales) to all the children. The only exception to this is for children who have a statement of special educational needs (SEN).

Like any other form of educational provision the National Curriculum is constantly being assessed and examined. Teachers are constantly assessing the children in their classes and more formal assessment is carried out in the form of Standard Assessment Tasks (SATs). Currently children take SATs at the end of KS 1 (Year 2) – in England only, but there are moves to drop these – and also at the end of KS 2 (in Year 6) and KS 3 (in Year 9).

Working with mixed age groups

Most home-based childcarers do not just care for one age group of children. For example, in any one working day registered childminders often care for school-age children before and after school, and also babies and toddlers. Nannies will often take care of siblings across different age groups. Planning and providing care for mixed age groups can be very stimulating; but at the same time it is important for the home-based childcarer to have flexible routines and practices that can accommodate the different needs of the children.

It can be quite a juggling act to organise the rest time for a baby, collect one child from nursery/pre-school, organise mealtimes, take a different child to nursery, do a school pick-up and remember important information to share with the parents.

Planning activities for mixed age groups can be challenging. How do you approach this?

It is important to remember that all children develop at different rates and that their care needs will change as they develop. Therefore, while care should be consistent and of the highest quality, the home-based childcarer must be prepared to adapt in order to meet children's changing needs.

Think about it

Registered childminders provide almost four times as many out-of-school places in England and Wales compared to the places available in clubs for school-aged children. Part of the NCMA's vision for 2015 is that registered home-based childcarers will provide at least one in three childcare places for children from birth to 14.

With the development of 'wraparound' care and extended schools, more and more home-based childcarers, particularly registered childminders, are becoming involved in the care of school-aged children. Some Children's Centres are actively seeking the support of registered childminders in providing this care. Get in touch with your local Children's Centre for more information about this service in your area.

As with any age group of children it is vital that the care that you offer reflects their individual needs. For example, school-age children will be able to take responsibility for many aspects of their personal care with minimal supervision from the carer.

Childcare practitioners must also take into consideration and support the growing need for independence, especially in older children.

It is helpful for the child if you can make yourself aware of the curriculum they are following in school. If you have some knowledge of the subjects within the curriculum, you will be in a better position to help with homework. This is not to suggest that activities and experiences that you plan are linked into a specific curriculum — that is the role of teachers in school — but you will be far better able to support the holistic development of school-age children if you have some understanding of what they are doing in school.

Outings can provide opportunities for activities involving mixed age groups.

Keys to good practice

Activities

Some suggested activities for before and after school are:

- preparing a packed lunch or snack if after school, breakfast if before

- a selection of resources and activities, such as hand-held electronic games, small construction sets and short stories to read, can be available; things that do not take much time to clear away or complete.

Plan to do some 'thinking games' such as:

- 'I-spy' – especially on the way to and from school

- asking each other questions to guess the identity of a famous person or place where they cannot answer yes or no.

These games and activities can be carried on after school.

- If a child wants to talk about their day, make sure that you can give them your undivided attention.

- Make sure that there is somewhere quiet where a child can recharge after a busy day, perhaps by watching the television or a DVD for a short time, listening to music or reading.

- If you have agreed with the child's parents that they will start homework activities, make sure there is a suitable place for the child to work. Do not forget to let the parents know what their child has done, or maybe needs help with.

Case study: Sharon's observation and planning

It was coming up to Bonfire Night and Sharon, a registered childminder, planned for the children – aged from 2 years 3 months to 5 years 6 months – to make firework pictures with glitter pens, sparkly paper, glue sticks and wax crayons. Sharon supervised the activity, but was able to make written notes on how one of the children, aged 2 years 10 months, used the materials. She observed that this child had difficulty using the glitter pens.

- It would be very easy to decide not to use glitter pens with this child again for a while, but Sharon felt that was not meeting his needs. Why do you think she felt this?
- How could Sharon use the information from this observation to inform her planning for future seasonal activities?

Find it out

There are several alternative curricula that offer appropriate experiences and activities for children. Find out about:
- HighScope
- Montessori
- Steiner.

The Common Core of Skills and Knowledge for the Children's Workforce

As a result of Every Child Matters a common set of skills and knowledge was developed for everyone working with children, young people and families. The Common Core sets out six areas of expertise for the whole of the children's workforce to practise within their roles. These are:

- effective communication and engagement
- child and young person development
- safeguarding and promoting the welfare of the child
- supporting transitions
- multi-agency working
- sharing information.

The Common Core reflects a set of values that promote equality, respect diversity and challenge stereotypes, helping to improve life chances for all children and young people and to provide more effective and integrated services. It acknowledges the rights of children and young people and the role that parents, carers and families play in helping children and young people achieve the five outcomes identified in Every Child Matters.

All the Common Core skills are covered in the full Level 3 Diploma for the Children and Young People's Workforce, and many of them are also covered in this book. For example, safeguarding and promoting the welfare of the child is covered in Chapters 4 and 9 and sharing information is included in Chapters 2 and 5.

Each of the skills has a clear definition and breakdown of the essential skills and knowledge required. You can find this information by accessing the website from the Hotlinks section (see page 3).

Case study: Chris's Common Core skills

Chris, a registered childminder, signed up for a course with his local authority called 'Supporting Children's Learning through ICT'. In the information that was sent about this course, Chris noticed that it was mapped to the Common Core skills and that it covered children and young people's development and sharing information.

- If you have signed up for training, have a look at the information about the course and see if it is mapped to the Common Core skills.

4. ESTABLISHING A SAFE AND HEALTHY HOME-BASED ENVIRONMENT

If you are to take your responsibilities seriously and be professional, it is essential that you understand how to keep all children safe at all times and how to prevent accidents. Accidents can, and do, happen — that is life — but there are important things you can do to reduce the chances of an accident happening to you or to the children you are caring for.

This chapter covers:

- supervising children
- risk assessment
- safe equipment and resources
- hygiene practices and waste disposal
- the storage and preparation of food
- the care of animals
- the appropriate responses to illnesses, allergies, incidents and accidents
- storage of medicines and other hazardous materials.

- This chapter links to Learning Outcome 2: Understand how to establish a safe and healthy home-based environment for children.
- All assessment criteria (2.1 to 2.5) for this learning outcome are covered, and guidance is given for CACHE Assessment Task 5.
- This chapter also links to Children and Young People's Core units CYP 3.1 to 3.7 of the Level 3 Diploma for the Children and Young People's Workforce.

Key terms

Environment – the surrounding, setting or situation in which you work and care for children.
Supervision – control, management or command of a situation or other individual(s).
Equipment – includes all toys, utensils, furniture, fittings and materials that may be used with or by children (or others).

Supervising children

Anyone who looks after other people's children under the age of 8 years, in their own home, for financial reward and for over two hours a day must be registered with the relevant regulatory body in their home country and they must meet minimum standards of care. In England, this is the Early Years Directorate of Ofsted; in Wales, the Care and Social Services Inspectorate (CSSIW); in Scotland, the Scottish Commission for the Regulation of Care; and in Northern Ireland, the local Health and Social Services Trust. This is a legal requirement under the Children Act (1989 and 2004). Any **environment** where children are cared for must be safe and secure, and the people caring for the children should have taken every possible action to prevent accidents and reduce risks.

As a registered childminder, responsibility for the safety and well-being of children in your care lies completely with you. In order to meet this responsibility – indoors and outside your setting, as well as out and about – you must understand how to supervise children. This does not mean that you are constantly watching every child, because that would be impossible. However, the amount of **supervision** you give a child depends on a number of factors.

- Their stage of development – a lively, curious toddler will need more supervision than an 8-year-old just back from school.
- What they are doing – a 3-year-old cutting pictures from a magazine will need a different level of supervision compared to a sleeping baby.
- Where they are – a visually impaired child may need more supervision when away from your home, such as in a park.

- Changes in the environment or surroundings – wet or icy weather may make outdoor play **equipment** slippery and so children playing outdoors may need more supervision than when indoors.

Supervision of children means that you are aware of what they are doing all of the time; in other words you can see and/or hear them. There are three types of supervision.

1. Constant supervision is when you are watching a child all the time, perhaps in close contact with them. You might have constant supervision of a young child when they are using scissors or a knife to cut fruit.
2. Close supervision is when you watch a child most of the time, but are not actually involved. However, you are ready to step in at any time should their well-being be threatened. You may have close supervision of a child on a climbing frame or in a paddling pool.
3. General supervision is when you are aware of what the child is doing and checking on them regularly, keeping an attentive eye from a distance. An example of general supervision could be when children are playing on the carpet together or when a baby is sleeping.

Supervision and safety outside the home

It is very important that the area outside the home where the children are cared for is safe. The regulatory body's inspectors will check the outside areas for safety and may make conditions on your registration. For example, it is possible to be registered as a childminder but only allowing children to access the inside areas of your house.

Case study: Supervision solutions

Caitlin, a registered childminder, cares for three 8-year-olds after school. When asked about supervising older children she says that she can open a hatchway between the kitchen and playroom so she can observe the children while she prepares a snack for them. When she needs to go to the toilet, she tells the children that she needs privacy, but leaves the door ajar so that she can still hear them. Think about your own practice.

- What do you do if you need to prepare snacks in the kitchen and the children are watching a DVD in a different room?
- What do you do if you need the toilet?
- How can you maintain constant supervision of children of different ages?

Keys to good practice

Supervision and safety in the garden

- Make sure that children do not play outside unsupervised.

- Make sure that all garden tools, equipment and any chemicals are stored away from children. These should really be in a locked shed, garage or other building.

- Make sure that all paving slabs, such as on patios and pathways, are firm and not loose or chipped.

- Make sure that any fences, especially wooden, are undamaged and firm.

- Children should not be allowed to climb on to fences or play equipment that is not designed for this purpose, such as play houses.

- Make sure that equipment and resources are not broken or damaged and cannot harm the children. For example, check for sharp edges, loose parts and missing pieces.

- Make sure that any large play equipment, such as swings, slides and climbing frames, are set up properly and that the ground underneath has safety mats or a safety surface so that children do not land on a hard surface.

- Make sure that children cannot get out of the garden. Is there a secure gate or fence?

- Make sure that the children cannot get at any rubbish, dustbins/wheelie bins or recycling containers.

- If there are pets, make sure that areas where the children play are free of pets' food and waste. Never leave children and pets together unsupervised.

- Cover or fence off any areas where there is water, including water butts and ponds.

- Cover sand pits when not in use, to stop animals getting into them.

- Do not leave a trailing clothes line outside; make sure it is securely fastened out of reach of children.

- Make sure that any plants are not harmful to children if touched or eaten.

Is this practitioner doing all she can to supervise the child?

Think about it

Check all plants that you have, both in the garden and in the house.

1. Find out which plants in the garden and indoors are poisonous to children.
2. Find out which plants have leaves, sap or flowers that could cause skin irritations.
3. Write down what you have found out and keep it somewhere safe so that you can refer to it in the future.

A good place to find out this information is at your local library or garden centre or from the Internet.

Poisonous plants in your garden and indoors should be removed, but many people find this aspect of safety a contentious issue. What can you do about any poisonous plants, shrubs and trees in a neighbour's garden that overhang into your garden? Discuss this with other course members, other home-based childcarers and the neighbours involved.

Supervising children when out and about

You may have to transport children in your own car or on public transport. If you are a nanny a car may be provided for your use. You may also want to take children out in buggies or prams or for a walk along the road to post a letter, go to a pre-school group or nursery, collect older children from school or go to the shops. In these cases, you could find yourself having to cope with a lively toddler and a baby in a buggy while trying to cross a busy road.

Permissions

Remember to obtain the parents' written permission to take children out. It is also good practice to tell them if you are planning a special trip, for example, during the school holidays, or going somewhere different from usual. Written permission is always the best practice.

Advance planning

Think about what you need to have with you when you go out with the children. This will depend on where you are planning to go and how long you plan to be out. You need to take with you some form of personal

How can this practitioner keep the children safe?

identification, relevant emergency telephone numbers, a mobile phone, a first aid kit and any other items you feel are necessary, such as the child's medication. A **risk assessment** should be carried out where possible.

> ## Key term
>
> **Risk assessment** – a risk is a possible danger or threat to safety. To assess means to measure, evaluate or make a judgement. Risk assessment therefore is about careful consideration of possible dangers or threats to safety and taking appropriate action.

If you are planning a trip to a park or outdoor play area, if possible choose one with special areas for younger children. Bark chippings or matting under play equipment is preferable to grass and you should check that the equipment is well maintained. Keep a look-out for broken glass, syringes, litter and dog mess. Parental permissions will be needed where large play equipment is involved.

Supervising and taking children in your own car

If you are going to use your own car you must be aware of the following points.

- Your car must have valid road tax.
- Your car must have a valid MOT certificate if appropriate.
- Make sure that the car insurance is valid for business purposes and that it is fully comprehensive – the National Childminding Association (NCMA) can advise you on this.
- All adults must wear seat belts, in the front and in the back.
- All children should have a seat; never allow a child to stand up in the car or sit on someone's knee.
- Children in the car must wear secure child restraints appropriate for the age, weight and size of the child.
- Never put a rear-facing baby seat in the front if there is a passenger airbag.
- Child locks should be used on the doors.

- Make sure that children get out of the car on the pavement side and not on the road side of the car.
- Think about how you drive – be careful and alert. Set a good example to the children when dealing with other road users.

You need to think very carefully about taking the children that you care for in someone else's car. Ultimately you are responsible for the children's safety and well-being and if you cannot be absolutely sure that the other driver has adequate insurance in place, and is a competent and careful driver, then you should decline to travel in that person's car.

Supervising children when using public transport

If you use public transport there are a number of points you will need to consider.

- Make sure that the children stand well back from the edge of the pavement if at a bus stop or on a station platform.
- Make sure young children are wearing safety harnesses (personal restraints) and that older children are taught to hold your hand.
- Plan your journey carefully so that you know where the bus stops are, which platform the train arrives at and leaves from, and how to get up and down stairs or across busy roads.
- Make sure that when on the bus or train the children sit next to you at all times; if there are no seats left, make sure that if the children are standing they are not in danger of falling over and that, if possible, they can hold on to you or to a safety rail.

Supervising children when out walking and road safety

When out walking with children you must be very alert and aware of their safety. There are many things that you can do to teach children how to keep safe; even young children can be made aware of dangers and begin to learn about keeping themselves safe. Walking along a road is a potentially dangerous situation for a child and all children will need constant supervision.

Think about it

Did you know that every day a child under 5 years old is killed or seriously injured on our roads? Brake is a road safety charity which aims to reduce the number of horrifying deaths and injuries of young children that happen every day. They organise special events to provide young children with their first road safety lesson and raise awareness among parents and practitioners. (Their details are in Useful addresses at the back of the book.)

Do you have an agreed meeting point with older children?

Keys to good practice

Supervising children out and about

It is good practice to use personal restraints on toddlers and young children. Many types are available, including reins, harnesses and straps that have a wristband at both ends for the child and the adult. Whatever you choose it should carry a Kitemark or other recognised approved safety symbol. (You can find for more information about safety symbols on page 69.)

Show the children how to cross a road safely and set a good example to them when crossing roads. Never hurry or cross in a place where you cannot see traffic coming in both directions. Always use a zebra or pelican crossing, if available. If there is no crossing, choose a safe place where you have good all-round visibility. Traditionally, children were taught to look right, left and right again, and, if clear, then it was safe to cross. However this does not work for one-way streets or for very busy roads in today's towns. The best thing to teach children when crossing a road is:

- stop, look and listen

- only cross when you are sure it is safe, and always use a pelican or zebra crossing if there is one nearby
- never run across the road.

Treat buggies and prams like all other equipment you use with the children. They should be checked regularly, especially the brakes and folding mechanisms, and kept in good working order. They should be fitted with harnesses, which you should always use. Do not have the buggy or pram sticking out into the road while you wait to cross. It could be hit by a vehicle, and the fumes from vehicles could affect the child.

In large places, such as parks or shopping centres, you should arrange with older children what to do if you get separated. Some practitioners and children look for a prominent building or special point, such as an information desk or a park bench, and agree to meet there. Young children should always be wearing personal restraints, such as safety harnesses, so that they cannot wander off and become separated from you.

Stranger danger

Children need to know what to do if a stranger approaches them. Talk to them about 'stranger danger' and work out what they should do. Help the children to understand that not everyone they meet, however friendly they seem, can be trusted. They should be taught not to speak to strangers and never to go off with someone they do not know. Do not frighten or scare the children, but firmly explain to them how to cope in such situations. Remember to discuss with the children's parents what you and the children have decided in such cases, so that the parents can use the same tactics with the children.

Organisations such as Kidscape produce useful leaflets and books to help teach children ways of keeping themselves safe. The National Society for the Prevention of Cruelty to Children (NSPCC) also has useful materials. (You can find details of their websites on pages 187–193.)

Case study: Feeding the ducks

Anna has been a registered childminder for six months. Apart from her own 6-year-old, she has responsibility for twins aged 2 and a half. During the school holidays Anna and all the children often walk to the local park to feed the ducks and play in the adventure playground.

- How can Anna make sure that the walk to the park is stress free for everyone?
- What can she do to make sure that all the children have fun and remain safe while feeding the ducks?
- What particular dangers should Anna be aware of in the adventure playground?
- What should she take with her in case of an emergency?

Think about your answers and discuss them with other childcarers.

Link to assessment

AC 2.2

Explain the principles of safe supervision of children in the home-based setting and off site.

CACHE Task 5
You are asked to produce a leaflet for carers, which has five sections. The **second** section is about the principles of safe supervision of children in the home-based setting and off site.

- Think about who your leaflet is intended for as this will affect the language and professional style that you use.
- How big should your leaflet be? Have a look at some of the information leaflets at your health centre or in a supermarket to get ideas on size and layout.
- A principle is a standard or a rule that you should follow in your practice, so identify the rules of safe supervision both inside and outside your home and away from your setting.
- Remember every setting is different; so, while it may be good practice to share ideas with your peers, what you actually decide to put in your leaflet may be different.

A professional discussion could take place between yourself and an assessor where you explain the principles of safe supervision. Your assessor could set you a series of questions for you to think about, and your answers would provide the basis of later discussions.

Risk assessment

It is good practice to undertake a risk assessment for each of the rooms the children will have access to and for your outdoor area.

Look at the following picture of a typical living room.

1. How many risks to children's safety can you spot?
2. Can you say why each one is a risk and what could you do about it?
3. How might you have to adjust the environment if you were caring for toddlers, children aged 5 to 7 and older children?
4. Walk around the rooms that the children will use. If you are caring for young children it is useful to get down on your knees and look at the room from a child's perspective; it can look quite different!

5. For each room complete a risk assessment exercise, listing the possible risks. Ask yourself: Why is this a danger? What can I do about it?

You may find it useful to record this information in a table or chart.

Think about it

You must remember that making your working environment safe is not just about checking for dangers and risks. It is also about being on your guard and aware of possible hazards at all times. It also involves teaching children ways of keeping safe by setting a good example yourself in the ways you work and behave.

Every room is full of potential risks to children. How many can you spot in this picture? How many can you spot around your setting?

Can you identify these symbols?

Safety symbols

The Kitemark is the symbol of the British Standards Institution to show that an item has been independently tested and certified as well as being of high quality and safe. Kitemarks can only be put on items that have been tested by BSI.

A safety mark in itself does not guarantee the safety of the person using the item; it only means that the item has met certain safety standards when manufactured. A Kitemark proves that it has been independently tested by BSI and is regularly re-tested to ensure it is consistently produced to high standards of quality and safety. You should always follow the manufacturer's instructions for any equipment you use.

The CE Marking means that a manufacturer has verified that the product complies with all relevant essential requirements of the applicable legislation, or, if stipulated in the legislation, has had it examined by an authorised third party. Only certain product categories are required to bear the CE Marking and these include toys, medical devices, measuring equipment, PCs, mobile phones and light bulbs.

Look out also for the Lion Mark. The Lion Mark

indicates that a toy had been made by a member of the British Toy & Hobby Association (BTHA) and shows the member's commitment to adhere to the BTHA Code of Practice, which includes rules covering ethical and safe manufacture of toys, toy safety, a ban on counterfeit goods, an assurance to market responsibly, a commitment to improving sustainability and a desire to promote the value of all play. Consumers can be assured that a toy which bears the Lion Mark has been made by a member who believes in making quality toys.

Before you buy any toy or piece of equipment it is good practice to look for one of the safety symbols or logos shown on this page. Some equipment or fittings in your home will have a BS number printed on it; for example, furniture that has glass incorporated into it should have a label with BS 73767 and BS 7449.8. This means that the glass has been approved to British Safety Standards.

Equipment for use with children

- Cots and beds
- Highchairs and baby seats
- Potties and toilet equipment
- Toys:
    - climbing frames, swings and large outdoor toys
    - wheeled, and push and pull toys
    - electric and battery toys
    - Computers
    - Other toys
- Televisions, DVDS, Blu-ray, iPods, Wii, Xbox
- Buggies, prams and car seats including booster cushions
- Baby harnesses
- Safety locks and gates

Do you have all the equipment you will need?

Preparing and making your home safe for children

Keys to good practice

Safety within the home-based setting

- Never allow children of any age into any room at any time without being supervised. (However, you must respect the privacy of older children when using the toilet.)

- Check furniture and appliances for sharp edges, such as the cooker, washing machine, table tops, shelving, and protect them if needed.

Continued

Continued

- Use short, coiled flexes on electrical equipment and fix wires and cables to walls, or to floors or skirting boards, so that they do not trail.

- Check that the plugs on electrical appliances are not cracked; replace them if they are.

- Make sure that wires or cables from electrical appliances are not frayed or worn.

- When checking any electrical appliance be extra careful. Do not put yourself at risk. Switch off at the socket before you touch the appliance. Make sure your hands are always dry before handling anything electrical. Never put your fingers or anything other than the plug into an electrical socket.

- Fit child-resistant socket covers on all power points.

- Make sure that all sharp and small objects are kept out of sight and reach of children.

- Have a fire blanket in the kitchen, and ideally a fire extinguisher in another part of the house. Make sure that you know how to use them.

- Make sure that safety gates used across doorways and stairs are fitted and fastened securely.

- Try to keep the floor space as free as possible, make sure that rugs and mats will not slip or cause a child to trip and fall. Mark big areas of glass with stickers, such as glass doors, and make sure that this glass is either safety glass or covered with safety film.

- Fit window locks.

- Make sure that there are no trailing cords from curtains or blinds.

- Make sure that all areas of the home are well lit, especially on stairs.

- Make sure that heat sources, such as electric or gas fires, have fireguards securely fixed around them.

- Fit a smoke alarm.

- Have a fire drill for the home and practise it regularly with the children at different times of the day.

- Buy toys and equipment that have a recognised safety symbol on them, such as the Kitemark or the Lion Mark.

How can you set about making your home ready for children and making it a safe place for them?

You need to work out a safety checklist for each room that the children will be using. Start with one room at a time and make the job manageable.

If you are caring for the child in their own home you will have to discuss safety issues with the parents and agree safe practices.

Let's start with some general suggestions to prevent accidents in rooms most frequently used by children in the home.

Safety in the kitchen

- Keep doors to washing machines and tumble driers shut at all times.
- Keep oven doors shut and make sure that children cannot touch the oven door if it is hot.
- Make sure that children cannot reach the hob and that pan handles are turned away from the edge.
- Make sure that children cannot get hold of plastic bags, cleaning materials and alcohol. These should be kept out of sight and reach.
- Make sure that all hot objects, such as mugs, kettles, toasters, are positioned well away from the edge of work surfaces and kitchen units.

Safety in the dining room

- Avoid using table clothes that hang over the edge of the table.
- Never leave the children unsupervised while eating.
- Do not allow them to wander around when eating or drinking.
- Never leave a baby propped up with a feeding bottle.
- Never leave hot food or drinks unattended.
- Make sure that children can use cutlery safely and correctly. Do not allow children to play with knives and forks.
- Make sure that children can reach the table safely by using a highchair with a harness, specially designed booster seats or cushions.
- Keep alcohol out of sight and reach of children or in a securely fastened cupboard.
- Keep cigarettes, matches and lighters out of reach of children. (Note: You are not allowed to smoke while working with children.)

Safety in the play room or sitting room

- Keep the floor space as free as possible.
- Do not use pillows for children under 18 months; use a firm mattress.
- Store toys carefully; do not allow children to climb up and reach for things.
- Check all toys regularly for sharp edges and missing or broken pieces.
- Secure any doors that lead to outside areas.
- Do not put anything that can be climbed on under a window.

Safety in the hall and on the stairs

- Use securely fixed gates to prevent children climbing the stairs unattended. It is recommended that you use gates with the safety standard number BS 4125.
- Remove any toys or objects that have been left on the floor or stairs.
- Make sure that the hall and stairs are well lit.
- Check that carpets are not frayed or loose.
- Make sure that bannisters and balustrades are strong and firm and do not have any footholds for climbing; consider filling in gaps between rails.

Do you have a safety gate on your stairs?

Think about it

When working out your safety checklists, try to think of all of the safety issues in each room. For example, did you know that it is illegal to leave a child under 12 in a room with an open fire?

Safety in the bathroom and toilet

- Lock **medicines** and tablets away in a high cupboard.
- Keep cleaning materials and air fresheners out of reach of children.
- When running a bath or water for washing, turn on the cold water tap first and test the water before letting a child use it; it is recommended that you use a bath thermometer.
- Use a non-slip mat in the bath.
- Wet floors can be slippery and therefore dangerous, so wipe and dry wet floors.

Key term

Medicine – a remedy, tablet, pill, lotion or liquid that can help alleviate a medical or health problem.

Find it out

Further information on children's safety can be found on the websites of RoSPA, Brake, the NCMA and the Health and Safety Executive (HSE), and in the welfare requirements of the EYFS.

Safe equipment and resources

The equipment that you use in the home with children is another very important aspect of keeping children safe. It is your professional responsibility to choose equipment and toys that are safe and appropriate for use with the children you are caring for. If you are working in the child's own home, you may want to discuss with the parents which toys and pieces of equipment are safe and appropriate. You will need to reach agreement on what to do about items that you are not happy to use or allow the children access to.

Link to assessment   AC 2.4

Know where to obtain current guidance on health and safety risk assessment of the home-based work setting.

CACHE Task 5
You are asked to produce a leaflet for carers, which has five sections. The fourth section is about where you can obtain guidance on health and safety risk assessment of the home-based work setting. The Find it out feature (left) gives some sources of information. You can also use your local library, health centre Early Years team or other appropriate publications and websites.

Find it out

Check the RoSPA website and find out about their recommendation for a five-point harness for highchairs.

Keys to good practice

Equipment

- High chairs and baby seats must have securely fastened safety harnesses. These should also be adjustable so that they can still be comfortably and safely fastened around a baby as they grow.

- Highchairs should not wobble, the legs should be level and the whole chair should be stable. Table-mounted highchairs are not recommended as they are not stable.

- Baby seats should not be placed on table tops or work surfaces. There should be no loose pieces of fabric, coverings or broken pieces. A young child could easily put small pieces into their mouth and choke.

- Children should not be left alone in either a highchair or a baby seat.

- Baby walkers can be very dangerous pieces of equipment as babies can easily overbalance in them. There is evidence that baby walkers actually hinder children's development and home-based childcarers are advised not to use this piece of equipment.

- Cots and beds are potential areas for accidents, especially as children can fall out

Continued

Continued

of them. Do not allow children to play on cots and beds – they should be considered as places to rest and sleep.

🔑 Cots with sides that slide down should have secure fastenings that cannot be undone by little fingers. Beds for young children may have side rails to prevent the child falling out, but these can often be used by children for climbing.

🔑 Young children should never be put into a top bunk accessible only by a ladder.

🔑 Mattresses for cots and beds should fit snugly around the frame of the bed or cot. Look for the Kitemark or BS number on the label to check if the mattress meets safety standards. The covering and filling of the mattress should also be flame retardant and should have a label to say so.

🔑 It is not good practice to use pillows for children and babies younger than 18 months; a firm mattress is usually enough.

🔑 Separate bedding should be used for each child.

🔑 There are many novelty potties and toilet seats available to encourage children to develop bladder and bowel control. Most of these are made of plastic, therefore you must check and make sure that the plastic has not cracked or split.

🔑 Toilet seats designed for children should fit firmly over the adult toilet seat, and do not forget that children using these seats will also need a step so that they can reach the toilet safely.

🔑 Safety gates and locks are a very important part of equipment. Gates across doorways and stairs make it so much easier for you and the children to stay together. All gates should fit securely and the fastening should be firm and childproof.

🔑 It is a good idea to fit window locks to all windows in the rooms that children will be using. There is a wide range of window locks available, in a range of colours and finishes, so you can match them to your décor. Locks can be bought from hardware and DIY stores. Most are fitted very easily. Remember to look for the safety standard labels. (Note: Keys must be accessible in case of emergency.)

🔑 Buggies, prams and car seats may not always belong to you, as some parents may bring their child to you in one and leave it at your home. Even so, you must check that there are no broken or damaged pieces or parts and that the harnesses are secure and will fasten and hold the child safely. You must let the parents know if their buggy, pram or car seat is putting their child at risk, because it is not safe.

🔑 Many childcare practitioners use television, computers, videos, DVDs and tapes to support children they care for, to help their learning and at times of rest and quiet.

🔑 The television, video and tape recorder, DVD player, computer or stereo should not have trailing cables or wires and should be put where they cannot be pushed or knocked over by a child.

🔑 Make sure that the battery compartments of remote controls for these pieces of equipment cannot be opened by children. Batteries are not playthings and can be very dangerous to a child if sucked or broken.

🔑 If you buy or rent DVDs, it is always good practice to watch or listen to them first, so that you know what they are about and to make sure they are suitable for the children in your care.

Toy safety

Toys can often be the cause of accidents. For example, toys left lying on the floor can easily be tripped over by someone. See below for information on toy safety.

Keys to good practice

Toy safety

- Make sure toys are safe. A European directive was introduced into British law by the Toys Safety Regulations 1995 as part of the Consumer Protection Act. Despite this, illegal and unsafe toys can still be found in many places, so shop with care. Look for the CE Marking and the Lion Mark (see page 69). If you are using toys in the child's home it is good practice to discuss toy safety with parents.

- Check regularly for possible hazards – some childcarers check every piece of equipment used by the children at the end of each working day. It will be up to you to decide how often you check but remember that accidents can happen when you least expect them.

- Make sure that toys are suitable for the age of the children. Toys that are designed for older children should be stored away from younger children when not in use, and toys with small pieces should not be within reach of younger children who might put things in their mouths and choke.

- Outdoor toys and other equipment, such as climbing frames, must be checked regularly for damage caused by the weather. Make sure that slides and swings are tough and will not collapse.

- Wheeled toys such as bikes, scooters and pedal cars must also be checked regularly to make sure that there are no loose parts, and that the toys have not become dangerously worn.

- Many toys are battery powered, which is usually safe, provided the batteries are used correctly. Batteries should always be fitted correctly and covered up. Spent batteries should be disposed of carefully, especially smaller mercury disc batteries. These could easily be swallowed by young children or find their way into ears and noses. Most batteries can now be recycled.

- All toys should be bought or borrowed from recognised outlets.

- Try to avoid toys with loose pile fabric or hair, as young children can choke on such material.

- If there are toys with many small parts or pieces, make sure that young children cannot get at them, so keep them in secure boxes or containers.

- Make sure children are supervised appropriately when using loose ribbons on toys and long ties on dressing-up clothes. Children can get ties and ribbons fastened tightly round their necks, with dreadful consequences.

If in doubt, do not use the toy.

Think about it

Have a look at the toys and equipment that you are planning to use. Can you decide which things are suitable for:

- all the children in your care
- children under 2 years old
- children between 3 and 5
- children between 5 and 7
- children between 7 and 11
- children above 11?

Make a checklist like the one shown here to write down your decisions. Note: You need to be aware of each individual child's stage of development when considering your list.

Toy/ equipment	Age group	Safety notes
LEGO™	4 plus	Keep away from the babies as they could choke on the bits. Keep in a plastic tub with a well-fitting lid

This will help you to become more aware of possible dangers and make your personal safety checklist more effective. If you are unsure about any toy or piece of equipment, it is always good practice to be overcautious, rather than take a chance that it will be all right.

Link to assessment

AC 2.3

Identify ways of ensuring that equipment is suitable for children and meets safety requirements

CACHE Task 5
The third section of your information leaflet should explain ways of ensuring that the equipment you use with children is suitable and meets safety requirements. You could include the safety symbols that you would look for on equipment and explain what they mean.

Look at the checklist suggested above; this should help you identify ways to make sure that your equipment is safe. Read again the section on safety symbols and ensure you understand exactly what they mean.

If you are not producing a leaflet to meet these assessment criteria, you will need to think how you could make sure that your assessor is aware that you can identify ways of making sure equipment is safe and that it meets safety requirements. You could make a list or a chart where you categorise your equipment and include a risk assessment.

Hygiene practices and waste disposal

As a professional home-based childcarer you and your setting are open to scrutiny. This may be from parents, Ofsted (or other regulatory organisation) or professionals such as health visitors, medical personnel or social workers.

It is very important that you have high standards of personal hygiene. It is also vital that your setting is a safe and hygienic environment for children and that you do all you can to prevent the spread of **infection**. As part of the registration process your workplace will be checked for cleanliness.

Key term

Infection – a disease, illness, virus or bug.

The children will copy and learn from the way you behave. For example, washing your hands after going to the toilet and before preparing food, or covering your mouth when coughing will teach the children good hygiene practices. You should be a positive role model at all times. You will need to establish routines that encourage personal hygiene and help children learn safe ways to care for themselves.

Hand washing

1 Massage palm to palm.

2 Rub right palm over back of left hand and vice versa.

3 Rub palm to palm with fingers interlaced.

4 Massage backs of fingers in opposing palm.

5 Rotate right thumb clasped in left palm and vice versa.

6 Rotate fingers of left hand in right palm and vice versa.

7 Rinse hands with water.

This is the best way to ensure you are washing your hands thoroughly.

Washing your hands and teaching children to wash their hands properly is one of the most effective ways of preventing the spread of infection.

- Wet hands thoroughly in hot water before applying soap. Ideally this should be liquid as soap bars retain bacteria if they sit in water.
- Vigorously massage both hands with the lather, paying special attention to the fingertips, thumbs and between the fingers, and also under any rings worn.
- Rinse your hands well under running water and dry them with a paper towel.

The hand-washing process should take no less than 30 seconds.

It is good hygiene practice to use disposable gloves when dealing with faeces, urine and blood, as well as washing your hands with hot water and soap.

Find it out

When do you wash your hands? Keep a written diary for one complete working day of how many times you wash your hands. Then check your diary with the figure on the following page and see if there are any times when you should have washed your hands and did not.

When you need to wash your hands.

Keeping the home environment clean

You must do everything possible to keep the home clean and hygienic to prevent the spread of infection. Children can easily pick up infections. Infection can be spread by transmission, such as touch, via droplets in the air (for example, coughs and sneezes) and movements of animals. It is also possible for infections to be carried on food, in water, on cuts and grazes and on fingers. The kitchen and bathroom are the rooms most likely to hide germs that cause infections and so must be kept thoroughly clean.

Keeping a clean home and workplace will stop germs from multiplying and reduce the spread of infection.

Using everyday things like soap and water and allowing in fresh air and sunlight will destroy many germs. Cleaning products will also help you to keep the home germ-free, but remember that many of these are harmful to children and pets and must be kept out of reach at all times, even locked away. Antiseptic cleaners and wipes are weak disinfectants and do help prevent germs from multiplying. However, they do not destroy germs and bacteria, and can be dangerous to children.

If you are caring for children in their own home you must discuss hygienic and healthy practices with the parents and make sure that the care and well-being of the children is paramount.

Keys to good practice

Keeping the home environment clean

- It is good practice to clean and disinfect floors, equipment and toys regularly. Many childcarers clean and disinfect kitchen and bathroom floors at least once a day.

- Make sure that you have good ventilation to help prevent the spread of infection.

- Highchairs and changing mats need to be cleaned every time they are used.

- Indoor rubbish bins must be kept covered and emptied at least once a day. Rubbish bins can be a source of germs and bacteria and for this reason it is very important to keep them thoroughly clean.

- Domestic pets and other animals should not be allowed in the kitchen. The much-loved family pet will bring in dirt and germs from outside no matter how careful you are.

- As well as keeping the bathroom floor clean, do not forget that germs can breed around damp towels and face cloths. It is good practice for each child to have their own towel and face cloth. These should be washed and thoroughly dried frequently. Many practitioners change the children's towels and face cloths each day.

- A soggy bar of soap can be a source of infection. Make sure any pieces of soap are clean and do not sit in a puddle of water on the wash basin. It might be better to use a dispenser with liquid soap. Remember to keep the dispenser clean as well.

- The toilet must be kept clean. Children should be taught to flush the toilet, each time they use it. They should be taught to put toilet tissue into the toilet carefully before they flush it. As children wash their hands after they have flushed the toilet, this means that the toilet handle is a source of potential infection, so make sure it is wiped and disinfected regularly. The toilet seat needs special attention, as does the actual bowl, both inside and out. If you have carpet around the toilet it could very quickly become smelly and a source of germs. Think about the flooring in the bathroom and consider a washable mat or floor covering around the toilet.

- Make sure that you wear disposable gloves when dealing with body fluids.

- Nappies and other soiled clothes or products should be disposed of hygienically. You can buy specially designed covered containers that wrap and seal nappies separately in anti-bacterial film. When the container is full the bag is lifted out and put in an outside bin. On the other hand, many practitioners use plastic bags for each item, fastened securely and then put in an outside bin. You need to decide what is best for you, as long as you dispose of nappies and other soiled items hygienically.

- Parents may decide that they want their child to wear terry cotton or other reusable nappies. Think about the pros and cons of using reusable nappies and talk to parents about how these will be kept hygienically when soiled and how they will be washed and dried.

Find it out

Imagine that someone in your family, or one of the children you are caring for, has developed cold sores.
How could you prevent the spread of the infection to others?
Make a note of your answer, and then read through this part of the unit again to check if you have the right answer.

The storage and preparation of food

Part of your job will be to prepare and give children food and drinks, whether snacks or full meals. The way that you prepare, cook and serve the food will help the children you care for to learn sensible eating habits, and should also encourage them to try out various foods.

If you are not very careful about how you prepare, store and handle food, you could pass on to the children many forms of food-borne illnesses. There are some very straightforward tips that you should always follow to ensure that the food you give the children is safe.

Keys to good practice

Storing food safely

- Cover all food that is left out.

- Check that the refrigerator is no higher than 5°C and that the freezer is set at ⁻18°C.

- Make sure that air can circulate around the refrigerator, and do not overfill it.

- Never refreeze food that has thawed out.

- Make sure that frozen food is completely thawed before using it.

- Never store raw meat or raw fish next to other food. Wrap it well and put it at the bottom of the fridge, preferably in leak-proof containers as it can leak or drip juices containing harmful bacteria on to foods stored below.

- Store cans and packets in a cool dry place (not above the cooker). Foods in cans should always be eaten within one year of purchase or before the expiry date on the label.

- Look carefully at the 'best before' dates on food, and do not risk eating food that is out of date. It is better to be safe than sorry.

- Do not keep food or juices in their cans once they have been opened as air can affect the quality of what is inside. It is good practice to transfer the contents to an airtight container and store in the fridge.

- Take care to protect fruit, vegetables and salads. Many people store salads in the fridge, but what about fruit and vegetables? These are often left out in the kitchen and can be touched by anything and anyone. This is a health risk, so always wash fruit and vegetables before eating if you are not going to peel them.

Preparing food

- Be careful not to cross-contaminate food. For example, do not use the same board to cut raw meat, chop vegetables and then slice bread. The juices from the meat can contaminate the other foods. In the same way do not use the same knives, plates or other utensils for different foods, unless they have been washed thoroughly.

- Do not thaw food on a kitchen work surface; use a leak-proof container and make sure the food is completely thawed through.

- Plastic chopping boards are easier to keep clean than wooden ones.

- You must follow the manufacturer's instructions on labels when thawing, heating or cooking food. Just as foods must be properly thawed, they must also be cooked thoroughly. Harmful bacteria are not destroyed until the food has been cooked to a temperature of 71°C (boiling point is 100°C).

The correct storage of food.

ncma
says...

The Food Standards Agency has produced a pack called 'Safer food, better business for childminders'. You can download a copy by accessing the website from the Hotlinks section (see page 3).

Keys to good practice

Safety at mealtimes

- You and the children should always wash your hands before preparing or eating food.

- Children should never be left unsupervised when preparing food or eating and drinking.

- If you are using knives and forks, make sure that you teach children safe ways to handle and use them. Do not let children wave cutlery around.

- Ensure children sit down when eating or drinking. This will reduce the risk of choking or tripping over.

Do you ensure children are sitting down when they eat or drink?

Case study: Tom's packed lunch

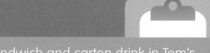

Jenny cares for Tom, aged 5, Ahmed, 3, and a baby of 8 months. She has to prepare Tom a packed lunch for school. Tom has decided that he wants a cheese sandwich, an orange that is peeled and cut up, and a carton drink. Jenny gets her wooden bread board and butters the bread; she uses the same knife and board to cut the cheese and the finished sandwich. She puts the sandwich and carton drink in Tom's lunch box. Jenny wipes the board with a cloth and then cuts up the orange, wraps it in plastic wrap and puts that next to the sandwich.

- How many times do you think Jenny has not followed good practice?
- Can you decide what she did wrong, and what should she have done?

Find it out

It is good practice to have a Basic Food Hygiene Certificate, which must be renewed every three years to make sure that you keep up to date. Check with your local authority what courses are available in your area.

General safety at mealtimes

Snack times and mealtimes can be very good learning opportunities for children, especially if they are involved with preparing the food. You must be a good role model so the children will learn good, safe practices.

The care of animals
Keeping children safe around animals

You need to make sure that the children in your care are not in danger from any animals kept in the home. There are often horrific stories in the newspapers about children who have been bitten and injured by dogs. In June 2010, sleeping 9-month-old twins were attacked in their London home by a fox. This was during a period of hot weather and the parents had left the patio doors open. Hamsters and rabbits can also bite, especially if children stick their fingers through the cage. Cats will scratch if play gets too boisterous.

Animals can be unpredictable in their behaviour, especially if provoked or hurt or if they sense danger. You can teach children how to care for and treat animals, but ultimately you are responsible for keeping the children safe.

As mentioned earlier, children should never be left alone with pets and other animals, no matter how tame and friendly you think the animals are, or how careful you think the children will be. Your elderly, much-loved dog might be the soppiest animal in the world around you, but might react violently to being touched by someone else when you are not there or to being among a lively, noisy group of young children.

- No childcarer should ever have a pet in the house that is not tolerant of children.
- You should teach children how to care for animals; encourage them, if appropriate, to clean out cages and feed the animals.
- Children should be taught to wash their hands after touching animals and not to kiss pets. It is not good practice to allow pets to lick faces.
- As with sick children, sick animals need time and special attention. You will need to consider this when caring for children. What will you do with the children if you have to take a sick cat to the vet? How would you make sure that a sick pet is properly isolated from the children you are caring for?
- Both children and pets need fresh air and exercise, so think about whether you have enough time to walk the dog and look after the children.
- Keep animal feeding bowls separate from those used by humans and wash them separately.
- Remember to clean up any 'pet accidents' straight away and dispose of everything hygienically.
- Check outside play areas for animal faeces before children have access. It might be neighbouring animals rather than your pet that use your garden as a toilet.
- If you or members of your household keep exotic pets, make sure they are housed securely and appropriately so that children cannot get access to them.

Case study: Hamsters can bite

Jenny, Tom (5) and Ahmed (3) are cleaning out the hamster cage on the patio. The telephone rings and Jenny tells Tom and Ahmed to wait until she comes back. While Jenny is on the phone, Tom runs in to tell her that the hamster has bitten Ahmed's finger and that he is crying.

- How could Jenny have prevented Ahmed being bitten?
- What should she have done about the telephone call?

The appropriate responses to illnesses, allergies, incidents and accidents

Children and babies can often become unwell with very little warning. Parents can leave their child with you in the morning and by lunchtime that child could be unwell. In most cases sick children and babies need to be with their main carer in their own home, if possible. Sometimes this can be a source of guilt and anxiety for parents and can cause conflict between the parents' employers, the parents and yourself.

One way that you can reduce any possible conflict is to make sure that your contract of childcare services covers circumstances when children and babies are unwell. Another way is to have a policy which covers the care of sick children and your responsibilities to the sick child, other children, parents and members of your family. It is worth noting that having such a policy is a requirement in Wales.

Children and babies who are ill have additional needs to healthy children and it is important that you understand how to meet these needs. As part of the registration process for registered childminders, you will have had first aid training. Nannies and registered childminders must ensure that they keep this training up to date, but it is good practice for nannies to undertake a specialised first aid course. First aid courses will be discussed later in this chapter.

How to recognise children's illnesses

There are some illnesses that need immediate action; the most common of these is meningitis. There are several strains of meningitis and a child can be immunised against some of them. However, if you suspect that a child has symptoms of meningitis you *must* get medical help immediately. The common signs in babies and young children are:

- high temperature (fever) with possibly cold hands and feet
- vomiting or refusing feeds
- whimpering cry or high-pitched moaning
- blank, staring expression
- pale, blotchy complexion
- being lethargic or difficult to wake
- a baby may be floppy, and dislike being handled.

Find it out

Your local health centre will have charts and leaflets showing the signs, symptoms and treatment of common childhood illnesses. Get a copy and keep it in a handy place for easy access. The Health Protection Agency has useful information about illnesses. You can find out more by accessing the website from the Hotlinks section (see page 3). Some parents may ask for your advice when their child is ill or seems unwell. It is good practice always to suggest that the parent takes the child to the doctor. It is better to see a doctor for a minor illness than to miss something important like meningitis.

Think about it

In all aspects of your childcare practice you are working in partnership with the parents. Together you want to ensure that the children are in reasonable health. You are helping the children in your care to develop and grow in a healthy and safe environment.

One way you can do this is to support the children's parents in the maintenance of regular health screening programmes and developmental checks. Encourage them to keep the appointments and share the information with you. Similarly, if you take the children to these appointments you must make sure that important information is passed on to the parents. Parents should have let you know, when you completed the contract together, whether their child has any **allergies** or sensitivities.

Keys to good practice

Your contract
You may want to include the following points.

- You must be able to contact the parents (or another appropriate person, such as a grandparent) at all times.

- If the parents are not able to collect their sick child from your home, or get home to support you, they must make alternative arrangements.

- You are not able to give permission for any treatment to be given to a child, other than in an emergency.

- You have the final decision to decide not to care for a child if doing so means the health of other children could be at risk, especially if you are a registered childminder.

Registered childminders may also want to remind parents that the terms and conditions of their registration do not allow them to care for children who have an **infectious** illness. You also have a responsibility to the other children in your care to make sure that you provide a safe and healthy environment.

If you find out that a child in your care has developed an infectious disease, you must inform the parents of all the other children. In nearly all illnesses children are at their most infectious before the symptoms appear.

Key terms

Allergy – an adverse reaction or sensitivity to a substance, food product, animal or other environmental factor.
Infectious – a disease or illness that can spread through the environment, such as flu.

Key term

Notifiable diseases – serious infectious conditions that must be reported to the public health authorities, for example, rubella, meningitis, measles.

Caring for children who are unwell

Young children can become unwell quite quickly and one of the first things you can do in these circumstances is to take their temperature. It is also very important that you make contact with the parents as soon as possible. The child will need somewhere quiet to rest – if possible away from other children – where you can keep a vigilant eye on them.

Your first aid kit should include a children's thermometer. There are three types of thermometer available, the most common being digital (which are easy to read), fever strips (which change colour) and mercury thermometers (which can be difficult to read). It is a matter of personal preference which one you use, but make sure that you can read it correctly.

Normal body temperature is 37°C, so a temperature above this should indicate that the body is fighting an infection. A child with a high temperature has an increased risk of convulsions and so you should help lower the child's temperature.

Keys to good practice

Practical ways to reduce a child's temperature

- Make sure that the room temperature is not too high; 15°C is about right.
- Remove the child's clothing (apart from underwear).
- Do not cover the child with a duvet or blanket.
- Give frequent drinks of cool water.
- You could possibly sponge the child with cool water, especially on the hands, face and upper body.

Allergies

Many children suffer from food allergies or intolerances. Some food allergies can be potentially fatal, such as intolerance to nuts or shellfish. These can cause the body to go into anaphylactic shock, when blood pressure can drop and airways swell up, often making it impossible to breathe. Children can die from anaphylactic shock. If a child has an allergic reaction to something when in your care, you must know exactly what to do.

Some common plants in your garden can cause allergic reactions if touched — for example, primulas. These plants are bright and colourful and could be attractive to young children.

Case study: Zak's fever

Alison left 18-month-old Zak with the registered childminder, Trish, at 8.30 a.m. Zak had not slept very well the night before, so Alison mentioned this to Trish just before she left. By lunchtime Zak's face was flushed and he felt hot. He did not want any lunch, which was unusual. Trish used a fever strip to take his temperature; it was 38.7°C. Trish phoned Alison at work and explained that Zak was not well. Alison's line manager was at lunch so she could not get away immediately. Trish agreed that she would start to try to cool Zak down and Alison said she would get to Trish's house by 3 p.m. Alison also said that she would make an appointment with their doctor.

Trish made sure that the playroom was not too hot and then took off Zak's jeans, sweatshirt, socks and shoes and left him in a T-shirt and his underclothes. She wiped Zak's head, face and hands with a cool, damp cloth and gave him a drink of cool water. Zak and Trish sat on the bean bags and looked at books together for a while, then Zak fell asleep. The other children watched a video in the same room. Trish left Zak where he was, but kept checking on him every few minutes to make sure he was not getting any hotter. When Alison arrived Zak was still asleep; his temperature had dropped slightly, but was not yet at normal body temperature. Trish had made a note of his temperature, how much water he had drunk and what she had done to make Zak feel comfortable. Alison took these notes with her to share with the doctor. Later that day Alison called to say that the doctor thought that Zak had roseola infantum (three-day fever), which is very common in under-2s, and had prescribed paracetamol. Alison's mum was able to look after Zak for the rest of the week at his home, and, hopefully, he would be back at Trish's the following week.

- Do you think that Trish did the right things?
- Was there anything else that she should or could have done?

Think about it

Do you have to have a bare, boring garden, or do you teach children not to touch?

Find it out

Asthma attacks can be quite frightening for children and you should try to find out as much as you can about this condition. The contact details for Asthma UK are provided in the useful addresses section at the end of this book. On their website you will find pages specifically relating to pre-school and school-age children.

Animal hair can also cause an allergic reaction, or even trigger an asthma attack. Make sure if you have an asthmatic child that you have their inhaler to hand at all times (although stored in a safe and secure place). If a child is having difficulty breathing, even after using an inhaler, or as a result of an allergic reaction you should call an ambulance. Make sure that your hygiene practices take into account your pets, as outlined on page 81.

Incidents, accidents and emergencies

Think about it

RoSPA research suggests that:

- most accidents at home occur in the living or dining room areas and that the most serious happen in the kitchen and on the stairs
- children aged 0–4 are most at risk from accidents in the home
- every year almost 70,000 children are involved in accidents in the kitchen and 66 per cent of these accidents involve children under 4
- most accidents happen between late afternoon and early evening in the summer and during school holidays
- boys are more likely to have accidents than girls.

Preventing accidents

As we know, an accident is something that happens that is not expected, or planned, and is not caused deliberately. Accidents can be prevented, or at least their effects can be limited. As a home-based childcarer your responsibility is to try to prevent accidents from happening; but if they do happen, then you must know what to do.

Table 4.1 gives examples of the most common accidents that can happen to children, possible causes and what you can do to prevent such accidents. Remember that accidents can happen anywhere, at any time and usually when you least expect them, so be prepared.

Potential accident	Possible cause	Prevention
Cuts and grazes	Sharp objects, such as scissors, knives	Make sure that sharp objects are out of reach of children
	Sharp edges on furniture and equipment	Protect furniture edges, especially corners
	Damaged or faulty toys	Remove or throw away damaged or faulty toys
	Broken glass	Mark large areas of glass, such as patio doors, with stickers, use plastic cups for children's drinks
Falls	Falling between two levels, such as highchair to floor, bed to floor	Use harnesses or personal restraints in highchairs. Fit safety rails to beds and make sure that cot sides are securely held in place
	Tripping over toys left on the floor	Make it part of your routines to encourage children to put away toys when they have finished playing
	Falling up or down stairs and steps	Fit secure stair and doorway gates. Never let children climb up and down stairs unsupervised
	Falling out of windows	Fit window locks and move furniture from underneath windows to stop children climbing

Continued

Continued

Burns, scalds and fire	Hot drinks being knocked over	Do not leave hot drinks within reach of children
	Matches and lighters	Keep matches and lighters out of children's reach
	Fires and heaters	Fit secure guards around any heating source. Have a fire blanket or extinguisher handy
	Water too hot	Domestic hot water should never exceed 54°C
	Kettles, irons and electrical	Fit coiled flexes to equipment equipment and do not allow flexes to trail over the edge of work surfaces
	Cookers	Oven doors can be fitted with protective guards or fitted with heat-resistant covers. Pan handles should be turned away from the edge of the hob or cooker
Poisoning	Cleaning materials	Store in a secure cupboard that children cannot open
	Plants – both indoors and garden plants	Either keep out of reach, or better still destroy poisonous plants
	Medicines	Store in a locked high cupboard
	Cosmetics	Keep out of reach of children
Suffocation and choking	Pillows	Do not use pillows for babies under 18 months
	Small pieces of toys	Keep toys with small pieces away from small children
	Skipping ropes	Discourage children from using ropes for anything else other than skipping
	Cord and ties on clothes and furnishings	Avoid clothes with ties. Make sure cords from furnishings and blinds do not hang down
	Plastic bags	Keep bags away from children. Store out of reach, preferably knotted, so that they cannot be easily opened
	Nuts	Do not give to young children
Electric shocks	Electric sockets	Fit covers to all electric sockets that are not in use. Do not overload sockets with too many plugs
	Damaged electrical equipment	Check equipment for frayed or damaged flexes and replace if necessary
Drowning	Bath	Do not leave children in a bath unattended and unsupervised
	Paddling pools	Do not leave children in paddling pools unsupervised
	Ornamental ponds	Cover or fence ponds
	Buckets or bowls of water	Do not leave any amount of water in a bucket or bowl

Table 4.1: Common accidents, causes and prevention.

First-aid kits

You can buy a first-aid kit from a chemist or supermarket that is already put together; however, some of the items in these kits are unlikely to suit your needs. Many practitioners make up their own first-aid kits, which mean they can put in what they need and know how to use. You may find that your development officer from the local authority, or the trainer from your first aid course, has a list of the suggested minimum requirements for a first aid kit; it is worth asking.

Every time you use the first-aid kit you should get into the habit of making a note of the items that you used and add them to your shopping list, if necessary; and

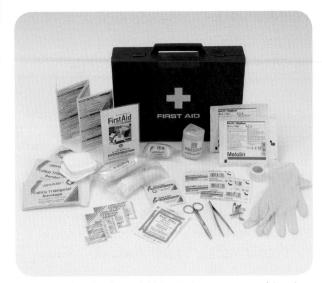

An example of a first-aid kit. Make sure everything in your kit is in date.

ncma
says...

You can obtain an approved first-aid kit via the NCMA website.

Think about it

What would you put in your first-aid kit? Make up a first-aid kit list that would be appropriate for use with the children you care for. See the photo above for ideas.

1.   Have you thought about possible allergies to plasters?
2.   What could you use instead of plasters?
3.   Have you thought about the different types of thermometers you would need, and which would be the easiest for you to use and read?
4.   Have you included disposable gloves, for both the children's and your protection? You should also be aware of possible allergic reactions to latex gloves.
5.   Where would you keep your first-aid kit?
6.   What sort of container would you use to store the items?
7.   How often would you check your kit?

when you have finished using the kit, do a quick check to see if everything you need is there and usable. You could stick a list of contents of the kit on the lid of the container, and simply do a quick check against the list.

Your first-aid kit should be used only for your childcaring business. Any medication that you keep to give to members of your own family should not be given to the children you are caring for. You must have written permission from the children's parents before you give any first aid or medication. The EYFS guidance suggests that this should be given each and every time it is needed. Any medication for children that you have been asked to give a child by parents must be stored out of the reach of children, and at the correct temperature (read the label), and disposed of carefully when the course of treatment is finished. Parents should give you written instructions about the dosage of the medication/time of last dose.

You should also record all accidents or incidents, with the date, time, the child/children involved and what action you took; parents should be shown this record and sign it to indicate that they have seen it.

Coping with an emergency

An emergency, like an accident, is unexpected. It can involve only you or several people. Emergencies often are the result of accidents. A fire on your premises would be an emergency, so make sure that you and the children in your care know how to get out of the house quickly and safely. Practise fire evacuation procedures regularly so that everyone knows what to do and remains calm.

Even though you cannot predict accidents and emergencies, you can be prepared. The best way to cope is to have a personal emergency plan, so that you are prepared for the worst. Such a plan will help you remain calm and more able to cope.

Emergency plan

You will need access to a telephone, either a landline or a mobile. If you rely on a mobile phone, make sure it is fully charged when the children are with you. Also, check that the mobile has good reception. In case of problems with your home phone, also make sure you know where the nearest public call box is and keep a phone card or coins handy.

(Remember emergency services can be contacted from landlines and public call boxes by dialling 999; many mobile phone services use 112 even when there is no signal for your network provider.)

Make sure that you have an up-to-date list of essential telephone numbers. This list should include:

- the children's parents and an emergency contact number if they are not available
- the children's doctors
- your own doctor
- the nearest police and fire stations
- the nearest hospital with an accident and emergency department
- the name, address and telephone number of someone whom you could call to cover for you if you have to leave your home.

You will have to reassure parents that you would never leave their children unattended and that, if possible, they would always be left with another qualified person.

You must make sure that your records of the children are up to date. When putting together an emergency plan you will need to decide what are the most important things to do first. These first actions are known as the 4Bs:

- Breathing – your first priority is to check that the child is still breathing
- Bleeding
- Breaks
- Burns.

It is very important that you do not attempt to resuscitate a child unless you have been specially trained to do so. Call an ambulance if you are in any doubt.

In case of an emergency

Mentally rehearse an emergency. This will help you plan what you need to do first and will help you feel more confident and more able to reassure the children in a real emergency.

A personal emergency plan could be something like this.

1. Do not panic, keep calm, take a few deep breaths.
2. Deal with injuries following the 4Bs outlined.
3. Check if it is possible to contain the emergency without harm to you or the children; for example, use a fire blanket or fire extinguisher if safe to do so.
4. Check the safety of all of the children and, if possible, remove them from the immediate area; never leave them unattended.
5. If necessary, phone the emergency services or doctor. Make sure you are talking to the correct person, identify yourself and explain clearly why you are calling.
6. Contact the children's parents. If you leave a message, make sure it is brief, but gives all the necessary information without causing the parents to panic. Remember to leave a contact number for them to get in touch with you.

Keys to good practice

Personal emergency plan
A personal emergency plan is exactly that – it is personal to you and it must work for you.

- It is good practice to write out your personal emergency plan so that other people can follow it if something were to happen to you.

- Look at your plan regularly and change it if necessary. This is especially important for keeping up-to-date records of the children.

The NCMA has produced a form that you and the parents can complete with addresses, telephone numbers, emergency contacts, medical details and other useful information. You could make up your own forms if you wanted, but make sure that you include all the details about the children that you need to know in order to keep them safe.

> " *I always do a fire practice at least once a month, and always when a new child starts. Sometimes I tell the children the fire is in the kitchen and we have to go out through the front door; sometimes I tell them the fire is in the playroom and we have to go out through the back. I try to make it a serious practice, not a game, because I think it is vital that all the children know what to do in case of a fire.* "
>
> *Sue, registered childminder*

Why do childcare practitioners need a relevant first-aid qualification?

One of the most effective ways to help make sure you are fully prepared for any situation, accident or emergency is to have an up-to-date and relevant first-aid qualification. It is very reassuring for parents to know you are professional and caring enough to get as many recognised qualifications as you can. A first-aid course is an Ofsted/CSSIW requirement and approved by Nestor (the approval agency for nannies). This qualification is very important and will teach you how to deal with emergencies and some first aid. Most qualifications last only for three years, so you will need to keep them up to date.

Having an up-to-date first-aid qualification is essential for all people caring for children. However, it is important that you are aware of your own limitations and in an emergency only carry out procedures that you are competent to do.

Emergency first aid

In an emergency situation where you have to give first aid, follow this routine.

- Stay calm — this helps you to assess the situation.
- Deal with a dangerous situation first.
- Remove the child, other children and yourself from danger.
- Talk to the injured child to see if they respond.

Remember **C D R T: C**hildcarers **D**on't **R**ush **T**hings. Then follow the **ABC** routine that you should have learnt on your first-aid course.

- Check the child's **a**irway.   A
- Check the child's **b**reathing.   B
- Check the child's **c**irculation. Is there a pulse?   C

Put the child into the recovery position — see the drawing on the following page.

If the situation you are dealing with is not an emergency or a crisis, you still need to remember C D R T. Many accidents can be dealt with easily provided your first-aid box is complete and you know what to do. Table 4.2 gives you a list of the sort of first aid to carry out when dealing with common minor accidents with children.

Accident	First aid/treatment
Grazes of all kinds	Rinse the area with plenty of clean, cool water to make sure the grazed area is dirt free
Minor burns	Run under a cold tap for at least 10 minutes; chemical burns need at least 20 minutes. Do not cover the burned area
Nose bleeds	Tip the child's head forwards and pinch just below the bridge of the nose
Bruising and sprains	Put something cold over the area (a bag of frozen peas wrapped in a small, clean towel is ideal)
Head injuries	Put something cold over the injury (a bag of frozen peas wrapped in a small, clean towel is ideal)
Objects in the nose or ears	Do not try to remove the object — get a doctor to remove it

Table 4.2: First aid for common minor accidents.

Put two fingers under the child's chin and one hand on the forehead.

Gently tilt the head well back. Straighten limbs. Bend the arm nearest to you so it is at right angles to the body.

Bring the other arm across the child's chest. Place the hand against the child's cheek – with palm outwards. Pull up the child's far leg, just above the knee, using your other hand.

Make sure the child's head is well back – to keep the airway open and to stop them from breathing in vomit or choking on their tongue.

Pull on the far leg and roll the child towards you, still pressing the hand against the cheek – until the child is lying on their side.

To stop the child rolling too far, use your knees as support. Bend the upper leg so that it is at a right angle from the body.

Make sure the upper arm is supporting the head.

The correct procedure for placing a child in the recovery position. Are you confident that you could do this?

Link to assessment — AC 2.1

Explain the key components of a healthy and safe home-based environment.

CACHE Task 5
Your information leaflet is to include information about the key components of a healthy and safe environment. Think about your understanding of how to deal with accidents and emergencies, and how this impacts on ways you make sure your home is safe and healthy.

Your emergency plan and accident policy and procedures could be used as evidence for this criterion if you are not doing the CACHE task.

The balance between safety and independence

It is often not easy to get the balance between keeping children safe and allowing them to learn and develop **independence**. Young children are naturally curious and love to explore, which is one of the ways that they learn. For example, older children want to be able to go the local shop on their own, and so gain confidence and independence; but you must always consult the parents and have their written permission before allowing children out alone.

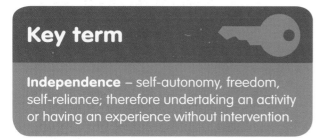

Key term

Independence – self-autonomy, freedom, self-reliance; therefore undertaking an activity or having an experience without intervention.

All children need to learn how to manage and assess risk for themselves. This helps to build their self-confidence and esteem. This can be done effectively by offering challenging play experiences and activities; allowing children to discover things for themselves, provided of course that they are not in danger.

Children need to be educated from an early age about safety and ways to cope in emergencies. Children learn about safety from you, their parents and other positive role models. Everyone in a home is relaxed, and often feels safe because they are at home. Yet most accidents happen in the home, and during the summer months. It is better to teach young children, when they are ready, a safe way to crawl up and down stairs than have them fall down if they gain access to ungated stairs. It is better to make sure an older child knows your address and phone number so that they can contact you in an emergency, rather than worry about their safety.

Storage of medicines and other hazardous materials

Medicines and prescribed drugs

There may be occasions when it will be necessary for you to store and administer medicines or **prescribed drugs** to the children in your care. This includes inhalers, Epi-pens, diabetes injections (insulin), tablets, syrups, creams, lotions and so on. You should only accept medicines that have been prescribed by a doctor, dentist, nurse or pharmacist.

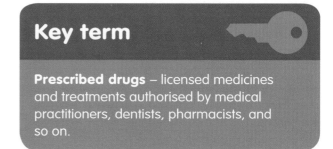

Key term

Prescribed drugs – licensed medicines and treatments authorised by medical practitioners, dentists, pharmacists, and so on.

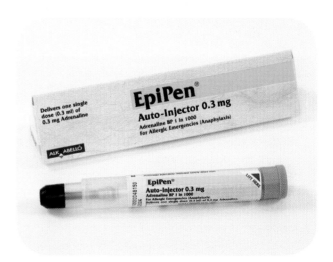

An Epi-pen.

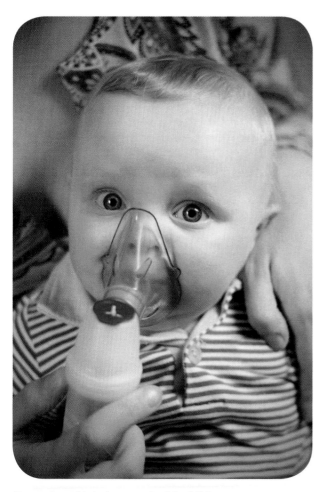

Examples of inhalers used with children.

Medicines and prescribed drugs must be stored according to the instructions on the packaging or labels. If the parents have not provided the packaging you must ask them about the correct storage procedures; for example, does the medicine or drug need to be kept in a fridge? All medicines should be kept out of reach of the children; if in the fridge they should not be in contact with foodstuffs.

Before you can give a child any form of medication, injection or other invasive procedure, it is essential that you have undertaken appropriate and up-to-date training that enables you to do such things competently. You must be trained by an appropriate medical childcare practitioner who can provide written confirmation of your competence. It is good practice to have written permission from parents for you to give their child a medicine.

You must follow the dosage instructions on the medicine or prescribed drug, to make certain that you are giving the child the correct amount. When giving a child medication, make sure that you know exactly when the child needs to have medicine or medication; for example, if before eating, how long before? Some children who take insulin for diabetes need to be injected about half an hour before eating.

You also need to know the purpose of the medication; in other words what is it supposed to do? If you do not have this information, you will not know if the medication is working properly. Make sure that you get this information from the parents, preferably in writing, and remember to ask if there are any side effects. Sometimes you might think that the medicine does not appear to be having the desired effect. Make sure that you know what to do if this the case. Remember that each child is different and so their reactions will vary.

Keys to good practice

Medication

- You must never give a child medication unless you have written permission from the parents.

- You should have a written policy for the administration and storage of medicines.

- Each time you give a child a prescribed drug or medicine you must record the time, date and dosage given.

- Medicines and other prescribed drugs should be stored in a locked, non-portable container (unless they are kept in the fridge).

- Make sure you know not only the correct dosage and how frequently the medicine should be given, but also if there is a particular way it should be given – for example, through a syringe, on a spoon, with water, with food.

- Make sure you know what to do if you forget to give the medicine.

Other hazardous materials

Other hazardous materials – such as cleaning fluids, powders, some make-up, deodorants, dishwasher or washing tablets and sprays, and alcohol – should be stored in places where no child can access them. It is good practice to have a childproof lock on the cupboard where these materials are kept.

Link to assessment

AC 2.5

Explain how to store and administer medicines.

CACHE Task 5

The last section of your information leaflet should explain to other carers how to store and administer medicines. This is important information and you should make sure that you are clear and precise. Look in your local health centre or doctor's surgery for additional relevant and useful information.

Your policy and procedures for administering and storing medicines could be used as evidence for this criterion if you are not doing the CACHE task.

5. WORKING IN PARTNERSHIP WITH PARENTS

Parents are the first educators of their children and it is very important that anyone working with children and young people makes every possible effort to establish efffective partnerships with parents. Children are more likely to reach their full potential if good lines of communication and sound partnerships with their parents have been established.

This chapter covers:

- the importance of the partnership with parents
- how to establish and maintain relationships with parents
- agreeing routines with parents
- making sure that each child and their family are respected, valued and welcomed.

- This chapter links to Learning Outcome 3: Understand the importance of partnership with parents for all aspects of the home-based childcare service.
- All assessment criteria (3.1 to 3.2) for this learning outcome are covered, and guidance is given for CACHE Assessment Task 6.
- This chapter links to Shared Core Unit SC1 (Communication) of the Level 3 Diploma for the Children and Young People's Workforce.

The importance of the partnership with parents

Parents and primary carers, such as grandparents or foster carers, are the most important people in young children's lives. It is from them that children will learn about their family cultures and religious beliefs. Parents and primary carers know their children better than anyone else. They are a child's first teachers and can powerfully influence a child's attitudes and development.

In recent years there has been a distinct shift in attitudes towards the role of parents in the education and care of their children. The Children Act (1989) gave parents definite rights, such as being able to express a preference about which school their child should go to and the right to information about their child's progress and achievements. Since 2008 the Early Years Foundation Stage (EYFS) in England has set out a clear framework for partnership working between parents and professionals, and also between professionals in all the settings a child may attend. This is important for childminders as many will be taking children to pre-school groups, nurseries and schools.

Most educational establishments and childcare settings have established policies that aim to make parents partners in the care and education of their children. As a home-based childcarer you should have a 'parents as partners' policy, which reinforces the importance of establishing positive relationships with parents, from

the first time you meet. The relationship between home-based childcarers and parents is often a close one. Parents come into a childminder's home regularly – a private nanny may live in the family home – so they also get to know one another very well.

It is important that you consider and respect parents' wishes in all aspects of their child's care and well-being. For example, it is important to make sure that wherever possible all your **routines** fit in with the parents' wishes. This does not just mean children's rest and sleep times, but could include how much time to allow for watching television and what programmes are suitable.

Key term

Routine – a custom, scheduled event or activity that is usually planned with regularity.

One of the main reasons parents choose home-based childcare is because they want their child to be cared for in their own home (in the case of employing a nanny) or in one that is as much like their own as possible. You will need to think about the different cultural practices that may be involved with care of children. It may be that in order to meet the needs and wishes of several different families, compromises will have to be discussed and agreed.

You may need to think about how you prepare food for some children. Some cultures have clear guidelines, and some quite strict rules, on handling and storing food and, for example, what meats or other products are excluded. Do not assume everyone eats what you do or that your way is right or best. You can find more information about common dietary habits on page 186.

If you care for African-Caribbean children you could find that their routines for hair and skin care are very personal, so your routine must take this into consideration. Some cultures have strong views about modesty and this could affect clothing worn by children when playing, or using the toilet. Again your routine must show that you have thought about these factors.

Do not assume that a family from a particular culture or group will follow all the practices of that culture.

Working in partnership with parents is an important part of childcare.

The only way to make sure that your routines give the child the care that the parents want is for you to ask them. Again you may have to reach a compromise, especially if certain aspects of a routine could affect other children. If you do reach an agreement in such cases, you must stick to it.

Case study: Paul and Shona care for six children

Paul and his wife Shona are registered childminders. They have only one son, who is 18 and still living at home – he is a full-time student at the local college. They live by the coast and often take their minded children to the beach, especially in the summer.

At the moment Paul and Shona care for four children each day. The youngest child is 3 months old and the oldest is 8. The others are 4 and 7 years old. Paul and Shona have been asked to care for twin girls, aged 18 months, whose parents are Trinidadian.

- How might the routines need to be adjusted to care for the twins?
- What good reasons can you give for the changes needed?

Link to assessment **AC 3.1**

Explain the importance of partnership with parents for all aspects of the childcare service.

CACHE Task 6
Your charter could be used to establish a relationship with parents. Think of it as a sort of contract (not legally binding) that will explain to parents your professional levels of service.

Make sure that the language you use is appropriate, unambiguous, clear and precise. Do not patronise or use jargon (terms that are specific to the profession). Explain why partnership with parents is important; you may want to link this to legislation and current good practice.

This assessment task may help you to put together a policy and procedures for working in partnership with parents. Your policy and procedures could be used as evidence if you are not doing the CACHE task, but you will possibly be asked also to write a short report which explains the importance of this aspect of your work.

Sharing information with parents

It is important to share information with parents effectively if you are to establish a positive working relationship. Older children often tell their parents what they have been doing and how they feel about their day. They can also tell a home-based childcarer what they have eaten and what they might need for their day at school. Younger children are not able to do these things yet and therefore it is essential that there are systems in place for parents and childcarers to exchange information.

Welcome pack

Many registered childminders find that an information sheet with a brief resume of their service is a useful starting point following an enquiry from a parent. Some set up a welcome pack containing more information that can be given to parents after the initial contact.

> *I found that to give parents an information sheet about my childminding business was a good opening as they could take it away with them. I put my name and telephone number on it, plus brief details of my experience, qualifications, when I was working and my rates. Later on, when a new family and I began to discuss the contract, I gave them my welcome pack, which was more detailed.*
>
> *Angie, registered childminder*

The welcome pack is a good starting point for exchanging essential information as parents can take it away with them and keep it for reference. Some nannies use their CV, with additional notes and letters from previous employers, to help potential new employers find out more about them.

Some childminders make a booklet about their business. What you give parents is up to you, but ideally you should include your:

- full name
- postcode (you may not want to give your full address at this stage)
- telephone numbers (landline and mobile)
- days and times when you are able to care for children, including details of your holidays
- rates for a full day, part-time/sessional, holidays and additional hours.

You should detail exactly what parents will get for their money – will your fees include nappies, food and drinks if you are caring for the child in your home? Remember to include any extras that you may wish to charge for and make it very clear who will pay for such things as pre-school sessions and after-school activities. You may also want to think about costs for late pick-ups, holidays, sickness, retainer fees and late payment.

- Arrangements if you are unable to care for children due to illness and/or an emergency.
- A brief outline of how you plan to organise your day. This helps parents know where you are likely to be and when would be a good time to get in touch with you.
- A brief outline of some of the activities you may do with the children.
- Brief details of when you were registered and inspected last.
- A detailed registration document for parents and you to complete before you start to care for the child. This can be your contract (see Chapter 1). It could also include child record forms and any other information forms.

Much of this information will have to be revised regularly and kept up to date, for example, your own holiday dates and any changes to the contract.

Parents will want day-to-day information about their child. This can be done face to face when the parent leaves the child in your care either at the beginning or end of the working day. Many childminders take photographs on their mobile phones or digital cameras and send them to parents during the working day. It is important for you to know, for example, if a baby or young child has slept well the night before. It is also important for a parent to know how much food, drink and rest their child has had during the day. However, remember that the start of the working day can be a busy time for parents; equally they may be tired at the end of the day.

Some childminders use a home/setting diary where they record important information for parents to read at home; parents can also include information for the childcarers. Some nannies find that exchanges of information happen after the children have gone to bed and through telephone calls and emails from the parents during the day. Whatever way you and the parents decide to exchange information, you must be very aware of confidentiality issues; so it is not good practice to discuss one child in front or in earshot of other parents or children.

Think about it

When compiling your own welcome pack, think about how you will make it and what you are going to include.
- Can you use a computer to compile some things, or devise your registration form?
- Will you use a child record form that is already made for you, such as the one produced by the National Childminding Association (NCMA)?
- Will it be in a hard or soft folder with individual pages that can be replaced as and when required?

How do the parents of the children you care for prefer to be contacted?

> " *I've lost count of the number of times a parent has asked their young child what they've done during the day and the child has said something along the lines of, 'Nothing, I just played.' This makes it so important that the parents and I share information at the end of each session.* "
>
> *Tony, registered childminder*

How to establish and maintain relationships with parents

The first meeting

Your first contact with parents will set the tone for the rest of your relationship with them. First impressions are very important and so you should be professional and welcoming. You should never agree to care for a child after just a hurried conversation between yourself and the parent, whether on the telephone or in the school playground.

Keys to good practice

First impressions

- Childminders – it is always good practice to invite the parents and the child to visit you in your home before the child starts coming to you.
- Nannies – visit the family in their home, preferably when the children are there. Agree a definite time for the first meeting so that you can organise your day to give time to the parents and the child.
- If necessary, do not forget to tell other children you care for – including your own, or other family members – that you have parents coming to visit.

Think about it

On a first meeting with parents you want to appear friendly, but at the same time professional and businesslike.
- Would you offer the parents tea or coffee?
- Think about the health and safety implications of hot drinks near children.

Case study: Sharing information

Sara is a nanny to two children, a girl of 2 years 4 months and a boy of 6 years 8 months. Both parents are doctors, working full-time and shifts. Sara lives in the family home. She realises that it is important to share and exchange information with the parents, but sometimes they leave or return from work when the children are in bed. They have worked together to establish regular opportunities for passing on information when they cannot meet face to face. They all have mobile phones and so find short text messages

very useful. Sara and the older child check the family's email before he goes to bed and he sends messages to his parents. It has been agreed that sticky notes on the fridge door be used for important messages.
- How can Sara and the parents make sure that the girl is not 'left out' of the exchanges of information?
- Can you think of more ways that Sara and the parents could use to pass on important information?

A first meeting can be a bit strained at first, so start by talking about everyday things such as the weather or something in the news that day. This helps to put people at ease and build confidence.

You should show the parents the rooms that the children will be using, and do not forget to show them the garden if the children will be playing there. Explain what kinds of activities you will be doing during the day. This is a good point to ask the parents and the children about what activities they like to do and their likes and dislikes.

It is a good idea to show the parents around the areas where their children will be.

Show parents your business documents such as certificates, registration and insurance documents. Explain to parents why you need them to complete specific information about their child and give them your information sheet or welcome pack. At this point you may want to talk about the importance of the contract (see Chapter 1) and agree when this will be completed and signed. They will need time to visit other possible providers before making up their minds.

Preparing yourself to meet new parents

As well as having to cope with parents feeling anxious and perhaps guilty about leaving their child, you will feel certain emotions yourself, especially if you are new to childminding.

- You will be concerned about the other children that you care for and any children of your own.
- You will need to think about how a new child could affect them.
- As a new home-based childcarer you may worry about what strangers will think about you and your home.
- You may even worry that you will not like the new child.

All of these worries are perfectly normal, but being able to recognise your own concerns and do something about them will in the end make you more professional and more able to offer a high-quality home-based caring service. Remember that you can learn from parents. Every parent will bring up their children differently. You must respect each parent as an individual and recognise that although their ways could be different from yours, they are equally acceptable and valid. Be open to new ideas and different ways of doing things.

Think about it

Think about the sort of questions that you will need to ask the parents about their child.
Write down your questions so that you will not forget anything important.
Write down the parents' answers as well, which will help avoid any misunderstandings.

Registered childminders should think about how they will introduce the new child to the other children that are cared for and also to the other people that live in the house. Remember to introduce the parents too. Ask them how they would prefer to be introduced; you cannot assume that everyone is happy for you to use first names.

Developing your relationship with parents

Developing any relationship has two features:

- exchanging information
- two-way **communication**.

Both are of equal importance in maintaining your relationship with parents. Often when problems arise it is because either the parent or the childminder has not exchanged information or communicated effectively.

Key term

Communication – an exchange of ideas, contact between individuals, consultation and interaction.

Exchanging information

Exchanging information regularly is essential for every aspect of your relationship with parents. Agree early on in your relationship what would be good times for you to share information about the child and what method you will use. Not every parent or childminder has time at the end of the day to chat, and may prefer an email, phone call or text message. However, if you have something important to discuss, such as concern or special achievement, you may want to ask yourself whether a text message is appropriate. If you find

that exchanges are becoming rushed, you may want to think about setting aside some time for a proper discussion, out of earshot of other children and parents, so that you can maintain confidentiality.

Many home-based childcarers give parents a brief verbal outline of what the child has been doing during the day as they arrive to collect their child. This is especially useful for parents of babies and young children as it can give information about what they have eaten and when, rest and sleep, the number of soiled nappies or how successful the toilet training has been that day. You can share information about things the child has enjoyed, as well as special or unusual occurrences or developments. If something has upset the child you must tell the parent so you can both reassure the child. In the same way, if something exciting has happened you can both share in the child's excitement and pleasure.

Some childcarers use daily diaries to record information and send them home with the child. This also provides parents, children and you with common information and helps to build and develop good relationships. Some parents use these diaries to share information with the childminder, some do not; but this does not mean that you should stop writing in the diary.

Two-way communication

The key to any successful relationship is communication, but this does not just have to be spoken – it can be electronic, written or in any other appropriate format. Communication is a two-way process, with a giver and a receiver.

For example, you are having a conversation with a child:

Child (giver) – *'Can you read this book with me please?'*

You (receiver) – *'Yes of course, let's sit down together on this cushion.'*

or

Text from parent (giver) – *'Has Toby settled ok cos he seemed a bit clingy this am?'*

You (receiver) – *'Yes he is fine, playing with blocks at the mo!'*

Case study: Beth's daily diary

Beth has a daily diary for each child she minds, which goes backwards and forwards between the child's home and Beth's. The entries vary greatly between each child but Beth always makes sure that she includes information on feeding and mealtimes, sleep and rest, nappies (for babies) and a general comment about the disposition of the child. Not many of the parents write back in the diary and Beth has begun to wonder if she is wasting her time. However, when she asked parents about their views on the diaries, all were very appreciative and **valued** this exchange of information.

- How do you share information with parents?
- Is it effective or are there other ways of doing this?

Key term

Valued – given importance, appreciated.

Communication requires time and effort from both sides. Lack of communication can lead to misunderstanding and misinformation. There are skills that you can learn to help you become a more effective communicator, not just with parents but also with the children that you care for — and indeed all the other people that you come into contact with in both your professional and personal life.

Communication is a two-way process. Are you able to get your ideas across clearly? Are you a good listener?

Communication can be non-verbal or verbal.

Non-verbal

- eye contact
- gestures such as pointing
- body language
- touch
- written language, including email, texts
- pictures
- symbols.

Verbal

- spoken language, including telephone conversations as well as face-to-face contact
- tone of voice.

We use most of these forms of communication every day. For example, have you calmed a baby by gently stroking their back and using a gentle tone of voice, used a different tone to manage a child's behaviour, or written a sticky note to remind you to tell a parent something?

Another thing to be aware of is that spoken words are often not as precise as written words. It is common practice to have to write things down — for example, when making a speech or giving a talk — to make sure that everything is covered accurately and nothing is missed out. It is good practice to make written notes beforehand if you are going to speak to a parent or another professional about a specific or important issue. In this way you can be sure that you remember everything you want to say, and that everything you say is accurate and factual.

Think about it

Effective communication is one of the Core Key Skills. If you decide to continue your studies and work towards more units of the Level 3 Diploma for the Children and Young People's Workforce, you will learn more about communication.

Agreeing routines with parents

Routines, whatever their length or focus, should be planned to meet individual needs. Care routines should be planned to give continuity of care, following the same pattern that has been established by the parents wherever possible. This will help the children feel more emotionally safe and secure while in your care. (You can find more information about routines in Chapter 7.)

It is important to discuss the planning of all routines with parents to ensure that the individual needs of both the child and the family can be met. Just as all children are different, so are parents and it is important to discuss care routines with parents before you start to care for their child so as to avoid any misunderstandings. How you organise your day, your daily routine, should also be discussed with the parents so that they have some idea of what their child will be doing while in your care, and also so they know where you are at any given time if they need to contact you.

Routines are usually planned with one specific age group in mind — for example, feeding a baby or toilet training. However, trying to put into practice a routine that does not cater for individual differences will result in a less than satisfactory situation. Some parents may want their child to be fed following a structured method, while others may be happy for their baby to be fed on demand.

Routines can also focus on one aspect of care or development, such as sterilising bottles, or the arrangements that you and the children have made to get to a gym club on time.

Food given at mealtimes can be an issue for some parents. Not only might their child have allergies or specific dietary needs, a parent may want their child to have only organic food, or vegetarian meals or meals that are appropriate to their culture or religion. (You can find more more information about common dietary habits on page 186.)

Some parents may want you to use disposable nappies, while others may prefer washable, reusable nappies, or may have a special way or place for changing nappies. In this case you should ask the parents to actually show you what they do.

Some parents may have established a routine for rest and sleep that they want you to follow, or a pattern of events when coming in from school, such as the child having a wash, changing their clothes, having a snack and quiet time, followed by homework and the evening meal.

Keys to good practice

Routines

Routines for babies and children that are important to their care and well-being include:

- care of skin, teeth and hair
- nappy changing, toileting
- feeding and mealtimes, including weaning
- cleaning/sterilising of feeding equipment
- prevention of infection
- sleep and rest, settling
- hand washing, bathing
- personal hygiene.

It is very important that you follow the best possible practice when planning your routines.

By making sure that you work with the parents in establishing care routines, you will enable the needs of the children to be met and will avoid misunderstandings. This is especially important if a child has a medical condition, allergy or a specific need relating to their religion or culture. Following the same routines as the parents will help you settle the child into your care, especially if you are not caring for them in their own home.

Find it out

If you have any doubts about your practices, find out how you can improve your routines. There are many sources of information available, including leaflets at your health centre, articles in professional journals and textbooks, information on the Internet and from talking to health care professionals.

Think about it

What do you do if the parents' care routines do not meet good professional practice? First, and of great importance, you will have to talk to the parents about why they want you to do things in certain ways or at a certain times. For example, they may want to start toilet training before a child is ready, because another baby is expected and they do not want to have two children in nappies. Another request might be to stop a child having a daytime rest or sleep, so that the child will go to bed at night earlier. These situations can be difficult to handle and, while you have to consider parents' wishes, remember that the child's needs and well-being are paramount. Good communication and positive relationships with parents are critical in situations like this and should avoid misunderstandings.

Link to assessment AC 3.2

Describe how partnership with parents are set up and maintained.

CACHE Task 6

Your charter should explain how you set up relationships with parents; this could include information about what you expect to share during the first meeting. You should explain how you meet children's needs through your routines and how routines change as the children grow and develop.

Instead of a charter you could engage in a professional discussion with your assessor about the ways in which you set up and maintain relationships with parents. You could use a welcome pack as a starting point, as well as your policy and procedures for working in partnership with parents.

Making sure that each child and their family are respected, valued and welcomed

Culture and religion

The United Kingdom is a multicultural society; but, while Christianity is regarded as the traditional religion and English the predominant language, there are large numbers of children who are bilingual or multilingual and brought up following other religions or no religion at all.

There are cultural differences between the types of family unit and structures in which children can be brought up. For example, children from families who are Jehovah's Witnesses will not celebrate birthdays, Christmas or Easter; one in ten Indian, Bangladeshi or Pakistani households consists of extended families where more than two generations live together, such as children, parents and grandparents. Cultural differences can affect interactions and communication, as many gestures and the use of eye contact do not have universal meaning and so can be open to misinterpretation. Childrearing can be affected by cultural variations, although there can also be striking similarities.

Think about it

In the late 1980s, studies in America, undertaken by Beatrice Whiting and Carolyn Edwards, compared the variations of parenting in such diverse societies as urban America, rural Kenya and Liberia. The studies showed that there were many overarching similarities, despite the vast differences in economic, social and political conditions. With infants and toddlers, the universal emphasis was on providing routine care along with attention and support. By the time the child reached 4 years of age, most parents shifted their focus to controlling, correcting or managing inappropriate behaviour. Finally, when children reached the age for formal schooling, parents became concerned with training their children in the skills and social behaviours valued by the group. The study concluded that parents around the world resemble each other in numerous ways because of the universal needs of children as they grow and develop.

Are you aware of cultural differences when communicating with the children you care for, and their families?

Family differences

It is important to remember that some children may live in two different households, moving from one to another at weekends and during school holidays. Many children can cope with this, but some may not. It is also important to remember that a change within any family unit or structure, such as moving away from family members, a death in the family, the birth of a sibling, or moving to another region or country, can be disruptive for children and families.

Again childcare practitioners should not make assumptions and should make every effort to find out about and respect the customs of other families. Also children will be gaining a rich variety of experiences outside the home, education and care settings. What is important is that children in any family are fed, clothed, sheltered and loved, and that they have the opportunity to learn and develop in a protective and caring environment.

It is vital to be non-judgemental and to avoid giving parents the impression that you disapprove in some way of what they are doing. However, you must remember that supporting parents can sometimes be emotionally very demanding and you can put yourself under a lot of pressure. It is never a good idea to become personally involved in other people's problems.

Everyone who works with children has to recognise that parents are the most important people in a child's life and all practitioners should constantly reaffirm this view to both parents and children.

Values and practices in parenting vary from one culture or social group to another and from family to family. There is no single 'correct' way to bring up children. Parents choose the methods and practices which are appropriate to their culture, traditions, beliefs and their own upbringing.

Sometimes parents' views about what they want for their children are different from your views, so you need to talk about the differences. You need to make it clear to parents that you do your best to care for children as the parents want; but if you are a job-share nanny or a childminder you may care for children from several different families. In such cases it will be necessary to compromise and negotiate.

> *I am a nanny and the way that the parents want to bring up their children is very different from the way that I was brought up. However, we have discussed their philosophy a lot and I can understand where they are coming from. If I have any doubts about how I deal with things, I talk to them. It is really important to me that I have the same consistent ways as the parents. After all, we all want what is best for the children.*
>
> *Kasey, nanny*

Case study: Maintaining a vegetarian diet

Cassie, a nanny to Jenny and Ryan, prepares vegetarian meals for the children in accordance with the parents' wishes. Ryan sometimes goes to his friend's house after school, where he is offered non-vegetarian treats by his friend's parents. Ryan's parents have asked Cassie to deal with the friend's parents and to make sure that Ryan sticks to a vegetarian diet.

- How should Cassie handle this situation?
- What could she say to Ryan and his friend's family?

Keys to good practice

Respecting and valuing others

- Find out how parents would like to be addressed – never assume that children have the same family name as their parents. Names are important.

- Because parents' views are different from yours, they are not wrong. Respect all views and wishes of parents.

- Comment positively to parents about what their child has done and reinforce the view that parents are central to the child's life.

- Be patient and use tact and understanding to recognise that some parents may feel quite guilty about leaving their child with you.

- You should not make the parents feel unskilled or lacking in information. Tell the parents about what their child has been doing; if appropriate share your plans for activities for the day.

- Think about establishing a home/setting diary if you are not caring for the child in their home. Encourage the parent to write in it – for example, about what the child has done after they left you, how they have slept.

- Take care not to appear an 'expert' in all subjects. If an inexperienced parent asks your advice and you do not know the answer, be honest and say so; but try to find out the answer.

- Remember that the needs of the child are paramount.

Find it out

There is much research into and study of partnerships with parents. Look on the Internet, or in professional magazines and relevant texts, to extend your knowledge about parental partnerships. You may find the CD-ROM in the EYFS pack a useful source of information. (You can find more information about the pack in Chapter 3.)

Link to assessment   AC 3.1

Explain the importance of partnership with parents for all aspects of the childcare service (inclusive practice).

CACHE Task 6
You have already written a policy and procedures for equal opportunities in Task 2 (Chapter 2) and will have considered ways to make your practice inclusive. Think about how you could explain to parents that all children are welcomed into your setting and valued. You may want to use specific case studies (while maintaining confidentiality) and practical examples of what you do. You may decide to write a report to explain the importance of this partnership.

This activity will also be relevant if you are not following the CACHE tasks.

6. CHILD DEVELOPMENT

Caring for children in home-based settings is not just about keeping them happy and safe; it is also about helping them to achieve their full potential. In order to do this it is important that you have a good understanding of children's development and the factors and influences that can affect their development.

This chapter covers:

- stages of development
- factors affecting development
- physical development
- intellectual (or cognitive) development
- language and communication development
- personal, social and emotional development.

- This chapter links to Learning Outcome 5: Understand how to provide play and other activities for children in home-based settings that will support equality and inclusion.
- This chapter covers all assessment criteria (5.1 to 5.5) and will provide information to help you complete the assessments for Learning Outcomes 4 and 5.
- This chapter links to Children and Young People's Core units CYP 3.1 and 3.2 of the Level 3 Diploma for the Children and Young People's Workforce.

Stages of development

Although knowledge of child development is not specifically assessed in this unit, it will underpin your practice. Promoting children's and young persons' development is a mandatory unit in the Level 3 Diploma for the Children and Young People's Workforce and if you decide to continue with your studies you will look at child development in greater detail.

While the Children Act (2004) considers children from birth to 19 years of age, it is unlikely that many home-based childcarers will care for children over the age of 16; most childminders and nannies look after babies and children under school age during the day, and older children (up to 14 years or so) before and after school. Many other settings care for older children and young people, especially in holiday play schemes and before and after school.

This chapter will give you an overview of child development from birth to approximately 11 years and it is strongly recommended that you research this subject in greater detail.

All children are unique and will develop at different rates. However, all children will pass through the same sequence (stages) of development. As children get older the difference in the rates of development will become greater, which can make it difficult to set out generalised statements about development at a certain chronological age.

Each stage in a sequence of development can be clearly defined — for example, a baby sits up before crawling and stands before walking. These are **milestones** or **developmental norms**.

Key terms

Milestones – quantitative measurements that provide typical values and variations in height, weight and skill acquisition. They are sometimes referred to as developmental norms.

Developmental norms – quantitative measurements that provide typical values and variations in height, weight, skill acquisition; can also be referred to as milestones.

Each child must pass through one stage of development before they can move on to the next, and this progress is often charted and measured through milestones or norms. While the use of milestones or norms can be very helpful it is important to remember that they are averages that have been recorded over many years. This means that there will always be some individuals who are quicker or slower to reach them.

Development is often looked at or approached in separate areas in order to make accurate measurements and assessments. There are five areas of development:

- physical
- intellectual (or cognitive)
- language
- emotional
- social.

It is important to remember that all aspects of a child's development are interrelated and impact on each other. For example, a child with a language delay may find it difficult to communicate with their peers, which may affect their ability to make friends and develop social relationships. It may make them feel frustrated and angry. The different areas of development are in many ways artificial divisions, as children develop as whole human beings and not in separate categories. This is usually referred to as holistic development.

While home-based childcarers are registered to work with children from birth to 16 years, many of you will mainly be working with children from birth to 5 years. This means that you will be following the Early Years Foundation Stage (EYFS) in England (or relevant early years framework for your country). The EYFS has six areas of learning and development which can be matched to the general five areas of development used in this chapter, as shown in the table below. However, it is important that you try to think of a child's development in a holistic way.

Area of development	EYFS Learning and Development
Physical	Physical Development
Intellectual or Cognitive	Problem Solving, Reasoning and Numeracy Creative Development Knowledge and Understanding of the World
Language	Communication, Language and Literacy
Emotional	Personal, Social and Emotional Development Creative Development
Social	Personal, Social and Emotional Development

Table 6.1: Areas of development.

Factors affecting development

There are many factors that can affect a child's growth and development. Some can be short-term, such as being temporarily hard of hearing after having a cold; some can be more long-lasting, such as food allergies; and in some cases they are permanent. It is almost impossible to list and consider all the factors that can affect a child's development. For example, in most cases a factor that affects physical growth and development will also affect other areas of a child's development and it can be difficult to separate them into developmental areas.

Some experts who study child development divide the factors that can affect development into three areas:

- Antenatal – from conception to birth. This would look at the condition of the mother before the birth, and includes such things as smoking, diet, alcohol intake, drug abuse and stress.
- Perinatal – the actual birth. This would include premature babies, those who are born between 24 and 37 weeks of pregnancy and are not therefore full-term. Birth difficulties can impact significantly on a child's future development. For example, a baby who is deprived of oxygen at birth can develop a wide range of developmental problems, such as learning difficulties and cerebral palsy.
- Postnatal – after birth. There are numerous factors that can impact on a baby's or young child's development. The most common are shown in the spider diagram on the following page.

Postnatal factors that can affect development.

Physical development

All aspects of a child's health and **physical development** can be met through appropriate activities and experiences; some will need forethought, structure and planning, such as diet and healthy eating; others could be in spontaneous, unstructured ways, both indoors and outside. Most activities and experiences that you plan will cover a range of physical developmental areas. For example, a 4-year-old riding a tricycle is developing **balance**, **coordination** and **gross motor skills**; a 7-year-old on a computer is developing hand–eye coordination and **fine motor skills**.

All children develop at different rates and sometimes it can be helpful to compare children's development to developmental norms or milestones.

However, while developmental norms are valued because they give us some indication of what a child should be doing at a certain age – for example, a baby can smile at 6 weeks, or a 5-year-old has good control of a pencil – they do not take into consideration different rates of development and any factors that may affect a child's development, such as illness or genetic influences.

As mentioned several times already, all children are unique, with individual differences and needs. Therefore to promote the health and physical development of the children in your care, you must take this into consideration.

It is not possible to cover all stages of physical development from 0 to 19 years within the scope of this book. Table 6.1 is only given as an approximate guide. It is suggested that you research further into this aspect of children's development, by looking in textbooks that have been written specifically on child development.

Key terms

Physical development is about how children get control of their bodies. It includes:

- **balance** – a skill that requires coordination, but not necessarily from the eyes or ears. The ability to balance is developed by the body as the movements use information received from the central nervous system

- **coordination skills** – control of hand, eye and foot, and the ability to combine more than one skill or movement at the same time. In this aspect of development a child may use their eyes to guide their feet when going upstairs

- **gross motor skills** – movements involving all of an arm or leg, such as throwing a ball

- **fine motor skills** – small movements of the whole hand.

Keys to good practice

Planning activities or experiences with the children

Before doing this, you need to ask yourself the following questions.

- What do I already know from parents?

- Have I undertaken an observation?

- Have I thought about this child's age? Is this activity appropriate or am I expecting too much? For example, is it realistic to expect a 2-year-old to stand alongside an 8-year-old while they dispose of a tissue after blowing their nose?

- Have I thought about this child's experience? For example, is it unrealistic to expect a 15-month-old to drink from a cup when they have only had a bottle in the past?

- Have I thought about this child's skills and abilities? For example, should I insist, for safety reasons, that a 7-year-old ride a bike with stabilisers when they clearly have good balance and coordination skills?

- Have I thought about this child's specific needs, including gender, cultural and religious issues? For example, have I got sun cream to protect their skin when outside (with parents' written permission to apply it)? Have I made a picnic that takes into account allergies and religious dietary needs? Can I provide privacy for a teenage girl when she needs to use the bathroom?

Approximate age	Main features of development
Newborn	Primitive reflexes should be present
	Moves legs less often than arms
	Sucks vigorously
	Sleeps for about 21 out of 24 hours
6 weeks	Can lift head
	Will follow a moving object with eyes for a few seconds
	Looks into space when awake
	Limb movements still uncoordinated
	Still spends most of time asleep or dozing
3–5 months	Waves arms in controlled manner
	Kicks and pushes feet against a firm surface
	Can roll from back to side
	Can hold head steadily
	Watches hands and fingers, clasps hands
	When lying on stomach can lift head and pushes upwards with arms
	Sleeps for about 16 hours a day
6–8 months	Can sit with support for long periods and for short periods without support
	Can grasp using whole hand (palmar grasp)
	Takes every object to the mouth
	Arms move purposefully
	Can roll from back to stomach
	Can pull themselves into a standing position if helped
	Hands and eyes are coordinated
	First tooth may appear
	Practises making different sounds
9–11 months	Very active, rolls and wriggles, begins to crawl or shuffle
	Can reach sitting position without help
	Can pick up objects with first finger and thumb (pincer grasp)
	Top lateral incisors may appear
	Sleeps for about 14 hours each day
12–14 months	Can pull themselves into a standing position
	May walk around furniture
	May walk with adult support or independently
	Can crawl or shuffle very quickly
	Can hold a cup
	Points and can put small objects into a container
	Uses hands and eyes to explore objects rather than mouth

Continued

Continued

15–17 months	Restless and active
	Stands alone
	Can walk unaided
	Can kneel
	Can go upstairs on hands and knees
	Can build a tower of two blocks
	Can make marks with crayons
	Can feed themselves with finger foods, tries to use spoon
18–21 months	Walks fairly well, can push and pull toys when walking
	Can walk backwards
	Can come down stairs with adult help
	Squats and bends from waist to pick up objects
	Canine teeth may erupt
2 years	Can run, kick a ball from a standing position
	Climbs on furniture
	Uses a spoon to feed themselves
	Can zip and unzip larger zippers
	Can draw circles and dots
	Will build a tower of five or six blocks
	Begins to use preferred hand
	Begins to develop bowel and bladder control
3 years	Walks and runs with confidence, can walk on tiptoes, can throw and kick a ball
	Jumps off low steps
	Can pedal and steer a tricycle
	Washes and dries hands with help
	Can put on and take off some items of clothing independently
	Turns pages in a book independently
	Can use scissors
	By the end of the third year usually has a full set of milk teeth
4 years	Can walk on a line, hop on one foot
	Bounces and catches a large ball
	Runs, changing direction
	Buttons and unbuttons own clothing
	Can cut out simple shapes
5 years	Skips with a rope
	Can form letters, writes own name
	Dresses and undresses independently
	Can complete a 20-piece jigsaw
	Can hit a ball with a bat
	Begins to lose milk teeth

Continued

Continued

6–7 years	Active and energetic
	Enjoys using large play apparatus
	Moves to music with understanding
	Can use a bicycle without stabilisers
	Hops, skips and jumps with confidence
	Kicks a ball with direction
	Balances on a beam or wall
	Handwriting is evenly spaced
8–11 years	Greater agility and control
	All physical activities carried out with poise, coordination and precision
	General health is usually good, appetite is good and food is enjoyed
	Energy levels can suddenly drop so may need a short rest and food, but usually recovers quickly
	Girls may be starting the process of adolescence
12 years plus	Boys may begin the process of adolescence
	Girls' periods have usually started and by 16 are, as a rule, regular
	Boys usually grow much taller than girls and may become less coordinated at times
	Boys usually stronger than girls
	Diet and exercise very important

Table 6.2: Some stages of development from 0 to 12 years plus.

Risk and challenge

Risk and challenge are essential aspects of physical development. Any activitiy that a child does, whether indoors or out, has an element of risk – even something as simple as playing with play dough. For example, a child might have an allergic reaction to the flour, or choke if a piece gets stuck in their throat.

It is important that you understand the risks involved in any activity and that you are able to balance these against the benefits to and the safety of the child. This is often referred to as risk assessment, which is an ongoing activity for all childcare practitioners. (You can find more information about risk assessment in Chapter 4.)

If you took the attitude that certain activities are too risky, the children would not develop and reach their full potential. Taking risks, meeting a challenge, having opportunities to explore and experiment with skills are part of a child's natural development.

Think about it

There is the danger that home-based childcarers may interpret risk assessment as not allowing the children to do anything that might compromise (threaten) their safety. So think about:
- the risks of riding a tricycle
- the risks of climbing up a frame in the garden
- the risks of using scissors.

Now consider the benefits of these activities in terms of developmental skills such as coordination or fine/gross motor skills.

Well-organised and planned environments in which you have overall control will minimise risks and at the same time give the children freedom to develop, explore and try out new skills. You should give children opportunities to develop their physical skills with adult support, but minimal **intervention**.

You will need to think about the space that is available to you when you plan activities that develop gross motor skills. Have you got room indoors for children to run, hop, skip or jump? If not, you will need to take children into the garden or to a local park or sports centre. You should also think about the safety of the equipment that you or the parents provide (You can find more information about equipment in Chapter 4.)

It is important that you discuss safety rules or boundaries with children and that the children understand the possible risks of not following those rules.

Intellectual (or cognitive) development

Intellectual development is sometimes referred to as **cognitive development**, but the two terms essentially have the same meaning. This area of development includes:

- how children learn
- sensory development
- imagination and creativity
- memory skills
- attention and concentration
- perception.

These are huge topics in themselves and it is not possible in this book to give them full consideration. Therefore each will be discussed briefly; you can then research and read more about each one. At the back of this book is a list of sources of further reading and useful websites which you may find helpful in your research, but do bear in mind that no such list can ever be complete.

Key terms

Intervention – action taken to prevent or change something, interference in another's actions.

Cognitive development – another term for intellectual development, involving thought processes, memory, problem solving and so on.

Case study: Safety on the climbing frame

The family that Bea, a nanny, works for bought a set of outdoor play equipment for their two boys. Bea was concerned that the boys might be at risk if they jumped from the top section of the climbing frame, especially as there was only grass underneath. Bea discussed with the parents that a proper safety surface was needed under the play equipment and they agreed to organise this. Bea also discussed with the boys the issues of safety and risks of the play equipment and why a proper safety surface was needed. The boys agreed that they would not jump from the top and talked about other things they could safely do, such as hanging upside down.

- Think about your own outdoor play equipment. Does it offer opportunities for challenging play?

How children learn

Learning is an individual process for everyone. You may remember being in school, in a class with others of the same age and all being taught the same thing.

- Some of the class will learn what is being taught the first time.
- Others will need to go away and think about it.
- Others will have to ask questions.
- Some may need to be taught the same thing again in a different way.
- Some children will never really learn what is being taught.

The teacher will find out whether any learning has taken place by testing the class in some way.

Learning does not just take place in schools. It can happen in any situation, at any age and everyone can learn something. Learning is not only about cognitive or intellectual growth and development. These areas are a fundamental part of learning, but not the only part. Physical development, controlling and coordinating movements, is also a form of learning. Knowing how to act and behave in certain places and situations is part of social development, but is also learning. Understanding how to talk and communicate with others is another form of learning.

There are many **theories** and viewpoints on how children learn. Some appear to be contradictory, others complementary, but all have valid points about learning. Children will learn in different ways in different situations and with different people; so you may find that part of one theory supports a child's learning in a certain circumstance, and another at a different time.

Key term

Theory – a well-researched and unique idea or perspective on a particular subject or topic.

Keys to good practice

Theories

- Do not dismiss theories you disagree with or do not understand.

- Understanding and reflecting on these theories are important to your own professional development.

Sensory development

The development of the senses is an important part of how children learn. Babies and young children explore and learn about their environment through their senses. Babies put many objects in their mouths in order to explore shape and texture – the mouth is very sensitive and can send innumerable messages to the brain about the object being examined. Many children, and adults, have to hold something in their hands in order to 'see' it properly, the sense of touch being an important way to send information to the brain.

Think about it

When buying fruit or vegetables do you just look before making your selection or do you touch, feel or smell the items?
When buying a pair of shoes do you try them on, walk up and down in them, look in the mirror; in other words do you use your senses to make a decision on whether or not to buy? Could this be the reason why some people find Internet shopping a bit lacking in something, other than convenience?

Sensory information that is sent to the brain helps children to stay attentive and to concentrate. Multi-sensory activities – those in which children can use sight, smell, hearing, taste and touch – can be very effective in helping children to develop concentration skills and learn how to differentiate between experiences. For example, a meal with others can be a valuable multi-sensory experience for all children.

Heuristic play and treasure basket play provide excellent opportunities for sensory development. This type of play is designed to stimulate a baby or young child's concentration and encourage exploration. Curiosity is stimulated and children develop an understanding of the properties of different materials, as well as developing fine motor skills and hand–eye coordination.

Key term

Heuristic play – a form of play that encourages babies and young children to explore everyday natural objects through their senses; usually attributed to the educationalist Elinor Goldschmied (1910–2009).

Toddlers and older pre-school children can explore natural objects through heuristic play. You will need to provide a range of clean tins in various sizes, boxes, cartons, tubes, plastic bottles, chains and other natural everyday objects that children can fit together, put inside each other, carry around, and can make different sounds with.

Sand, water, clay and dough are also play materials that will promote sensory development. 'Gloop' —

cornflour and water — has a unique texture and feel and encourages exploration. Some home-based childcarers use cooked or uncooked pasta; jelly or dough containing different textures (such as sawdust, sand or uncooked rice); or dough that has been perfumed with essential oils, such as peppermint, rose or almond.

The list of natural things that you can use to promote sensory development is almost limitless; let your imagination run riot! However, do check for allergies or adverse reactions to certain substances, and be aware of health and safety issues.

Imagination and creativity

Imagination could be described as making mental images or pictures and it is an important aspect of developing the ability to become a symbol user and represent things. We need to be able to use symbols in order to read and write.

Babies show imagination in the ways that they respond to people and the world around them. They imitate and copy facial expressions, movements and sounds, especially of their main carers. Playing imitative games, such as 'round and round the garden', will help develop imagination.

Heuristic play provides excellent opportunities for sensory development.

From about 18 months old imaginative play seems to come almost naturally. Toddlers and young children imitate adult actions, such as putting a teddy to bed, talking on a telephone. Children recreate their recent learning and develop a sense of control and power where they can safely explore and express feelings, both negative and positive.

Older children can use role-play and acting to repeat events in their lives, to express complex feelings and emotions, or to develop and understand relationships.

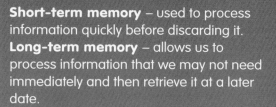

Key terms

Short-term memory – used to process information quickly before discarding it.
Long-term memory – allows us to process information that we may not need immediately and then retrieve it at a later date.

Keys to good practice

Developing imagination and creativity
Babies and children need a supportive adult who can:

- provide a rich range of materials

- provide a range of experiences that stimulate and interest children

- encourage them to explore, make decisions and choices

- provide personal space for them to develop their own ideas

- balance the need for exploration with the need to keep them safe

- communicate effectively, giving full attention and eye contact

- be sensitive to their moods and interests.

Memory skills

Memory and attention are fundamental components of how children learn. We have a **short-term memory** and a **long-term memory**. Psychologists believe that short-term memory is only about 15 seconds, but this can be extended through rehearsal, or repeating something several times. Young children are not capable of rehearsal, which is why they often quickly forget instructions.

Babies remember sensory experiences, such as hearing their mother's voice, and will know that she will feed or comfort them. They remember the smell and touch of their mother or main carer and again will learn that this person will meet their needs. Later, babies will remember and repeat sounds that they have heard and so begin to develop verbal communication skills.

We can help a child to develop memory skills by sensitive questioning to encourage them to remember events, experiences and activities. Often asking a child how they feel may help them to recall something, as emotions will trigger a memory. Asking open-ended questions, such as 'What happened next?', will help children learn to sequence and order events.

Attention and concentration

Attention and concentration are skills that the brain uses to focus on specific information and so filter out distractions, such as noise and smells. This does not mean that we can only direct our attention to one single activity; as humans we are quite skilled at multi-tasking. For example, when having a nappy changed, a baby can concentrate on the adult's facial expressions, conduct verbal interchanges and enjoy the sensation of freedom all at the same time. For many childcarers multi-tasking is part of the job!

If a child cannot concentrate for periods of time they will not be able to store information long enough to process it and therefore will not learn how to interpret their sensory experiences and learn new skills and knowledge.

Perception

Perception and vision are not the same thing: our brain receives an upside-down flat image from our eyes, yet what we perceive is a three-dimensional picture. Research has shown that in order for babies to develop perception they need stimulation of the senses.

Language and communication development

This aspect of a child's development is not just about talking. It is about all the ways in which we can communicate – from the different cries of a baby, indicating 'I am hungry', 'I am wet' or 'I am bored', to having a conversation with someone or sending a text message.

Everyone uses language in many different ways. We use it to express feelings and make our needs known, to find out more information through questioning others or reading. We describe events and situations to others and use language to get reassurance and confirmation.

Think about it

How many different forms of language do you use? For example, do you ask questions, give instructions, directions, guidance? Do you share information? Do you use language to start or develop relationships, to show how you feel and so on?
Try to recall all the different forms of language that you have used in one day; you might find it helpful to make a list. Then ask yourself whether you provide opportunities for children to develop all these different forms of language.

There is a clear sequence in which children learn to communicate with others, and adults play a key part in this learning. It is through hearing language and seeing gestures and by imitation that babies and young children are encouraged to learn. It is important that you remember that, while all children will at some point develop language, the rate at which they do so will be different for each child. Table 6.3 outlines the main stages in language development.

Stage	Age (approx.)	Features	Comments
Pre-linguistic stage			
Cooing	6 weeks	Cooing sounds show pleasure. Babies also cry to communicate needs	These early sounds are quite different to later sounds as the muscles of the mouth are still developing
Babbling	6–12 months	Blends consonants and vowels to make strings of sounds; later with intonation that copies the pattern of adult speech	Babbling makes up about 50 per cent of non-crying sounds; by the end of this stage babies can usually recognise 15–20 words
Linguistic stage			
First words	12 months	Babies will repeat words that have most meaning to them	Words may be unclear at first and can be mixed into babbling
Holophrases	12–18 months	One word can be used to express more than one meaning	Tone of voice and context of a situation is used to supplement holophrases; most children now have 10–15 words
Two words	18–24 months	Two words put together to communicate meaning, for example, 'me down'	Sometimes known as telegraphic speech

Continued

Continued

Language explosion	24–36 months	Rapid increase in vocabulary, plus greater use of sentences	Children begin to use plurals and negatives, but can make errors, for example, 'doned it'
	3–4 years	Longer sentences and imitation of adult speech; speech can be understood by non-family members or close carers	Use language in more complete ways, but can still make grammatical errors
Fluency	4 years onwards	Language is refined and a child understands that language can be written symbolically	Have mastered basic grammar rules and are usually fluent

Table 6.3: The main stages in language development.

The importance of children's development of **oracy** and **literacy**

In the early days adults talk to babies in simple, repetitive ways; this is called 'Motherese' or 'Baby Talk Register'. At these times it is essential to maintain good eye contact with the baby and give praise and recognition when the baby makes attempts to communicate, such as babbling.

Whatever the child's age, it is important that they feel they are being understood and listened to. It is important that childcarers give children time to answer or use language and not try to speak for them. You can, however, correct grammatical errors and mispronunciations by modelling, repeating the child's words but correctly. For example, a child says, 'I've doned it' and the adult could reply, 'I am really pleased that you have done it.'

You need to provide opportunities to extend and stimulate a child's language and communication through the use of:

- questions, especially open-ended ones
- repetition
- naming objects
- playing listening games appropriate to the child's age and stage of development.

It is also important to remember to listen carefully and with interest to what the children are saying. This shows that you respect and value their views.

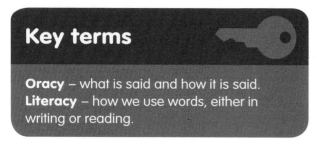

Key terms

Oracy – what is said and how it is said.
Literacy – how we use words, either in writing or reading.

Reading together can be a pleasurable activity.

Case study: Expression through dance and mime

Chris, a registered childminder, is very interested in dance and mime and plans many opportunities for the children in her care to share her interest. She finds dance helps the children express their feelings, and sometimes the older children plan dance and mime routines together to tell a story or recall a past experience.

- Think about the communication opportunities in some of the activities that you provide, such as cooking or going for a walk.

Personal, social and emotional development

Many **theorists** believe that there are very close links between language and cognitive development. There are also close links with physical development; children need to be able to control the muscles of the face, throat and tongue in order to make sounds. Children also need to be able to communicate in order to establish and develop social relationships; and a lack of social relationships can affect emotional development.

Key term

Theorist – an individual who has extensively researched a subject or topic and produced a unique and original view.

Personal, social and emotional development are the three building blocks of future success in life. They are very closely linked and often referred to as one area of development. Personal development is about how a child understands things about themselves. The Early Years Foundation Stage (EYFS) is clear that this aspect of a child's development is extremely important. For example, one of its commitments concerns positive relationships. One of the National Strategies for the Early Years is known as Social and Emotional Aspects of Development (SEAD) and another national strategy for school-aged children is Social and Emotional Aspects of Learning (SEAL).

What is social development?

Social development is about learning how to be with other people, how to build relationships and make friends, and understanding who you are. It is also about knowing how to look after yourself, for example, using a toilet independently or getting dressed. These skills are often referred to as self-help skills and may involve aspects of physical development. Often children who have difficulty with language and communication also have problems developing relationships with others.

What is emotional development?

Emotional development is about how children learn to deal with and express their feelings. It is also about how children learn to bond with their carers, or make strong relationships with important adults. This area of development also includes the development of self-confidence, self-control, self-image and self-esteem.

It is often quite difficult to separate emotional development from social development as aspects of one affect the other. Sometimes problems with emotional development can be far-reaching and have long-lasting effects; unfortunately, in some people, into adulthood.

Table 6.4 gives an overview of emotional and social development. It is important that you research these aspects of a child's development to develop your knowledge and understanding.

Approximate age	Main features
Newborn	Seems most content when in close contact with mother or main carer Needs to develop a strong bond or attachment
6 weeks	Seems to sense presence of mother/main carer Responds to human voice Watches primary carer's face Can swing rapidly from pleasure to unhappiness
3–5 months	Smiles and shows pleasure Enjoys being held and cuddled Still has rapid mood swings
6–8 months	May show anxiety towards strangers Eager and interested in everything that is going on around them Laughs, chuckles and vocalises when with mother or familiar people, generally friendly Shows anger when a plaything is removed but is easily distracted
9–11 months	Can distinguish between familiar people and strangers Will show annoyance and anger through body movements Begins to play peek-a-boo games Begins to wait for attention
12–14 months	Affectionate towards family members and primary carers Plays simple games Growing independence can lead to rage when thwarted Mood swings less violent Shows little fear and much curiosity
15–17 months	Emotionally more unstable than at 1 year Can show jealousy Swings from being independent to dependent on an adult Has more sense of being an individual
18–21 months	Can be obstinate and unwilling to follow adult suggestions Very curious, but short attention span Mood swings
2 years	Shows self-will and may have tantrums, nightmares and irrational fears Tries to be independent Has strong emotions Copies adult actions and activities Parallel play and begins to engage in pretend play
3 years	Becomes more cooperative, adopts attitude and moods of adults Wants adult approval Asks lots of questions Shows concern for others Begins to share playthings
4 years	Confident, shows purpose and persistence Shows control over emotions Has adopted standards of behaviour of parents and family members Develops friendships with peers

Continued

Continued

5 years	Self-confident
	Shows desire to do well and will persevere at a new task
	Still seeks adult approval
	Shows good control of emotions
	Cooperative play with both boys and girls, usually has a best friend
	Enjoys stories of strong people
6–7 years	Emotions can be more unstable than at 5, can be moody
	Independent and may be solitary for short periods
	Father's or male authority not usually questioned
	Teacher's standards often accepted over mother's standards
8–11 years	Emotionally independent of adults
	Needs to be accepted by peers
	Usually good control of emotions
	Intolerant of weak adults
	Enjoys team games
	Towards the end of this period sexes begin to socialise separately
12 plus	A time of great change as moving from childhood to adulthood
	Can be a time of pressure to gain qualifications, fit in with peers, experiment, take risks and face challenges
	Still need meaningful praise and to know that they are valued

Table 6.4: Key features of emotional and social development.

The formation and quality of relationships in a child's early life can have a direct impact on how they socialise and build relationships in later life. The term **attachment** is often used to describe how young children make relationships, especially with an adult.

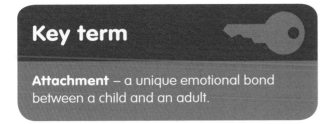

Key term

Attachment – a unique emotional bond between a child and an adult.

Why are friendships so important to children?

As well as developing attachments, children need to learn how to make friends with their peers (children of similar age). The older a child becomes the more important their friends are to them. By the time a child is 12 or 13 years old their friends can be more important to them than their family members.

Case study: Katie fears losing her friends

Katie is 15 years old and has a small, close group of girl friends, whom she has known for several years. One of her friends wants the others to take drugs when they are out. Katie does not want to take drugs as she is worried about the effects they will have on her, such as losing control. However, Katie believes that if she refuses to take the drugs her friend will not want her to go out and Katie fears she may lose all or most of her friends.

• How would you help and support Katie?

Children under 3 are social beings but are not usually cooperative in their play and interactions with others. They are aware of and respond to other children and by the age of two will play alongside another child, rather than with them. By the time a child is 3 years old they will begin to play more cooperatively and can perhaps share.

The school years are times when children develop friendships (often of the same sex). Girls often have fewer closer friends than boys. By the time a child is in their teens, friendships can be of either sex and sometimes can be a source of dilemmas for the young person, especially if the values of their friendship group are at odds with what they believe, for example, issues around drugs, alcohol and sex.

Link to assessment

AC 5.1–5.5

Learning Outcome 5 is concerned with providing play and other activities that will support a child's development and learning. It is important that you have an understanding of child development so that the activities and play opportunities you provide are appropriate to a child's age and stage of development.

7. ESTABLISHING ROUTINES

Being a professional childcarer is a busy and demanding job; it can seem sometimes that there are just not enough hours in the working day. If you can establish routines for daily, weekly and longer events you should make your life, both professionally and personally, run more efficiently and smoothly.

This chapter covers:

- how to establish routines
- how to make sure that your routines are based on agreement with parents
- how to make sure that your routines are planned with the participation of children
- how routines need to change as children develop and grow
- routines for arrivals and departures
- routines for taking children to and from other settings
- routines for meal and snack times
- routines for sleep and rest
- routines that include play and other activities
- routines for outdoor activities
- routines for homework and evening activities for school-aged children.

- This chapter links to Learning Outcome 4: understand the principles of development of routines for home-based childcare.
- All assessment criteria (4.1 to 4.3) for this learning outcome are covered, and guidance is given for CACHE Assessment Task 6.
- This chapter links to Shared Core Units SC1 (Communication), SC2 (Equality and Inclusion) and SC3 (Personal Development) of the full Level 3 Diploma for the Children and Young People's Workforce.

How to establish routines

In any business, time management is something that should be thought about very carefully. If not planned properly, a lot of time can be wasted, or not used well. If you are caring for other people's children in your home you are running a business. Admittedly it

is unlikely you will employ large numbers of people; even so how you manage your time is very important if you are to be successful and enjoy what you are doing. If you are caring for children in their own homes, time management is equally as important.

Routines are everyday events and activities that happen regularly in the home setting. Routines can be set up for daily, weekly or monthly activities and events. They are usually planned things, such as watching a favourite television programme, having a haircut, collecting children from school at the same time each day; or they may be activities around a child's care, such as meal and snack times, nappy changing and sterilising bottles. Daily routines often happen around the same time each day, such as getting meals ready and going to school.

Routines can sound rather dull, repetitive and sometimes boring, especially for adults. However, this is not the case for babies and children. Routines provide emotional security and stimulation. Care routines such as nappy changing are excellent times for stimulating a baby. Routines can provide consistency and continuity for the children and for you. Routines

Routines provide continuity and security. What routines do you have?

can help children feel emotionally secure. Children who feel secure and have consistency and continuity in their lives develop well, especially emotionally. An established, well-thought-out routine can help a child settle into their new care environment, or with a new carer, and help promote their emotional well-being.

Daily routines give a pattern and a structure to the working day, so that everyone knows what is going to happen and what they are expected to do. Routines can help you cope better with a busy, hectic working day or week.

> " *We have to have a routine in the morning or else we wouldn't get to nursery on time. Bethany has a chart that we made together with her routine in pictures so she knows what is going to happen next. Even Thomas knows that after he has got dressed he has his breakfast.* "
>
> *Bea, nanny to Thomas, 10 months, and Bethany, 4 years*

Routines can also involve physical care, such as having meals at certain times, brushing teeth and teaching children about hygiene. A good routine, for example, when sterilising bottles, can make effective use of your time and allow you more time to spend playing with the children. A routine for nappy changing can make sure that you spend time talking to the baby as well as allowing them the freedom to kick and stretch their legs, both important aspects of their development.

It is impossible to describe routines in a specific way as each routine will depend on the individual circumstances, such as:

- the ages and number of children being looked after
- the needs of the parents, the children and your own family
- personal likes and dislikes.

A routine should be planned to help you. It should make your working day easier and, within reason,

should be flexible. For example, you may have to decide whether it is more important to the overall well-being of the children for you to go outside to play with them during a dry spell on a wet day, or to prepare vegetables for the evening meal because that is your usual routine at this time.

Think about it

Routines need to change as children grow and develop. Remember, whatever routine you plan, it must be right for you and the children in your care.

You should try not to change your routine too often. If you do regular activities, such as getting ready for a meal, a different way each time or with no set pattern, then the children may become confused. They may not be able to predict what will happen next and this, together with feeling confused, could affect their emotional development and possibly their behaviour. (You can find more information about children's development in Chapter 6.)

Obviously there will be times when you will change things for good reasons, and you need to be flexible enough to accommodate these cases. However, there is a danger that if you change your routines too often, or make them too flexible, you could become overwhelmed by events and lose control. Some routines should not be changed, such as sterilising bottles, as you could put the children's health at risk. You should be managing your time and activities, not letting activities control you.

Routines also play a part in establishing good standards of care and hygiene, and teaching children to look after themselves, for example, going to the toilet, and helping them become independent. You should discuss your routines with parents and make sure that you take into consideration their wishes and have their agreement. This is especially important when establishing care routines, such as feeding and changing, as it will ensure continuity for young children and therefore make them feel more emotionally secure.

Case study: Emma's busy routine

Emma is employed by working parents to care for three children – a baby of 12 months, a boy of 5 years and a girl of 7 years. The girl goes to gym classes twice a week from 5 to 6 p.m. The boy is sometimes invited to play at his friend's house and needs collecting at around 6 p.m. and also at this time the baby is starting to get grumpy and tired. Emma has the use of a car and drives the children to their activities.

- How can Emma make sure that the needs of the baby are met?
- How can Emma organise the pick-up times of the older children so that no one is left waiting and possibly put at risk, or misses out on part of an activity?

If you are caring for children in their own home your routines may be different. You may have more contact with the parents; you may have more demands on your time. For example, you may have to get the children up, washed and dressed, sort out breakfast and get to school on time – not forgetting that you also need time to get washed and dressed yourself.

How to make sure that your routines are based on agreement with parents

You must work in partnership with parents at all times and this has been discussed in Chapter 5. The ways in which you work and the routines you establish will be developed around the children that you care for. This will ensure that you meet their individual needs. Everyone who works with children must recognise that parents are the most important people in a child's life and all practitioners should constantly reaffirm this view to both parents and children.

Values and principles in parenting vary from one culture or social group to another and also from family to family. There is no single correct way to bring up children; the only decisive factor is that children should be protected from harm and safeguarded. Parents choose routines, methods and practices which are appropriate to their lifestyle, culture, traditions, beliefs and their own upbringing.

> *I have worked with many parents over the years and they all have slightly different values and principles, but they all want the best for their children. I spend a lot of time at the first meeting discussing routines and how we can best meet the needs of the child and the parent; I believe this is really important.*
>
> *Jan, registered childminder*

Sometimes a parent's views about what they want for their children might be different from your own, so you need to talk about the differences. You need to make it clear that you do your best to care for children as the parents want, but if you are a job-share nanny or a childminder you will be caring for children from several different families. In such cases it will be necessary to compromise and negotiate. This means that you must have good and effective communication skills. (Find out more information about communication skills in Chapter 5.)

Keys to good practice

Care routines

If you are caring for a child in their own home and do not have previous experience of care routines you will need to:

- spend time with the parents and learn from them

- check your knowledge by looking at recognised publications and texts. It is always good practice to try to follow as closely as possible the routines that the parents have already established.

How to make sure that your routines are planned with the participation of children

If you are a home-based childcarer, you need to show all children that they 'belong' and are welcome in your home. Remember, each child is an individual, unique and different from any other child. Even children from the same family — siblings, twins or triplets with similar physical appearances — are different; they have their own personalities, likes, dislikes and abilities. You cannot treat every child the same; you need to give them the same opportunities but still treat them as individuals. This is what is often referred to as **inclusive** practice.

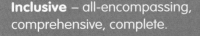

Key term

Inclusive – all-encompassing, comprehensive, complete.

This inclusive approach should be applied to your routines and, where appropriate, children should be involved in establishing the patterns of their day. For example, if you are caring for school-aged children, their needs as they arrive from school could be very different.

- One child may be hungry and need a snack.
- Another might be tired and just want to rest and be quiet for a while.
- Another may want to get stuck into homework as soon as possible.
- Another may want to talk to you about their day.

These different and individual needs have to be met and the only way you can do this successfully is to discuss it with the children and involve them in the daily routine at that point in time. All children can be involved in establishing your routines. For example, 3-year-olds who want to go to the park on the way back from nursery will then be able to understand that if this is going to happen then they may have a shorter time to play at your home before being collected by a parent.

How routines need to change as children develop and grow

All children benefit emotionally from structure and routine, regardless of their age. Older children are gaining in independence as they grow and develop, and this needs to be encouraged. They need opportunities to make responsible choices about what they do, and when and how they do things. However, the duty of care still remains with the childcarer and older children may find this restrictive at times, especially if you are caring for younger children as well. You have to be sensitive to the needs of older children while allowing them independence and privacy at times. This means that you will need to adapt and modify some of your routines to accommodate the changing needs of children.

Case study: Anwen involves the children

Anwen runs a busy home-based childcare practice, with an assistant, which includes seven school-aged children between 5 and 14. After school two of the older children take themselves to the far end of the room and either play a computer game or listen to music before they have something to eat. The younger ones are often hungry and need a snack before they go and play. One of the children likes to talk about her day as soon as she comes in, so Anwen prepares a snack for the other children with that child and is able to listen to her and meet her needs.

The assistant supervises the hungry ones, making sure they have followed hygiene routines before they eat. This routine has been discussed with the school-aged children and they agreed that they all needed different things at almost the same time of day. One of the older children has agreed that when he has 'chilled' for a while, he is happy to go into the garden and play with the younger children; one says she does not need a snack but is happy to help prepare something for the others.

- How can you involve children in establishing your routines?

> *I had a routine for walking home from school with several children. This routine made sure that all the children were safe and we all stayed close together. As the two older schoolchildren got more familiar with the route and wanted to be more independent, we talked about how we could change the routine. The older children and I decided that they could walk as far as the corner of the road and then had to wait for me. I talked to the parents and they were happy about this change. It gave the girls a bit more independence but at the same time made sure that they were safe.*
>
> *Sara, registered childminder*

If you start your childcare career looking after for a baby and a toddler you will probably have planned care routines for such activities as sterilising bottles, nappy changing and cleaning potties, as well as routines that allow enough time for play and rest. As these children grow and develop you will find that bottles will be used less and less, and eventually the routine for sterilising bottles will not be needed. It might be replaced by another care routine that is more suitable for the age and needs of the children. You may find that your daily routine will include just one quiet time for rest and sleep.

In the same way you may start off by caring for a child who goes to a morning pre-school session, so your daily routine will involve taking and collecting the child. When the child starts school, your daily routine will have to change. Older children in your care may join after-school clubs as they become more independent and again this could affect your daily and weekly routines.

As children develop and grow they will want to help you or do things for themselves. It is often quicker to put a child's coat on yourself. However, letting the child do it for themselves may help them learn how to cope with buttons or zips, and so aid independence. Allowing children to do things for themselves and independently will probably take longer than doing it for them, so you will have to adjust your routine accordingly. Another example is a child wanting to help you prepare food or help find things in the supermarket. Again these are valuable learning experiences but do take more time. Remember to allow for this when planning your day.

How do you help children do things for themselves?

Find it out

Think about your own daily routine.
List three things that are part of your routine today that will have changed by this time next year.
1 _____
2 _____
3 _____
Why will they have changed?
What impact will these changes have on other daily events?

Routines for arrivals and departures

It is good practice to encourage parents to develop and use their own special routine for saying goodbye to their children. This is something you should raise at the first meeting. You may also have a policy for settling a new child into your setting and this should be shared with the parents.

Keys to good practice

Departures
Encourage parents to make their goodbyes quite short and to say the same thing each time they leave (i.e. to follow their own routine). By doing this the child will begin to understand what to expect and what is going to happen next. They will then settle into your care better, and will feel emotionally secure and safe.

If young children show signs of distress at being separated from their parent, it might be useful for the parent to leave a small personal item, such as a scarf, 'accidentally on purpose' with the child when they leave. The child may then understand that the parent will come back to collect the item and the child (if not in their own home). However, during the settling-in period, the parent should be encouraged to stay with their child until they are settled.

Find it out

Being anxious about being separated from their main carer is a very common feature of a young child's development. Much research has been done into this subject, most notably by John Bowlby (1907–90). Bowlby developed the theory of attachment, which stated that babies need to form one main attachment that would be special and of more importance than any other. This theory has been highly influential in social care policy and childcare practices and has inspired further research into attachments.
Find out more about Bowlby's theory of attachment and the work of others, such as Mary Ainsworth (1913–99) and Elinor Goldschmied (1910–2009).

Separation can be a distressing time for parent and child. Encourage the parents to say goodbye with a comforting smile.

Long drawn-out goodbyes can be stressful for everyone. They take up more time than necessary, and if a child is already unsure about their parent going, delaying the actual parting will not help. Parents should remember to give their child a kiss (assuming the child wants one)!

Keep it short and simple (or sweet) – KISS

A suggested routine for settling a child into a home other than their own and saying goodbye could be something like the following:

- Parent and child arrives at the house.
- You greet both child and parent.
- They both come in.
- Parent removes child's outdoor clothing.

- If appropriate, both you and the parent take the child through to the room that they will be in.
- Parent says that they are going now and that they will come back at lunchtime or teatime, or at another agreed time.
- Parent and child say goodbye in their own special way.
- You pick up the child or hold their hand.
- Go with parent to the door.
- Child and parent wave goodbye.
- Close door and immediately start to occupy the child with an activity.

A routine for parents leaving and collecting a child cared for in their own home is equally important. Parents should be encouraged to have a leaving and returning routine. This will benefit the child, the parents and the childcarer. It is important to remember that some parents may need space when they arrive home and the initial greeting might be quite brief.

The time of day when parents return to their child is very important. It is a time for exchanging and sharing information. Sometimes adults and children can be tired and grumpy at the end of the day, so it is important that you have a routine that allows time for you and the parents to talk and also time for the children to talk to their parents. Some childminders find their routine is to welcome the parents and then let them talk to the children before there are any exchanges of information.

> " *The routine in my workplace is for the children and I to have tea as their mother returns home. Mum gets changed, by which time we have finished our tea and then we all spend time together.* "
>
> *Heather, nanny*

Routines for taking children to and from other settings

It is important that you establish routines for taking children to and from settings to make sure that everyone has plenty of time to get ready and that there is no last-minute rush. Remember that things often take much longer than expected and you may become harassed and forget something. Before leaving, make sure that:

- everyone has time to go to the toilet if needed
- the children have got their coats and any items they may need for school or to take to pre-school or nursery
- the children have got everything they need for the day ahead.

If something does get left behind in the early morning rush, reassure the child and, if necessary, let their teacher know.

Keys to good practice

Establishing routines

- Try to make time to talk to the child about their day ahead. It is good practice to try to remember what you talked about, so that you can ask them about it when you meet them.

- Try not to rush or hurry the child.

- Help them to start the busy day ahead in a calm and relaxed way; in other words be a good role model.

- Use care routines for washing hands and cleaning teeth before leaving for school. This will help develop emotional security and can reduce anxiety.

Children of school age need to learn how to become independent, while still remaining safe. The journey to school is a good time to talk about 'stranger danger' and road safety.

Children may also want to talk about problems they have at school with friends and peers. Listen to what the children say and speak to their parents if you have any concerns.

School-aged children might only be in your care for a relatively short time before school, but this could be a very busy time for you. You may have other children to care for, parents arriving and leaving, and possibly your own children to consider. This makes the need for routines very important.

Each child in your care has an equal right to your care and time. Just because a child is older and perhaps more independent than others, it does not mean they do not need your time and care. Do not leave school-aged children to fend for themselves before school because you are too busy dressing, or sorting out younger children, or talking to parents.

If it is appropriate and does not distract you if you are driving, or from caring for other children, you could use the journey to school to play 'mind games' such as 'I

Case study: Tina's travel dilemma

Tina has to walk to school with her own two children and a toddler in a buggy, and also take a 3-year-old to nursery. At 11.30 a.m. she collects the 3-year-old plus another child. At 3 p.m. Tina, the two 3-year-olds and the toddler in the buggy go to collect her own children from school. Tina has been asked to care for a child after school, who goes to a different school from her own children. Tina has had to turn this job down as her routine did not give her enough time to get to two different schools.

- What would you have done in Tina's position?

spy', or have older children make up words from car registration number plates, or you could just talk to each other.

If you are walking with the children remember to take the opportunity to reinforce road safety and stranger danger. (Find out more about this in Chapter 4.)

Routines for meal and snack times

All mealtimes should be social, happy times and a positive experience for all. Meal and snack times are also very good learning opportunities for all children. It is important to teach children good personal hygiene routines when preparing, handling food and eating. (You can find more information on hygiene in Chapter 4.)

Routines for babies

It is highly likely that the mother will have established some sort of feeding pattern for her baby. This can be very varied, from feeding whenever the baby is hungry to feeding at set times of the day. Whatever pattern has been established by the mother, you should not try to change it without talking to her first.

If the baby is still being breast-fed you will need to make sure that your routine considers the needs of the mother. You may have to help the mother and baby transfer from breast to bottle, and later you may have to wean the baby on to solid foods. Routines will help you manage all these things better.

Routines for toddlers

Toddlers will be fully weaned and many will have made serious and determined attempts to feed themselves. Most toddlers will eat a normal balanced diet and drink from a cup or training cup. It is also quite normal for toddlers still to have a bottle, especially just before a nap or at bedtime. It is good practice to sterilise bottles and training cups.

Toddlers are very active and use up a lot of energy, and boys usually need more calories than girls to keep up

Case study: Keeping the baby happy

Pam has agreed to care for a 3-month-old baby boy in his home from 8.30 a.m. to 5.45 p.m. for three days a week as his mother has returned to work. The mother has breast-fed her baby and has tried to gradually introduce him to formula milk and bottles over the last three weeks. At the moment the baby has a combination of formula milk and expressed breast milk at different times of the day when he is hungry. He is beginning to get colic, often cries and Pam feels that he is not as content as he could be.

- What would you suggest to the mother that you both could do to try to sort out these problems?
- What else mght be causing the baby distress?

their energy levels. It is good practice to give children regular small meals or snacks every two to three hours rather than three big meals; for example, children could have breakfast quite early before coming to you and be ready for a mid-morning snack and drink. All children should be able to have water whenever they are thirsty, especially in hot weather or after physical, vigorous play activities.

Routines for older children

Routines for snacks and meals will change as children develop and grow. School-aged children may be independent enough to organise their own snack when returning from school and this is an important aspect of their emotional development. You may need to remind them about personal hygiene routines before preparing food and also what to do with the crockery and cutlery they have used. These routines also provide good learning opportunities for discussing healthy diets.

Routines for sleep and rest

It will help you and the children if you can establish a pattern for rest and sleep times; but this does not mean that you should become inflexible in your routine, insisting, for example, that all children must rest or sleep after a midday meal. Children and babies should be able to sleep and rest when they are tired. Babies who are over-tired are often difficult to settle and can become distressed. This could upset and distract older children. When a baby is asleep during the day, do not creep about and prevent other children from making any noise. Carry on as normal as the baby should be able to sleep through a normal level of noise.

All babies are different in their needs for rest and sleep and in the ways that they settle to sleep. You must ask the parents how much sleep their baby needs during the day, what position they are put in and how they are settled. These questions should be part of your first meeting with parents, especially if you are not caring for the baby in their own home. It is important that you follow the routine that has been established by the parents for rest and sleep, but at the same time be flexible. By the time a baby is about 9 months old a

routine or pattern for rest and sleep should have been established, otherwise it might be difficult for you to settle the baby.

Find it out

- Find out from the parents where they put the baby to sleep during the day; if possible use the same piece of equipment, such as a cot, Moses basket or baby seat.
- Find out from the parents how they settle their baby. This could be by cuddling or rocking; using comfort objects such as a blanket, special toy or soothers; making a special noise; playing music; or stroking or gently patting.

As babies get older they will begin to learn the sequence of some events in their lives. For example, they will get to know that they will have a nappy change after waking from sleep.

Many young children still need to take a nap at some point during the day, often up to the age of 4. Toddlers are very active and need time to 'recharge their batteries'. Some children do not want to sleep, but you should still encourage them to rest and be quiet. You can plan activity that is restful, such as watching a DVD, listening to music or a story. Establishing a routine for naps or rest and quiet will help parents, as their toddler should then be ready for bedtime at home.

It helps to have a quiet moment before going to bed.

Some school-aged children may also need to rest and have a quiet time when they return from school. Again you need to establish a routine to meet their needs. If, for example, they want to listen to music, watch a DVD or read a book, they should be able to organise a routine for themselves, such as first putting away their school bags and outdoor wear and washing their hands.

had planned to do finger painting — it would be much more fun to go outside and feel and experience the snow; or you and the children may hear a fire engine's siren outside and want to watch through the window and leave the construction set on the floor for the time being.

School holidays should be fun times for children, but it is still important that all children have a structure and routine to their day at any age. You will need to have routines for care and mealtimes during school holidays as well as routine times for play experiences, rest, sleep or quiet activities.

Children can be given responsibility for planning their own day and building into their plan routines to encourage good personal hygiene, for example, they could use charts to help them plan a week's activities, drawing or writing daily details. This helps them develop a sense of time as well as giving them independence and responsibility — both important aspects of a growing child's emotional development.

Routines that include play and other activities

These routines could be part of your overall daily schedule in that there will be set times for meals, feeding, tidying up and collecting other children from school, so play and other activities will fit in around these events. Some practitioners work out a timetable for the day to help them plan in advance how long they will have for certain activities. For example, it is not worth setting out a cooking activity that will take about 45 minutes when you only have 30 minutes before you have to collect a child from nursery. A timetable could help a newly registered childminder to plan the working day.

One of the main benefits of being a home-based childcarer is, however, that you can be flexible and spontaneous. While planning a day's activities can be very useful it is also important to remember that there will be times when you will want to drop your planned routine and take your cues from the children. For example, it may have started to snow and you

Routines for outdoor activities

Routines for outdoor activities include being away from your setting as well as in your outdoor area, such as a garden, patio or decking. The safety of the children must be your major concern at all times, regardless of where they are. Ofsted (or the regulatory body for your country) will check the outside areas for safety at the time of your inspection, but you should have your own regular and frequent routine for checking the equipment and outdoor areas. It is good practice to implement this routine every day. Look again at Chapter 4 to remind yourself about keeping children safe when outdoors.

It is very important that older children have an understanding of road safety and stranger danger. Your routines should make sure that all the children are safe; for example, if you expect children to hold either your hand or the handle of the buggy when walking down the road, be firm and do not compromise. You can use these situations very effectively to teach road safety and establish a routine for crossing a road safely. You also need to establish a procedure for what to do if children become separated from you. Some practitioners suggest that they and the children look for a prominent landmark, for example, a well-known shop in a shopping centre or a large building in a park, and children are taught to head for the agreed place. (You can find more information about safety routines in Chapter 4.)

Your routine should also include a personal safety check, for example:

• Have you got a first aid box?
• Have you got emergency phone numbers?
• Is your mobile phone fully charged?

You need to get into the habit of regularly checking your car if you are planning to use it with the children. Ask someone else to check your tyres, lights, oil and battery for you if you do not feel competent to do it yourself.

Routines for homework and evening activities for school-aged children

At the end of the school day many children are tired. Their concentration and energy levels will be low and they may not want to talk or be bothered by other children. On the other hand, some children will come out of school bursting to tell you about what they have done. Some may want to get stuck into homework straight away. Whatever the needs of the child, you must respond appropriately.

For the quiet child, allow them time to recover, sit quietly and perhaps play a game that does not require much effort. Do not push them into doing an activity if they are clearly tired, as this will only lead to upset and possible confrontation. Provide a snack or drink that may help to restore their energy levels.

Do you always allow children time to recover after school?

For the talkative child, give them your attention and let them tell you what they have been doing. Do not just 'hear' what is being said; actively listen, by giving eye contact while the child is talking.

Most children come home from school hungry and so you will need to give them a healthy snack and drink. Many parents like children to change out of school clothes into something more casual; this is a good time for the quiet child to have space as they change their clothes independently. Many children will have homework to do and you should agree with the parents when this is to be done. If it is your responsibility to make sure that homework is started, if not finished, then you will have to provide the child with a quiet place to work but where you can still supervise them.

Case study: Winding down after school

Caroline and Laura are in the same year at school and walk together to a nearby childminder's house after school. Laura wants to talk about her day as soon as she gets through the door; Caroline on the other hand likes to be left alone and be quiet. The childminder prepares a snack before the girls arrive so Caroline takes hers and goes to sit down; Laura has hers after she has finished talking. When Caroline has finished her snack she sometimes starts to talk about her day.

• How would you meet the needs of these two children?

Many children attend after-school or early evening activities. It could be part of your job to take the child to these activities, so you will need to adjust your routine in order for you to do this. It could be that taking a child to an early evening activity will affect the pick-up times and collection of other children. You will then have to decide what is most important or arrange with other carers or parents going to the same activity to car-share if possible. If this is what you decide, you must get the parents' written permission for someone else to take their child. If there is an accident and you have not got the parents' permission, you could be held responsible for the child.

Link to assessment

AC 4.1–4.3

Explain how routines are based on meeting a child's needs, agreement with parents and participation of the children.

Explain how they would adapt routines to meet the needs of children at different ages and stages of development.

Explain how they ensure that each child is welcomed and valued in the home-based work setting.

CACHE Task 6
The information in this chapter covers the task in several different places and so you will need to check that your charter contains all the details required but does not become repetitious.

8. PROVIDING PLAY AND ACTIVITIES TO SUPPORT EQUALITY AND INCLUSION

To play can mean to amuse yourself, to have fun (either on your own or with others) or sometimes just to 'mess about'. You can probably think of other meanings, such as to play an instrument or a sport. Some educationalists and theorists think play is one of the most complicated ideas to try to understand. For a child, play is one of the most important ways to learn.

This chapter covers:

- children's rights and responsibilities
- how to treat children as individuals
- how to plan play and activities that are inclusive
- how to be a positive role model
- how to challenge stereotypes
- how play promotes children's development and learning
- why it is important to observe children at play
- how to extend your play opportunities through the use of toy libraries and equipment loan schemes.

- This chapter links to Learning Outcome 5: Understand how to provide play and other activities for children in home-based settings that will support equality and inclusion.
- All assessment criteria (5.1 to 5.5) for this learning outcome are covered, and guidance is given for CACHE Assessment Task 7.
- This chapter links to Children and Young People's Core units CYP 3.1 to 3.7 of the Level 3 Diploma for the Children and Young People's Workforce.

Some people think that children play naturally, but in fact children learn how to play. Children will learn from their parents and family members, from you, from older children and from doing the same things over and over again. We all like to play, whatever our age. Everyone should be able to play, in some shape or form, regardless of their age or whether they have an additional need. Play should be fun and relaxing as well as stimulating. It is a very important part of children's lives. When children play they are in control; they can put right their mistakes and can experiment and explore.

Play underpins every aspect of the Early Years Foundation Stage (EYFS) and the guidance clearly states that children should have opportunities to play, both indoors and outside, and that those opportunities should offer times for **spontaneous play** in a secure and challenging environment. It is your responsibility to plan inclusive play opportunities that extend and support a child's learning and development.

Key terms

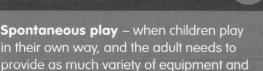

Spontaneous play – when children play in their own way, and the adult needs to provide as much variety of equipment and resources as possible, with opportunities and time for exploration and experimenting.
Rights – constitutional entitlements, privileges and/or civil liberties.

Children's rights and responsibilities

In order for you to be inclusive and promote children's **rights**, you will need to have an understanding of children's development. (You can find more information on development in Chapter 6.) Through this understanding you can plan and provide appropriate activities and experiences which will meet individual needs, and will stimulate and promote development and growth.

The rights of all children are paramount and it is essential that all home-based childcarers protect and promote those rights. It is also important that your setting is inclusive, one where everyone is welcomed, and that you think about your attitude towards all children and their families.

To try to explain what is a 'right' people sometimes talk about the difference between 'wants' and 'needs'. Wants are idealistic things that are not vital to our lives, such as a plasma screen television. Needs are the things that we must have or be in order to thrive and live well, such as fresh, clean water. Rights are like needs. They are basic things that we must have or be able to do in order to live a healthy and secure life. Other people have a duty to respect and meet these needs or rights. It is the government's responsibility to make sure that people's rights are met and it also has a responsibility to help parents, childcare practitioners and guardians meet the needs and rights of children and young people.

United Nations Convention on the Rights of the Child

The United Nations Convention on the Rights of the Child (UNCRC) was drawn up in 1989; the UK is a signatory and the Convention was approved in 1991. It gives children and young people under the age of 18 their own rights. The 54 articles contained within the UNCRC state that all children must be shown respect and that their well-being is the principal factor. The rights can be divided into three main areas:

- provision (for example, access to food, clean water, housing, education, health care)

- protection — for example, being safe from **abuse** and **discrimination**
- participation (for example, having their views heard and participating in making decisions).

Key terms

Abuse – suffering or considerable harm from physical, emotional or sexual ill-treatment, neglect or bullying.
Discrimination – treating someone differently and unfairly because of their race, gender, religion, disability and so on.
CSSIW – Care and Social Services Inspectorate Wales, the Welsh regulatory body.

Of the 54 articles the following primarily affect childcare practitioners. These are:

- **Article 2** — children have a right to be protected from all forms of discrimination
- **Article 3** — the best interests of the child must be the primary consideration in all activities and actions concerning children
- **Article 7** — the child shall have 'full opportunity for play and recreation, which should be directed to the same purposes as education; society and the public authorities shall endeavour to promote the enjoyment of this right' (note that this comes from the 1959 Declaration of the Rights of the Child)
- **Article 12** — a child has a right to express his or her views freely and that view is to be given appropriate weight in accordance with the child's age or maturity
- **Article 13** — a child has a right to freedom of expression and exchange of information regardless of frontiers
- **Article 16** — children have a right to privacy
- **Article 28** — a child has a right to education with a view to achieving this right progressively on the basis of equal opportunities.

These articles are relevant and important for home-based childcarers because they should make you think about the way you relate to children, how you listen to them and recognise and respond to their comments and

views, and how you plan inclusive play opportunities and activities. These articles reinforce that all children are special and that each one is unique and entitled to be treated with dignity and respect. (You can find more information about children's rights in Chapter 2.)

Think about it

Think about the different ways that you can support and encourage Article 7 of the UNCRC (the right to play) for children:
- under 2 years old
- between 2 and 5 years
- between 5 and 11 years
- over 11 years.
How might your practices and routines have to change to meet the needs of different-aged children?

Link to assessment   AC 5.4

Identify how and why it is important that children receive equal treatment and access, based on their individual needs and acknowledging their rights.

CACHE Task 7
Write a report which will explain to parents and regulatory bodies (such as Ofsted and **CSSIW**) how you make sure that children's needs and rights are met in your setting. You also need to explain why this is important and show your understanding of inclusive practice.

Find out more about children's rights; you might find sources such as Rights4Me a useful starting point. You can find it by accessing the website from the Hotlinks section (see page 3).

If you are not following the CACHE tasks, this criterion could be evidenced with a written section in your portfolio, a poster, a leaflet or anything else that you think is suitable.

How to treat children as individuals

It is a requirement of registration for anyone who offers home-based childcare that they comply with the Children Act (2004) and its guidance. The Act has the requirement 'to treat all children as individuals and with equal concern' and links to Articles 2, 12 and 13 of the UNCRC.

Treating children as individuals is not the same as treating all children in the same way. This is impossible to do, as all children are different. What is important is that practitioners understand how to treat all children and their families with respect in a fair way, do not discriminate; have inclusive practices.

We know that everyone learns in different ways; this is a feature of our individuality and therefore children learn through play in different ways. How we learn can be influenced by many things, such as:

- who the child or young person is with during the play opportunity
- the number of children and adults around the child
- where the child is
- what resources are available to the child and whether they access them independently.

Children can use different **learning styles** in different situations, at different times of their development, or they may combine more than one learning style at a time. This is explained in more detail in Table 8.1.

If you are familiar with differing learning styles you will find it easier to plan play activities and experiences that meet the individual needs of children in your care.

Key term

Learning style – the way in which we process information. Most people will have a preferred learning style.

Recognising children's individuality is the basis of inclusive practice and this should underpin all your work with children and their families. Inclusion is often used in combination with anti-bias practice and in the case of home-based care, should mean an environment where everyone is welcomed and respected.

All children are unique; they have different personalities, needs, interests and abilities. They should be valued and respected for who they are. Children who feel valued will enjoy being in your company, they will respond positively to you. Home-based childcarers should always try to meet children's individual needs and develop positive relationships with children based on trust and respect.

Could you do any more to make sure every child feels welcomed and respected?

Learning style	Features
Auditory (concerned with hearing)	Talkers and listeners Talkers have to hear information Listeners have to retain and recall information Both: • prefer the spoken word • love different voices • enjoy explanations • enjoy communication with others • when reading often mentally hear what they are reading
Kinaesthetic (concerned with spatial awareness in relation to senses)	Need to sense position and movement in relation to the situation in which they are in Like and need to touch, examine and feel something in order to learn
Tactile (concerned with tangible concrete experiences)	Want or need to touch, handle and experiment in a sensory way Can sometimes be perceived by others as being disruptive
Visual (concerned with what is seen and perceived)	Enjoy pictures in books Enjoy visual descriptions of things Like to watch people speak as well as listening to them Look for shapes and forms in pictures and words

Table 8.1: The features of different learning styles.

This view is reinforced in the Early Years Foundation Stage (EYFS) which is followed by all practitioners in England. One of the principles of the EYFS is 'a unique child' and on Principles into Practice card 1.1 A Unique Child it states, 'Every child is a unique individual with their own characteristics and temperament.' (You can find more information about this and frameworks for other UK countries in Chapter 3.)

All children will pass through the same stages of **development** but the rate at which they develop will vary according to each child. On this basis it can be misleading to say, for example, that all babies can sit without support at 8 months; some will, but some will sit at 7 months, while others will do it at 9 months. This depends on many factors. All of these babies are probably developing quite 'normally' but differently and in their own individual way. (You can find more information about child development in Chapter 6.)

> ## Key term
>
> **Development** – ways in which children grow and acquire skills and competences. Areas of development are sometimes categorised as physical, intellectual (or cognitive), language, social and emotional. All of these areas are interrelated and interdependent.

Children from the same family will have different and individual personalities; they will have different physical characteristics and will react differently in some situations. It is important that children know that you respect them as individuals regardless of their strengths and weaknesses.

Keys to good practice 🔑

Using names

🔑 One very positive way of helping a child understand that you respect them as an individual and not as some other person's child, brother or sister is to use their name. Make sure that you pronounce the name correctly and when writing a child's name make sure that it is spelled correctly.

Link to assessment   AC 5.4

Identify how and why it is important that children receive equal treatment and access, based on their individual needs and acknowledging their rights.

CACHE Task 7
Look at the previous link to assessment for guidance (page 143). Think about your policy and procedures for equal opportunities; maybe you need to think about a policy and procedures for inclusive practice as well.

How to plan play and activities that are inclusive

One very effective way to encourage children to develop positive attitudes and respect for other people is to create a positive learning environment in your setting and plan activities that are inclusive. This is not just about putting 'different-coloured dolls' out for the children to play with. It is more about having materials, toys and resources that reflect the diversity of our society. It is about having materials in the home that do not just reflect the background of the children that you care for, but that are inclusive. It is about you having an open mind, a flexible approach and a positive attitude to your work.

There is a danger that some home-based childcarers may fall into a 'multicultural trap' and inadvertently plan activities or provide children with materials, activities and images that do not accurately reflect

ncma
says...

Using your observations will allow you to plan and offer activities to meet the individual needs of children, which is one way of offering an inclusive setting.

other cultures, for example, giving the idea that all Inuit people live in igloos, when in fact many live in towns and cities. In the same way having a length of material in the dressing-up box and calling it a 'sari' does not show respect or understanding of women who do wear this form of clothing.

How you use and work with your equipment and resources is very important. You should avoid the potential danger of teaching children a little about a culture and then presenting a **stereotype**, implying that

Case study: Chris and 'the twins'

Chris is a private nanny and has just started to care for twin girls aged 7 and a 3-year-old boy. Chris notices that the parents rarely use the twins' individual names, referring to them collectively as 'the twins'. They talk about their son as 'the twins' brother' to other people. One

of the girls can be quite defiant at times and Chris wonders if she might feel resentful.
- Why do you think the girl might be feeling this way?
- What could Chris do?

everyone is the same. It is like believing that the British culture is only about Big Ben and Christmas and that everyone in Britain celebrates Christmas and uses Big Ben to set the time.

Key term

Stereotype – to label, put into artificial categories, to typecast.

During your childcare career you will probably care for children from a wide variety of backgrounds. You need to show that you value and respect each family and, if appropriate, you should ask parents to help you acquire suitable resources and toys. This could include sharing a new song, rhyme or story, or trying a new recipe together. Books and photos in your setting should also reflect different family groupings. This will not only make individual children feel welcome and valued by you, but will also extend the knowledge and understanding of other children that you care for.

Think about it

It is possible to buy small-scale toys of people in wheelchairs, on crutches and with physical impairments or disabilities. Ask yourself whether these help make children with disabilities and impairments feel more welcome, included and more respected.

Planning any activity is a very individual process. As you get to know the children you care for, you may start to plan play opportunities in advance so that you can meet their individual needs.

You will probably receive lots of advice and suggested ways to do your planning, but essentially it is up to you. Many local authorities have standard planning documentation that is used across all registered settings, and this can be invaluable. You may want to amend these documents to make them individual to

your setting. However you decide to plan, in order to make your practice inclusive, you will need to take into account:

- each child's stage of development and learning
- each child's needs
- their individual likes and dislikes, strengths and areas to be developed
- what interests and motivates each child
- next steps.

You will be able to find out all these things through careful observations of each child, which are factual and should be used to inform your planning.

Link to assessment   AC 5.1

Explain the importance of play to children's learning and development and the need for an inclusive approach.

CACHE Task 7
Produce a written section in your portfolio which gives information on:
- why learning through play is important
- how your practice reflects learning through play
- how you make sure that your practice is inclusive.

You could use photographs (with parents' written permission), case studies and examples of good practice to support this section in your portfolio. Make sure that you cover all three points and it may be a good idea to start with a short explanation of what you understand by 'play'.

This criterion requires quite a lot of information and so even if you are not completing this unit with CACHE you may find it useful to produce written evidence. You could also include copies of your own plans with an explanation of how you ensure that your practice reflects learning through play.

How to be a positive role model

One very effective way to encourage children to develop positive attitudes and respect for other people is from your own example. Children notice how you behave and react towards others and will take their cues from you. You should give each child equal opportunities to develop and grow in their own unique and individual way. It is essential that you are able to make adaptations to your work practices and routines so that children can be treated according to their individual needs.

Children learn how to behave, react to others and manage their feelings from the adults around them. If children see adults behaving in an aggressive way towards each other they will learn that this behaviour is acceptable. If at all possible children need to see adults managing their feelings appropriately and understand that feelings can be talked about and shared.

Children need to have accurate information about every aspect of their learning and development, with honest and truthful answers. Being a positive role model means that you do not pretend differences do not exist; instead you talk openly about them and encourage children to do the same.

Think about it

You are driving your car along a busy road, with children in the back. The driver in front of you does not indicate that they are turning left. What do you do?

- Shout at the driver about their bad driving, even though the driver cannot hear you.
- Say nothing, but make a rude gesture.
- Say nothing, but just shake your head to show your disapproval.
- Do nothing.

Keys to good practice

Being a positive role model …

- does not mean that you will be perfect all the time; you are human and we all make mistakes

- means that you will admit your mistakes and learn from them

- means that children see that you are open-minded and that you treat children and their families with respect and care.

Case study: Children learning from adults

Sheila, a reception class teacher, was observing a group of 4-year-olds playing in the role play area. One of the girls was busy organising everyone and said, 'I'll be the mummy, you can be the baby and you can be the one next door.' She then turned to the only boy in the group and said, 'And you can be the lazy b***** that sits on the settee all day watching telly.'

- How do you think this 4-year-old girl had learnt her understanding of gender roles?
- How could you extend her ideas and play?

How to challenge stereotypes

Prejudice and prejudicial views are often based on incorrect judgements and in many cases lead to stereotypical assumptions, for example, the idea that looking after children is not a 'proper job'. The view that childcare is not a proper job could result in the carer giving a poor-quality service because they do not feel valued or respected.

 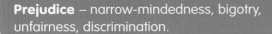
If you hold prejudicial or stereotypical views you may find that these will affect your work practices, the activities you plan, the resources you provide – in fact every aspect of your work. Prejudicial attitudes and stereotypical views can be obstacles to children reaching their full potential.

Stereotypical attitudes, labelling individuals and prejudice all will lead to discrimination and negative effects on children and their families. Labelling takes away a person's individuality. For example, saying that all football supporters are hooligans does not take into consideration the many families and children who regard supporting their local football team as a great way to spend time together.

Think about it

When deciding to begin a career in childcare, did you encounter any prejudicial or stereotypical views? Did people ask you when you were going to go 'back to work', implying that you were not really working at the time?
- How did you feel?
- How did you respond?

Prejudice and stereotyping lead to discrimination. This may not always be obvious, but may result in children's and parental rights being ignored.

> " *I encountered negative discrimination when a parent in the school playground asked me, in front of other children, if I was going to get a proper job now that my youngest has started school. One of the other children asked me later why I wasn't doing a proper job and was quite upset about it.* "
>
> *Kath, registered childminder*

Gender discrimination is in effect here. How do you make sure you do not discriminate?

Keys to good practice

Dealing with discrimination

- Make sure that within your framework or policy for promoting positive behaviour you include rules or guidelines about children playing together and not excluding another child for any reason.

- Get involved immediately if you hear a child make a discriminatory or prejudicial remark and talk to the child who made the remark about the hurt and distress that they could have caused.

- Comfort any child who has been on the receiving end of a discriminatory remark. Make sure they understand that you will care for them unconditionally. Help the child to respond positively to such remarks.

- Be aware that sometimes children repeat things that they have heard adults say. When discussing what children have said, do not devalue or undermine the child's parents or family members. It is better to explain that everyone has different views and opinions, and without being judgemental try to explain to children how you wish them to behave when they are in your care. Hopefully the good example you set will help the child form positive attitudes themselves.

- Be assertive and protect the children in your care from prejudice and discrimination. Point out that prejudice and discrimination are hurtful and politely give accurate information to any individual who makes a prejudiced or discriminatory remark.

- Answer all children's questions about why some people look different, wear different clothes or behave differently from them, with accuracy and honesty. Do not ignore their question or change the subject.

- Think before you speak! 'Engage the brain before the mouth.' Use language that is positive and does not give stereotypical impressions. For example, get into the habit of saying 'police officers' rather than policemen.

- Everyone in your setting must comply with your equal opportunities policy and procedures – and this includes the parents. If a parent made a comment or remark that was discriminatory you should challenge it.

How play promotes children's development and learning

All children play in some way, whatever their age. Babies play with 'toys' such as their own fingers and toes. Some experts say that a baby's first toy is the mother's breast as the baby becomes familiar with the smell of the mother's skin, learns to find the nipple, suck and get satisfaction while being fed. When children play they behave in different ways. Sometimes their play will be noisy and energetic; sometimes it will be quiet and thoughtful. Sometimes children will describe what they are doing and discuss and plan how to play and what to do next.

Playing with a baby gym is more than just fun.

To help children get as much as possible from play you must understand how valuable play is. Play is how children learn; it offers opportunities for children to explore, investigate, develop new skills and master and improve existing skills. You will need to know how to plan and organise play opportunities for all children and understand how you can get involved with, or stand back from, those activities. As a childcarer you should give all the children in your care activities that you know they will enjoy, that will stimulate them and help them to learn. You will have to plan into your routines opportunities and time to play, and sometimes things to play with and the space to play. You will have to learn when to become involved in the children's play and when to step back and let them get on with it.

Some home-based childcarers think that if they are planning and supporting children's individual learning and development, through play, they have to write lots of things down in a formal way and 'teach' children in the same way that teachers do in schools. This is not the case.

As professional childcare practitioners, childminders and nannies plan activities and support children's learning in many valuable ways. Many experienced practitioners do this almost instinctively and do not always appreciate the full extent of their work in this area. They can and often do provide children with an excellent start to their formal years at school, and also support all aspects of a child's growth and development in ways that could not be achieved in schools. This is one of the many benefits for parents when they choose a home-based childcarer for their child.

Implementing your plans involves some form of teaching or educating. As a professional home-based childcarer you will be 'educating' the children that you care for all the time. You will be helping them to learn, to grow and to develop in every way. You probably will not set aside times of the day when you make a conscious decision to 'educate' the children, but you may include in your daily routine time to play with them. You do not have to provide worksheets and special educational toys to 'teach' the children. You will talk to the children and play with them, help them to do things that they could not do before, such as feed themselves or fasten their own coat.

All the things you do as part of your childcare service are your inclusive teaching methods. If you wanted to list your methods you might include:

Think about it

The German educator Friedrich Froebel (1782–1852) set up a kindergarten (nursery) in Germany where he was able to test his ideas about play. He believed in outdoor and indoor play and is recognised as inventing finger play, and many songs and rhymes. Many of Froebel's ideas still influence modern thinking about play.

- **talking**, as all children learn through talking and other forms of communication
- **providing a safe environment and equipment** for the children to play in and with, as children learn through play and first-hand experiences
- **offering a wide range of inclusive activities and experiences**, as children learn through exploring the world around them
- **playing with** the children and guiding them
- **joining in** and supporting their play.

Play is all about encouraging the children that you care for to develop and learn in every way possible. Play can be spontaneous and require little or no planning or preparation. On the other hand it may be necessary for you to plan ahead for some play activities, to make sure that you have appropriate resources.

Making use of domestic routines and household items

It is not necessary to buy expensive toys and play equipment to encourage development. There are many things around the home, and routine things you do that will help children of all ages develop through play. You must remember that whatever you give the children to play with must be safe, hygienic and not likely to harm them in any way. (You can find more information about safety and hygiene in Chapter 4.)

All the activities in Table 8.2 are things that you probably do every day in the home. This list could easily be extended; only the main ones have been included. They are also excellent play activities and opportunities for children's development.

Routine activity	Learning opportunities for young children	Learning opportunities for older children
Cooking	Sequencing – cognitive Counting, measuring, weighing – cognitive Using a range of tools and utensils – physical New words, and asking questions – language Awareness of healthy diet – cognitive Sharing, taking turns and playing in a group – personal and social Having fun – emotional	Sequencing – cognitive Addition, time, weighing, measuring – cognitive Science, how things change – cognitive Greater fine motor control coordination – physical Vocabulary development – language Understanding a healthy diet – cognitive Sharing, taking turns and playing in a group – social Having fun – emotional
Preparing food	Counting, matching, sorting – cognitive Colours – cognitive Sensory development Using tools – physical Likes and dislikes – emotional	Understanding of quantities – cognitive Awareness of needs of others, diets and allergies – social and cognitive Using tools – physical Personal preferences – personal, emotional
Setting the table	Counting, matching, sorting, patterns – cognitive Following instructions, new words – language	Developing independence – social and emotional Understanding 'house rules' – social and cognitive
Getting dressed	Learning names of different part of the body – language and cognitive Developing fine motor skills – physical Self-help skills – personal, physical and social	Making choices and decisions – emotional and social Developing independence – personal, social and emotional
Helping to tidy up	Counting, matching, sorting, patterns – cognitive Developing an understanding of 'house rules' – emotional and social Developing an understanding of caring for equipment and toys – social	Awareness of needs of others – social and emotional Understanding 'house rules' – social and emotional Understanding how to care appropriately for toys, resources and equipment – social
Washing hands and face	Developing an understanding of good hygiene practices – personal, physical, social and cognitive Self-help skills – personal, physical and social	Understanding good hygiene practices and preventing the spread of infection – personal physical, social and cognitive
Making shopping lists	Understanding symbols carry meaning – language and cognitive Memory skills – cognitive	Writing for different purposes – language Memory skills – cognitive Valuing opinions of others Making choices and decisions – personal, social and emotional Developing independence – social
Putting shopping away	Counting, sorting, matching – cognitive Recognising different shapes and colours – cognitive Following instructions – language and cognitive	Developing an understanding of safe food storage – cognitive and social Developing independence – personal, social and emotional How to dispose of packaging and waste – cognitive and social

Table 8.2: Opportunities for play and learning in everyday routines.

All the play activities in Table 8.2 can be fun and enjoyable for all children. None of them need special or expensive equipment, but they are still play activities. It is up to you to make the play activities experiences from which the children can learn and develop.

Think about it

Some childcarers think that helping to sort clothes before putting them in the washing machine could be unhygienic, but it is a matter for discussion and also depends on what you are planning to wash. Others may think that getting children to help with domestic activities is almost like making them into domestic workers.
Can you think of some other domestic routine activities that might be contentious?

Setting the table provides many learning opportunities.

Link to assessment

Plan a challenging and enjoyable learning environment in the home that includes using everyday domestic routines and household items.

CACHE Task 7
Think about some of the domestic activities that you do with children.

Make a note of short activities that you and the children could do together, such as sorting the washing or setting a table for a meal. These are ideal opportunities for learning and playing.

Decide which activities need planning beforehand and which could be spontanteous. You could make a game of sorting washing by colour and 'accidentally on purpose' put a red sock in with whites, before washing of course! (Some parents and practitioners may not like the idea of children sorting your dirty washing, so maybe sort dolls' clothes or sort after washing when the clothes are dry.)

Children love to point out your silly mistakes and as well as helping them recognise colours, doing something like this is fun and helps to build their self-confidence.

In your portfolio write about how these domestic events form part of a child's learning. You could present this information in the form of a chart as in the example below.

Activity	Resources	Possible learning
Breakfast	Bread, toast, butter, spreads Toaster, plates, knives	Independence, self-help skills, decision making Physical skills (fine motor and coordination) Language – vocabulary
Building dens	Old curtains, sheets, pegs	Problem solving Creativity, imagination, role-play

Why it is important to observe children at play

When you observe, you are making an observation. As you know, to observe means to watch, study, examine or scrutinise. These are things that you will do every day as part of your childcare practice. You will watch children to make sure they are safe. You will watch them so that you can tell their parents what they have been doing with you. You will do this almost automatically, because you are a professional and care about children. There are, however, other reasons why you need to observe children.

Do you know what to look for when observing children?

Some reasons why you need to observe children. Can you think of any others?

Making specific time to observe and watch children is very valuable and important. We all watch children play and observe them, sometimes in a formal way, but often intuitively. You may, for example, notice that a child can complete a 10-piece jigsaw puzzle very quickly, so this will tell you that it is time to introduce a 15-piece puzzle. A toddler may be dry when you go to change their nappy and so it might be time to think about potty training. These kinds of observations will help you plan appropriate play activities that will stimulate and extend a child's development and learning. Observation can help you identify particular strengths or weaknesses, or perhaps confirm your suspicions if you think there may be cause for concern. Information that you get from watching children can be passed on to parents, keeping them updated on their child's progress and development.

Think about it

Look at your daily routine.
- Can you identify specific times when you can watch and listen to the children?
- (These times do not have to be very long; it is better to observe for frequent short sessions of 5–10 minutes than one long session.)
- Can you identify one specific skill, or aspect of development, that you could focus on for each child that you care for?

It is good practice to get into the habit of having a pen/pencil and notebook or sticky notes to hand so that you can make quick jottings to refer to later.

> *When it was suggested by my tutor that I did observations of the children I thought that I would never find the time, but I do, I am watching them constantly. Observations are now something that I do all of the time.*
>
> *Zoe, registered childminder*

Observations and assessment

There will be times when you are observing when you will want to record something that a child has done very informally and quickly. On the other hand, there will be times when you will want to record something in a more formal, organised way. There are several different ways, or methods, that you can use to record information about children. No one method is better than another; it depends on what you are observing and what you want to find out.

Some practitioners think that writing down observations adds to their workload and therefore takes them away from caring for the children. It is very important that you see observing children not as an additional workload, but as a central and fundamental part of providing the best possible care for the children. The more accurate information you have about the children, the more able you are to provide appropriate and inclusive activities for them and therefore improve the quality of the service you offer.

You need to include in your daily routine times when you can watch and listen to the children and so get information about their progress and development. This will also help you to assess and evaluate the activities that you have provided. Doing observations has the added advantage of giving children time and space to play as they choose and guide their own activities, while still being supervised by you.

Observation, assessment and planning are covered in greater detail in the Early Years Mandatory Pathway unit Promote learning and development in the Early Years of the CWDC Level 3 Diploma for the Children and Young People's Workforce.

The information, or evidence, that you collect when you do an observation can be invaluable for several reasons.

1. It can show that you understand how children learn, grow and develop and that the activities you provide take this into consideration.
2. Observations will give you information so that you can check whether the activities are at the right level and whether the children have learnt or progressed in any way. This is called **assessment**.

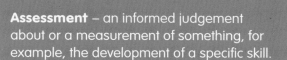

Key term

Assessment – an informed judgement about or a measurement of something, for example, the development of a specific skill.

Case study: Extending Daisy's vocabulary

Marie, a nanny, lives in the family home and cares for a 9-month-old baby and Daisy, aged 2 years 10 months. Daisy loves to dress up and pretend to be a princess, queen or fairy. Marie listened carefully to Daisy's language when she was playing and realised that in some ways her vocabulary was quite limited. Marie decided to look for books and DVDs in the library that were linked to Daisy's interests but would at the same time introduce new situations and extend her vocabulary. Marie did not think that she would have been aware of Daisy's limited vocabulary if she had not made a conscious decision to observe her.

- Can you suggest possible reasons for Daisy's limited vocabulary?
- What else could Marie do to extend Daisy's vocabulary?

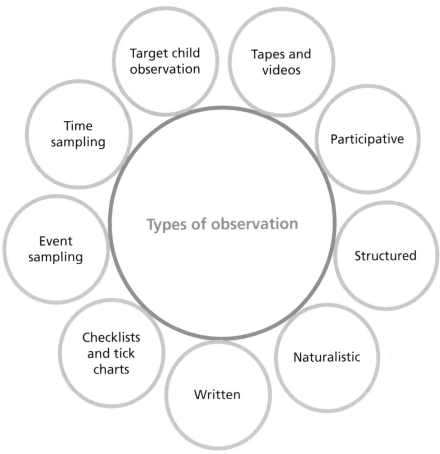

Types of observation.

3. The information you gain, together with your own knowledge and experience, will help you to plan appropriate inclusive activities. Your observations may have made you more aware of a particular need of a child. You will then be able to plan a suitable activity to help that child.

4. As a professional childcarer you have a busy workload and you want to make sure that everything you do is for the benefit of children. Sometimes, when you are working very closely with children, it can be difficult to decide whether the activities you are providing are really meeting all the children's needs. In other words, you need to be able to reflect on and evaluate what you are doing. One way that you can reflect on and evaluate the activities is to make observations of the children while they are playing. This will then provide you with evidence that you can look at in a quieter moment and decide whether the activity really did what you intended it to do.

Assessment of a child's needs must be objective and impartial if it is to be meaningful. You will need to think about the information that you have gathered in your observations in several ways.

*   Did the method/format you used provide the information you needed?
*   Have you sufficient evidence to make an assessment? One observation is rarely sufficient to provide enough information.
*   Have you recorded everything you saw or heard, or have you got gaps?
*   Is your information accurate and factual, not based on speculation or guesswork? Did you write down what actually happened, not what you think happened?
*   Can you draw a sound conclusion from your evidence or do you need to do more observations?
*   Whom do you need to share this information with and why?

The reason for assessment is not to label a child at a particular age, but to give you help on how you can best meet that child's needs and help them to progress and achieve. You should not compare one child with another because each child is an individual and will develop and progress at their own individual rate.

Any observation that you carry out will give essential and valuable information about that child's individual needs from the assessments that you have made. These assessments will allow you to make informed decisions about the activities and experiences that you provide and plan to provide.

You need to decide what you would like to accomplish with any child, what you and their family want them to be able to do, and what goals to work towards. These could be new skills and new ways of behaving, and should be related to the results of the assessments. Then you will need to decide how you are going to achieve these goals: this is your strategy or plan. You will need to think about how much time you have realistically to give to each child in order to meet their needs and how you may have to change your routines.

It is important that you reflect on what you are doing with the children in your care. This can sometimes be quite different from what you had originally planned, but because you are flexible in your approach you can take into consideration individual needs and interests. For example, you might have planned to collect natural materials to make a seasonal collage, but one child finds a woodlouse under a log and you all get involved in finding out more about mini beasts!

While your plans might have to change it is important that you evaluate and **monitor** them. You may need to think about:

- why some things were more successful than others
- what you could have done differently and why
- what resources you used and whether they were suitable.

Key term

Monitor – check or keep an eye on something.

Case study: Helping Jalah's development

Ameera noticed that Jalah, aged 7 months, was trying to roll over from her back to her stomach, but not quite making it (Ameera's observation). Ameera thought (her planning) that if she placed interesting toys and objects just out of Jalah's reach, she would be encouraged to roll over. Ameera observed that Jalah made several attempts to reach the objects before she finally rolled over. Ameera made written notes in a notebook about what Jalah did and in doing so reflected on her provision of play activities in relation to Jalah's needs.

- How else could Ameera have stimulated Jalah's development?
- Think about how you have changed your play activities in response to observing children. It may be that you did not write down your observation, it was almost instinctive. However, it is good practice to try to record your observations of significant development milestones.

How to extend your play opportunities through the use of toy libraries and equipment loan schemes

Drop-in sessions for childminders and their minded children are often informal arrangements between childminders, or can be organised through a Children's Centre. Drop-in sessions can be invaluable in providing support and an opportunity to share ideas, good practice and resources.

No one can expect you to have every toy, book and plaything for every situation. There will be times when you may only want to have a plaything for a short time and for a specific purpose.

- You may be caring for a child with a special need and so may need adapted toys or equipment.
- A child in your care could be going into hospital, so you could get storybooks from your local library about hospital visits and stays.
- You may want to have a dressing-up area of uniforms worn in hospitals and have play stethoscopes.

For situations like this, toy libraries are invaluable. They will lend toys and equipment to childcarers for agreed lengths of time at a nominal charge. In most cases you have to collect and return the toys to the library. Toy libraries also have toys that are more accessible for children with disabilities. Ask your local Family Information Service (FIS), Children and Families Service Children's Centre or library whether you have a toy library in your area. If you have difficulty contacting them, their addresses are at the end of this book.

Some childcarers also share toys and equipment informally amongst themselves. This is another good reason to meet up with other childcarers in your area. Some groups of childcarers have got together and successfully applied for funding from the National Lottery to set up their own toy libraries. Again the addresses should be available through your local library or on the Internet.

Some local libraries give tickets to professional childcarers so that they can borrow larger numbers of books. Ask in your local library for this service.

If you are caring for a child with special or additional needs, the relevant association can sometimes offer advice and support about playthings. Some of the larger organisations have regional offices that run their own toy libraries. It is a good idea to ask the parents of the child whether they are members of the association; if they are they could give you a contact name and number, which always makes it easier. You can find details of some of the organisations for children with special or additional needs on pages 187–193.

Case study: Tracey helps with homework

Tracey is a registered childminder and as well as her own two young children has three 8-year-olds after school. The older children have told Tracey that they are learning about the Egyptians at school and have homework that involves making a model of an irrigation tool. Tracey does not have any books at home to help with this and so goes to the local library where she is able to borrow five books linked to this subject to help the children with their homework.

- What other sources of information could Tracey have used?
- What would you do in such a situation?

Keys to good practice

Other opportunities for home-based play activities

- Try a 'keep-fit' session in a suitably open space or cleared room. This can involve all the children, whatever their age.

- Use a roll of wallpaper for children to draw or paint on. Older children could be encouraged to draw a story that develops along the roll of paper.

- Make dens with old sheets, curtains and boxes, then prepare a picnic to eat in them.

- Get together with other home-based childcarers and organise mini sports events, treasure hunts or picnics if the weather is good.

- Encourage older children to get together with their friends and put on shows to entertain you and the younger children.

- Plan special days out to local parks, museums and places of interest. Take a camera and let children take pictures of things that interest them. These pictures can then be made into a scrapbook or copied later.

Remember to let parents know of your plans and get their written permission before you take the children out.

Link to assessment — AC 5.5

Compare how other resources available for children support their play.

CACHE Task 7
If you compare something you are making judgements about what is good and what is not so good, or strengths and weaknesses. What other resources do you use to support play?

You could make a chart to consider and compare some resources, as in this example.

Resource	Strengths	Weaknesses
Lego	Encourages fine motor skills and coordination, problem solving, designing	Not suitable for younger children
Play house	Encourages role play, imagination, turn taking, sharing	Older children not interested in it
Climbing frame	Encourages gross motor skills, challenge and risk	Not suitable for all children

As well as the chart in order to complete the CACHE task you may need to add written details of how you could make comparisons.

9. SAFEGUARDING CHILDREN

There could be times when, despite all your good work and care, children may need protecting from harm and ill-treatment. It is important that you have a basic knowledge of types and signs of abuse and that you know what to do if you suspect that a child is in need of protection. Many practitioners find dealing with any issue about child protection very difficult, so it is also important that you know where you can get support and help.

This chapter covers:

- types of abuse
- the signs and symptoms of different forms of abuse
- the regulatory requirements
- your role and responsibilities
- ways of protecting yourself from allegations of abuse.

- This chapter links to Learning Outcome 6: Understand how home-based childcarers can support the safeguarding of children in their care.
- All assessment criteria (6.1 to 6.4) for this learning outcome are covered, and guidance is given for CACHE Assessment Task 8.
- This chapter links to Children and Young People's Core unit CYP 3.3 of the Level 3 Diploma for the Children and Young People's Workforce.

Throughout this book it has been stressed that you should do everything you can to make sure the children in your care are safe at all times. You will have looked at the possible risks and hazards in the home and garden and thought about how your practice ensures that children are protected. It is also vital that you understand how you can help **safeguard** the welfare of the children in your care.

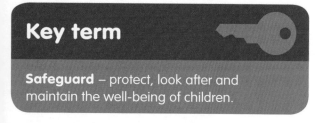

Key term

Safeguard – protect, look after and maintain the well-being of children.

Abuse can happen in any family, whatever the family structure or parenting style. Abuse does not only happen to children in poor families, or in lone-parent families. It does not discriminate; it can happen to any child. You must not assume that children of 'respectable' families will not be abused and will be automatically protected.

It is very difficult to get accurate figures about how many children are in need of protection at any time. Charities such as the National Society for the Prevention of Cruelty to Children (NSPCC) work unceasingly to protect children and raise awareness, but children are still abused. When the NSPCC

suggested that as many as one in six children may have been abused, some people felt that this was overstating the true picture. Many children who are abused or in need of protection do not talk about their experiences, for many reasons. The abuse may not be obvious to other people that they come into contact with and so it can be very difficult to do anything about it, sometimes until it is too late.

Types of abuse

It is generally accepted that there are four forms of child abuse.

The four types of abuse. Do you know what signs to look for?

Neglect

Another word for neglect is 'abandon', and this sums up, in a way, this type of abuse. The child does not receive the appropriate care needed to grow and develop; they are literally abandoned to look after themselves. It can be that the child does not receive medical care and attention when they need it, or that they are not given enough food, or appropriate clothing, or kept clean. Parents who leave their children unattended can be considered to be neglecting them. They are therefore abusing that child.

Case study: Home alone

It was reported in the press that a mother had gone on holiday to Spain for a week and left her two children, aged 7 and 9 years, alone at home. She had left some food in the fridge and a small amount of money. When she returned from holiday the mother was arrested and charged with neglect.

In another case a couple was charged with neglect after their child was rushed to hospital having taken methadone, which the parents had left in reach of the child.

- Why are these both cases of neglect?
- What might be the effects on the children?

Parents of neglected children often have personal problems which can have a negative impact on the overall well-being of the child. Many parents of neglected children will love their children, but are unable to care for them adequately.

Physical abuse

Physical abuse can occur when an adult injures a child by hitting, shaking, using excessive force, burning with cigarettes or giving a child something that could harm them, such as alcohol or drugs.

Smacking

There is a very fine line between smacking, in order to discipline a child, and physical abuse. A gentle smack on the hand could be considered acceptable by some people, whereas hitting a child with an object would be regarded as a criminal offence. In recent years there has been much controversy about the rights of parents to smack in order to discipline their child. In some countries, such as Sweden, parents are not allowed to use any form of physical punishment on children. Many educationalists and childcare experts believe that smacking a child is an ineffective form of discipline. They feel that it teaches children to be violent and that it is acceptable to deliberately hurt another person.

At the present time, parents can still use 'reasonable chastisement' to discipline their child. However, all members of the National Childminding Association (NCMA) agree, as part of the NCMA's Quality Standards, that they will not 'slap, smack, shake or humiliate' a child and it is against the law for any childcare practitioner to use any form of physical punishment. It is also clearly stated in the EYFS Statutory Framework that providers must not threaten or use corporal punishment.

Think about it

What do you think about smacking? You will have your own personal views about this. You may have been smacked yourself as a child. You may use or have used smacking as a form of disciplining your own children. Talk to other course members about both sides of the smacking issue. If you do not have other course members to talk to about this, ask a family member, neighbour or a friend.

It is good practice to talk your views and opinions through with other course members. This can help you gain more knowledge and understanding and make you more aware of the issues. You may also want to do some further reading around this subject.

Discuss:

- the view that smacking teaches children that bigger people can hurt smaller people
- the opinion of some adults that 'I was smacked as a child and it didn't do me any harm. I learnt what was right and wrong. If more parents smacked their children today, we would not have as much juvenile crime.'
- smacking encourages children to be violent.

Sexual abuse

Whenever an adult uses a child for their own sexual gratification they are said to be sexually abusing that child. This can be anything from rape, penetration and sexual intercourse, to fondling the genitals and other parts of the body, such as breasts, by people whom the children may or may not know. Sexual abuse also includes adults involving children in pornographic activities. It can begin gradually and develop over a period of time. Sometimes children who are sexually abused believe that this is a way of pleasing adults and so gaining their love and approval.

Emotional/psychological abuse

When an adult fails to show a child love and affection, the child will lose confidence and can become withdrawn and nervous. This is a form of emotional abuse. In the same way, continually threatening, verbally abusing or shouting at a child can have long-term damaging effects.

Bullying

Bullying is also a form of abuse and can be physical, emotional and psychological. These days bullying can be done by mobile phone, social networking sites and Internet chat rooms – cyberbullying – as well as face to face. Children have a right to feel safe and protected and to have people they can tell if they do not feel safe. To be able to protect themselves from abuse and bullying, children need to feel good about themselves, they need to have a good level of self-esteem and a positive image. Very often children who are abused or bullied do not have good self-esteem or self-image.

Children need:

- lots of praise and encouragement to raise their self-esteem
- opportunities to encourage independence
- opportunities to develop assertiveness
- opportunities to make choices
- opportunities to express their feelings and wishes
- opportunities to succeed without fear of failure or 'getting something wrong'
- activities and experiences that are appropriate to their needs and age and stage of development
- positive role models who encourage tolerance, respect and cooperation between children
- to be respected and valued as individuals
- a good understanding of their own bodies, using correct anatomical language through age-appropriate activities
- a trusted adult whom they can talk to.

Find it out

The charity Kidscape has devised the Keepsafe Code, which has nine straightforward pointers, such as saying 'No' in an assertive way, to help children protect themselves.

The code can be accessed from the Hotlinks section (see page 3).

Case study: Tom's emotional problems

Tom is 12 years old; he attends a small school for children who have severe emotional and behavioural problems. He often displays violent and abusive behaviours towards his peers and staff, and can be very uncooperative and unwilling to participate in class activities. One morning he arrived at school more distressed than usual and spent a lot of time sitting on the floor with his head in his hands. A staff member who had developed a reasonable relationship with Tom tried to talk to him about how he was feeling. Tom told the teacher that his mum hated him because she was always telling him that she wished he had never been born.

- Why is this a form of emotional abuse?
- What do you think the teacher could do to help Tom?

The signs and symptoms of different forms of abuse

There are definite indications of each form of abuse. Sometimes practitioners suspect that a child is in need of protection without having seen any physical signs of abuse. This could be through a child's behaviour, for example, if they have become withdrawn or distressed for no apparent reason. It is important that you are alert to changes in a child's behaviour, as well as being aware of the physical signs of abuse.

In all cases of abuse the signs and symptoms fall roughly into two categories: behavioural and physical.

Signs and symptoms of neglect

Behavioural

- Parents can often be difficult to contact or fail to make appointments.
- Children tell you about looking after younger siblings and taking on responsibilities not normally expected of children of their age.
- Children talk about being left alone.
- Children stealing food from cupboards/other children's lunch boxes.

Physical

- Children generally show an unkempt and uncared-for appearance, perhaps with dirty, unwashed clothes.
- Children look underweight.
- They are always hungry.

- They are frequently tired due to lack of sleep and irregular sleeping habits.
- A child has lots of accidental injuries that could be caused through being unsupervised or left unattended.
- They have lots of minor infections and ailments, such as colds, coughs and earaches, that are not treated.

Signs and symptoms of physical abuse

Most children will at some point in their life suffer an accidental injury. Children fall, bump their heads, become bruised and grazed or cut in the normal rough and tumble of everyday activities and play. These are true accidents, and while you offer sympathy and support, you would not necessarily become concerned.

The time to become concerned is when the injuries are frequent, do not have a good and acceptable explanation, or if the part of the body that is affected is not where you would normally expect a child to have an injury, for example, bruising on the back or stomach.

The signs again are behavioural or physical.

Behavioural

- A child being withdrawn and quiet, when in the past they have been sociable.
- Aggressive play, often towards other children and in role play.
- Aggressive responses to the childminder.
- You receive messages from parents asking that the child is not changed or undressed for any reason.
- A child is unable to sit comfortably or does so with unusual stiffness, and is reluctant to join in vigorous play.
- A child flinches if someone makes a sudden movement.
- Children not crying/showing distress if they fall and hurt themselves.

Physical

- Unexplained bruises, cuts and grazes.
- Unusually shaped bruise marks.
- Frequent broken bones.
- Unusual scalds and burns, such as cigarette burns.
- Bite marks.

Sometimes parents feel under tremendous pressure at certain times in their lives, and a baby or young child can add to their stress. At such times an adult may physically abuse a child or baby. A baby who is difficult to feed or who cries incessantly at night can put some parents under an intolerable level of stress, especially after a long day at work.

Such adults may lose control of their actions, and often feel they are also losing control of other aspects of their lives. They may lose control to the point that they violently shake their child. Shaking a young baby can cause a great deal of internal damage; for example, the damage to the brain is much the same as dropping a baby head first on to a concrete floor. The symptoms of this type of brain damage can be:

- loss of vision
- loss of hearing
- fits
- lack of response.

If you know that the parents are under stress, you should offer support and advise them to seek help (for example, counselling) from appropriate organisations and other professionals. You could direct them to their local Children's Centre. You should be concerned if a child or baby starts to show the following signs:

- not interested in feeding
- unable to settle to rest or sleep
- unusually tired and not interested in what is going on around them
- poor muscle tone.

Remember that these signs could also indicate that the child is not well, possibly in the first stages of an illness or infection. However, it could be related to physical abuse such as shaking.

Signs and symptoms of sexual abuse

It can be very difficult to notice any signs and symptoms of sexual abuse. Sometimes there are no visible marks, especially in the case of showing or involving children in pornographic materials. Sexual abuse in children is possibly easier to detect from changes in their behaviour rather than physical signs.

Behavioural

- Using sexual language and having knowledge of sexual behaviour not normally associated with a child of that age.
- Showing insecurity.
- Clinging to trusted adults and at the same time indicating an unwillingness to be in the company of particular adults.
- Immature actions for their age, for example, comfort habits such as rocking, thumb sucking, wanting a comforter.
- Using imaginary play to act out sexual behaviour.
- Undressing themselves at inappropriate times or exposing the genital area.
- Drawings or paintings of a sexual nature.

Physical

- Injuries such as bruises and scratches that are non-accidental, especially around the genital area.
- Bloodstains.
- Vaginal discharge.
- Difficulty in urinating or having a bowel movement or having frequent 'accidents'.
- Difficulty in sitting down or walking.
- Frequent urinary and/or genital infections.
- Showing distress or signs of fear when needing to pass urine or have a bowel movement.

Signs and symptoms of emotional/psychological abuse

It can be very difficult to see any signs or symptoms of emotional abuse, especially physical signs. Children who are subject to this form of abuse are very vulnerable. They lack self-esteem and crave attention from anyone. Any person who shows them attention, in almost any form, will get a positive response and trust from the child. Some unscrupulous individuals abuse that trust. Children who are subject to emotional abuse will have a very low opinion of themselves, very poor self-worth and very little confidence.

Behavioural

- Attention-seeking, such as deliberately being uncooperative, troublesome, telling lies or clinging to an adult and craving attention.
- Immature behaviour, such as tantrums at an age when normally they would not behave in that way.
- Poor social skills with children of their own age.

Physical

In older children the signs may be:

- extreme eating habits and dieting caused by very low self-esteem and self-worth
- deliberately hurting themselves to gain attention (self-harm).

Link to assessment — AC 6.2

Outline the possible signs, symptoms, indicators and behaviours that cause concern in the context of safeguarding.

CACHE Task 8
An information document can be in a range of formats, but as with a leaflet think carefully about whom it is aimed at. This will influence the type of language you use, whether you use diagrams and charts and how much information you include. Remember that you are required to give only an outline and you may want to include sources of further information, reading and support.

If you are not following the CACHE task, you may still want to produce an information document as outlined above.

The regulatory requirements

The welfare requirements of the Early Years Foundation Stage (EYFS) in England, the Childminding and Day Care regulations in Wales or the equivalent requirements and standards of your country must be met by all Early Years providers. These are legal requirements and it is an offence not to comply with them. Safeguarding and children's welfare is a general requirement. Specific details relating to this requirement can be found in the Statutory Framework for the Early Years Foundation Stage (2008) published by the DfE (formerly DCSF) and available to download by accessing the website from the Hotlinks section (see page 3). (You can find more information about the EYFS in Chapter 3.)

You must have a written policy in place for safeguarding children. As with all other policies and procedures, it must be regularly reviewed and shared with parents. You will also need to have an enhanced Criminal Records Bureau (CRB) disclosure; anyone else in your family over the age of 16 who comes into contact with the children must also have a CRB disclosure. (You can find more information about policies and procedures in Chapter 2.)

There are very clear procedures for responding to suspected cases of child abuse. The Local Safeguarding Children Board (LSCB) is a multi-agency body working within each local authority. The LSCB has the responsibility for producing safeguarding procedures. The LSCB team will contact other relevant professionals and the child's parents after you have raised a concern.

ncma says...

It is always helpful to access Local Safeguarding Children Board training wherever possible.

Children who are subject to emotional abuse will crave attention.

Once you have contacted your representative LSCB in the first instance or Social Services, they are required to investigate. This may involve talking to you, the child and their family. A case conference is then set up to decide what will happen next in the best interests of the child. After the case conference an action plan is agreed.

The case conference aims to gather as much information as possible about the child. Parents are often invited to case conferences and can bring legal representation if they wish. There will also be social workers, medical professionals (such as the child's GP), and possibly the child's teacher and carer. This can sometimes result in a multi-agency approach to caring

for the child – often referred to as a Team Around the Child (TAC).

If you are invited to attend a case conference you must make sure that any information you give is accurate, factual and can be backed up with evidence. All of this information is completely confidential and to breach this is very serious for you. This is a situation where your observations could be vital, so it is important that they are factual.

ncma says...

It is a good idea to document any concerns in the incident, accident and medication book.

Keys to good practice

Disclosure

 In the case of a **disclosure** – if a child discloses to you something that causes concern, or you see some of the signs and symptoms or behavioural changes outlined previously – you should make a written record which you keep secure and confidential.

 Take your cues from the child; do not question them, but let the child tell you things in their own time and way.

 In the first place you must keep your concerns confidential. You should not discuss your concerns with any other person – definitely not the parents of a child you suspect may need safeguarding if you feel that doing so would put the child at risk.

 The next step for registered childminders is to contact your local LSCB. You should have this telephone number to hand. You could also contact Social Services instead of the LSCB.

 Seek support for yourself if you find the situation distressing and hard to deal with, but maintain confidentiality.

Link to assessment

AC 6.1, 6.3

Explain the concept of safeguarding and duty of care that applies to all practitioners

Outline regulatory requirements for safeguarding children that affect home-based childcare

CACHE Task 8
These criteria will be included in your information document, so read again the earlier Link to assessment on page 167.

If you are explaining something you should make the main points clearly, using plain words, and give reasons for the actions that you would take.

Key term

Disclosure – a child has told an adult or another child what has been happening to them. This can also include evidence of abuse or neglect.

Case study: Kerrie's concerns

Kerrie is a very professional registered childminder with extensive experience of living with children who have been abused and in need of protection, as her mother is a foster carer. Kerrie suspected that one of the children in her care was being sexually abused. She found this very distressing. Kerrie sought advice, support and reassurance from her mother, also a registered childminder, and her college tutor, both of whom advised her to report her concerns. Kerrie was very careful not to breach issues of confidentiality when seeking advice and support. Kerrie said later that this was the most difficult telephone call she had ever had to make.

- How do you think you would feel in such circumstances?
- Do you know whom to contact in the case of suspected abuse? (If you answer no to this question, then find out!)

You must inform Ofsted (or the regulatory body for your country) of any allegations of serious harm or abuse by any person who is living with, working with or looking after children in your setting, regardless of where the alleged abuse has taken place. If you fail to do this you have committed an offence. Make sure you follow your LSCB procedures as there could be a requirement to notify staff at your local authority.

Your role and responsibilities

Every childcare professional, in whatever capacity, has a duty and responsibility to put the child's needs and welfare first. It therefore follows that if you suspect that a child is in need of protection you must do something about it. Rather than regarding safeguarding as something that, hopefully, you will not have to deal with, it should be part of your everyday practice to protect children.

Some home-based childcarers find it very difficult to report parents whom they suspect of abuse. They feel they are betraying the trust and relationship that they have with the parents; but this is not the case. You should be aware, however, that parents are not the only adults who may be suspected of abusing a child. You have a duty of care and a legal responsibility to report all suspicions. The well-being of the child is paramount.

In general terms there is a possibility of abuse when a child has a number of the signs described earlier or any one of them significantly. It should also be remembered that a child can be the victim of more than one form of abuse, such as neglect and sexual abuse.

Children who are possible victims of abuse can be very vulnerable and your dealings with them should be sensitive at all times. You must take your cues from the child and make sure that you do not upset them any further.

Why are children abused or bullied?

This is a difficult and emotive question to answer fully as the reasons can be complex and perhaps not really fully understood. Abuse can be an isolated incident in a child's life; on the other hand some forms of abuse can last for years. Abuse and bullying can take place anywhere, for example, bullying by text messaging is increasing and the bully can be miles away. Abuse and bullying can be carried out by anyone, but most cases of abuse and bullying are instigated by someone whom the child knows.

If you suspect any form of abuse, you must proceed with care and caution and be certain of your facts. It is not good practice to question or probe a child about what has happened, but once a child does begin to talk to you, gently and sensitively encourage the child to continue talking to you – and you must give the child your full attention (see overleaf).

- Take your cues from the child.
- It is always good practice to make a written record of any conversation you have with a child if you suspect that they need protection.
- Make a note of any signs or symptoms.
- Be factual and precise; do not make assumptions. For example, do not assume that because a child has a black eye that they have been hit by someone: they may well have accidentally hit their head on the edge of a cupboard.

Keep your eyes open, but be careful not to jump to conclusions.

Abuse can have long-term effects. Children who are subjected to repeated abuse can suffer severe psychological damage and be seriously affected for the rest of their lives. Many adults who suffered abuse as children or young people have great difficulty forming relationships and can have problems parenting their own children. Bullying and **harassment** can happen to all individuals but research shows that older children can be more at risk. This form of abuse can last for a long time. It can be carried out by one individual or by groups and can take many forms.

Key term

Harassment – torment through constant bothering, interference, intimidation and so on.

Think about it

- There is a stronger likelihood of a parent abusing their child if there are difficulties in their attachments.
- The risk of abuse increases if the parent has been separated from their child, for example, in premature births or severe neonatal/maternal illness.
- Postnatal depression can sometimes affect how a mother reponds to her child and this can sometimes lead to abuse.
- Lack of parenting skills can mean that some parents are unable to respond to their child.
- Children with disabilities can be very vulnerable to abuse as they may not respond to the parents' attempts to bond.
- Stress can be a major factor in abusive situations and factors such as poverty and relationship breakdown can be highly significant.
- Abuse can be like a vicious circle; an adult who was abused as a child can go on to become an abuser.

Think about it

Jeff was sexually abused by his mother's boyfriend between the ages of 8 and 12 years. Jeff became a father at the age of 18 and when the child was 4 years old, Jeff began to abuse him. Jeff's girlfriend realised what was happening and reported him to the police. Jeff's experiences as a child came to light during the court case and he began counselling to help him.

This does not make Jeff's abuse of a young child right or acceptable but it goes some way to explaining why it happened.

Ways of protecting yourself from allegations of abuse

All childcare practitioners are in positions of trust and great responsibility, given that they care for other people's children. In such positions they are vulnerable to allegations of mistreating children and accusations of abuse. In this respect, childminders and nannies are no different from other childcare professionals. In some ways, however, you are even more vulnerable as you can be working alone and may not have the support of colleagues and other people. For people working in an organisation with several employees there is a process whereby they can air their concerns about bad practice, usually referred to as 'whistleblowing'. The Public Interest Disclosure Act (1998) protects staff from victimisation provided they make their claim in good faith. But home-based childcarers do not have such protection and are therefore vulnerable to accusations. It is therefore essential that you make sure you have a support mechanism in place for yourself.

Apart from behaving in a totally professional way at all times, there are other things that you can do to protect yourself from false allegations.

Keys to good practice

How to protect yourself from allegations of abuse

- Maintain confidentiality at all times.

- Make sure that all your records, registers, incident report forms, accident forms and other documents relating to the children in your care are kept up to date and are stored in a safe place. You should get into the habit of completing records for each child every time that you care for them.

- Report any suspicions you have about ill-treatment or abuse of a child to the LSCB (see comments above regarding making referrals) or Social Services. You should also keep a written record of your conversations or contact, including the name of the child or individual you spoke to, the date of the conversation and what was agreed.

- Make sure that you tell parents about every incident, accident or event that has happened to their child that could result in a mark or injury on the body, while they are in your care, regardless of how insignificant it may seem. Keep a written record of such conversations and record the incidents or accident and get parents to sign to say that they have seen what you have recorded.

- Never leave the children unattended or in the care of unauthorised people.

- Encourage the children to be independent as soon as they are able, especially when carrying out personal hygiene tasks.

- Make sure that you do not handle a child roughly when managing unwanted behaviour.

- Make sure that you always use appropriate language when with the children.

- Take your cues from the children and do not ask for cuddles and so forth if the child is reluctant to respond.

- Be open and honest with the children and do not ask them to keep secrets.

- Help children learn how to protect themselves.

- Attend child protection courses and keep yourself well informed and up to date.

- Remind your family members that they too could be accused of abusing a child in your care.

- It is essential that you keep accurate, factual written records so that the reporting of suspected abuse is based on honest, observed evidence and not rumour or gossip.
- It is vital that these records are kept secure and confidential at all times and only disclosed to the appropriate professionals.

There have been cases of childcare practitioners being accused of abuse. This can be a most distressing time and experience for all concerned. If this happens to you, you must remain calm and professional. Keep records of all conversations that you have regarding the accusation, and keep copies of all letters that you write. It would be sensible to seek legal advice as once an accusation is made there is a legal requirement that it be investigated. Organisations such as the NCMA offer legal help and advice to its members, or you can seek independent advice from the Citizens Advice Bureau (CAB). You can find details of the NCMA and the National Association Citizens Advice Bureau on pages 187–193.

As mentioned earlier, child abuse is an emotive topic. It is likely that if you are working with children who have been abused, or suspect that a child is being abused, you will experience a range of emotions and feelings. This could be anger at the abuser, shock at what has happened to the child, a feeling of helplessness, or feeling that you have failed the child because you did not notice that something was wrong sooner. All of these feelings are perfectly normal. You may of course react in different ways.

It is important to remember that you should not expect to deal with all your emotions on your own. You should not try to pretend that you do not feel angry or frustrated or have a sense of failure. The most professional way to act is to recognise your feelings, and seek the support of another adult. It is essential to remember that you must maintain confidentiality at all times, so select your supporting adult with care.

Childminders who are working in a community childminding network may be asked to care for children who are already on the 'at risk register' or subject to a protection order. In such cases there will be a range of other professionals that you could turn to for support, such as:

- social workers
- general practitioners (GPs)
- health visitors
- child protection police officers.
- network coordinators.

Organisations such as the NSPCC and Kidscape will often lend a 'listening ear'. The contacts for these organisations are at the back of the book. The NCMA will also offer support and advice in such situations.

Link to assessment   AC 6.4

Explain procedures that need to be followed by lone workers in home-based settings when harm or abuse is suspected or alleged either against them or third parties.

CACHE Task 8
You will need to have written evidence in your portfolio of what procedures you need to follow when harm or abuse is suspected. Include relevant telephone numbers and contact details of appropriate agencies. In addition you must show clearly that you understand what you must do if an allegation is made against you. It is important that all of this information is presented clearly, with an appropriate level of detail, and uses plain language; avoid using jargon (professional/technical terms) or abbreviations.

This task is appropriate whether or not you are following a CACHE programme of study.

10. PROMOTING POSITIVE BEHAVIOUR

Every society has its rules and social boundaries, with behaviour that is considered to be acceptable or unacceptable. You will have your own views, formed by your upbringing and culture. These views may have changed over the years, or been altered by where you live and whom you live with. Deciding what is acceptable behaviour is not easy and we must remember it is important to accept different behaviours from children of different ages.

This chapter covers:

- typical behaviours linked to a child's stage of development
- how to develop ground rules to promote positive behaviour.

- This chapter links to Learning Outcome 7: Understand the principles of supporting positive behaviour in home-based settings.
- All assessment criteria (7.1 to 7.2) for this learning outcome are covered, and guidance is given for CACHE Assessment Task 9.
- This chapter links to Children and Young People's Core unit 3.5 of the full Level 3 Diploma for the Children and Young People's Workforce.

Typical behaviours linked to a child's stage of development

Children are not born with an understanding of what is acceptable behaviour. This is something they learn as they grow and develop. Adults play a very important part in helping children to learn acceptable forms of behaviour that will help them become useful members of society. Childminders play a vital part in promoting positive behaviour. In the past, adults often expected children to obey without question and be compliant (submit) to adult requests. Children's behaviour was managed through control, with little or no consideration of children's rights or needs. Today we manage behaviour recognising that children have rights and are entitled to be valued. We actively promote positive behaviour, which stems from children being **empowered**, valued and respected.

Key term

Empowered – having/being given the opportunity to be in control of situations.

Factors that influence behaviour

There are numerous factors that can influence a child's behaviour. Some influences are quite short-term, such as feeling under the weather or being very tired; other factors can be long-term, such as the effects of abuse. (You can find more information about abuse in Chapter 9.)

Overall development

A child could behave in a certain way because they have emotional difficulties, or because some aspect of their development is delayed. It is often the case that children with some form of developmental delay will show behaviour that is not normally associated with a child of a certain age. A child with either a temporary or long-lasting physical impairment, such as hearing loss, will not be able to hear other children and adults, follow instructions or join in play. They may have difficulties communicating with other children, which will affect their relationships, so they could become frustrated and angry, and this will be reflected in their behaviour.

Self-image

The way a child feels about themselves can affect the way they behave. Their self-image is in turn affected by many things, as shown in the illustration.

Factors that contribute to self-image.

Changes in a child's life

A change in a child's circumstances is often reflected by a change in their behaviour. These changes can immediately affect the child or their family. It must be remembered that all children are unique and may react in very different ways to change.

The changes can be:

- the arrival of a baby in the family
- the death of a family member, close friend or pet
- moving house
- illness within the family
- divorce or separation of parents
- change in work pattern of parents, or unemployment
- adapting to a stepfamily following the remarriage of one parent
- moving to another setting, changing classes, moving to another school.

Think about how a young child could react to the birth of a sibling.

A child's personality

Think about how a child's personality develops. Is it inherited or does it develop as a result of experiences and environment? This is often referred to as the 'nature/nurture debate'. Does it follow that because Granny had a bad temper one of her grandchildren will also have a bad temper? Or did Granny's temper come from the fact that she was short of money, always tired and did not have a good standard of living?

Think about it

- Do you believe that the child of 'well-behaved' parents is also 'well-behaved'?
- Does it follow that if a parent of a child is always breaking the law, the child will 'follow in their footsteps'?
- Will shy quiet parents have a shy, quiet child?
- Think about your personality. How many of your personal traits or behaviours have your children inherited from you?
- Think about your mother's or father's personality.

A child's school

A school, nursery or pre-school group will have its own behaviour expectations that the child will have to learn to adapt to. This can affect how they behave before or after attending the school. Children who have been inactive and quiet for a period of time in school will obviously need to 'let off steam' and use up surplus energy when they get to your house or to their home.

Peer groups

Some peer groups will set their own 'rules' and expectations for behaviour, which can have both positive and negative effects on an individual child. The influence of the peer group, and the need to belong, is very strong in older children, although research has shown that peer group pressure can impact on a child's behaviour at a very young age. The desire to fit into the group can bring a child into conflict with their carers and parents at times.

Case study: Carlie's peer pressure

Carlie, aged 4 years, refused to go to nursery unless she could wear her branded designer trainers that were like everyone else's. If she could not wear them she had screaming temper tantrums. Her mother became so weary of the tantrums that she gave in and let Carlie wear the trainers.

- How is this an example of peer pressure?
- What would you do in a similar situation?

The influence of the media

Children may copy the behaviour of people they see on television, for example, well-known footballers spitting during a game, or questioning the referee's decisions. A child who sees the way these 'stars' behave may believe it to be acceptable and may copy them.

We must also remember that young children can be influenced by the way the media reports major world events (often tragedies), such as the Asian tsunami in December 2004, the effects of flooding in Cockermouth or the earthquakes in Haiti in 2009. How do you know if the children are frightened or worried by such events, especially if they do not talk about it? Sometimes how the child feels can be reflected in the way they behave.

All children will respond and react to these influences in a unique and individual way. Their response will depend on their age and stage of development; for example, a 2-year-old may become very frustrated with the arrival of a new baby in the family. They may find they are not getting as much attention, and not be able to understand why and will do the only thing they can do – which is to have a screaming temper tantrum.

While this behaviour may be acceptable for a 2-year-old (although not exactly to be encouraged), we should feel concern if a 5-year-old expressed their frustration in the same way. Similarly you could accept uncommunicative behaviour from hormonal teenagers, who do not regard adults as 'cool' and prefer to be with their peers. You would not reasonably expect a 5-year-old to be uncommunicative but you might expect them to tell you about an exciting event or recall what they did at the weekend. Uncommunicative behaviour in a teenager can be a developmental stage, whereas in a 5-year-old this should be cause for concern.

Look again at the common features of stages of development in Chapter 6. There Table 6.3 highlights some of the common behaviours that you may identify at certain ages, for example:

- 12–14 months – growing independence can lead to rage when thwarted

Case study: True stories

September 2004 – just after the attack on a school in Beslan, Russia, by terrorists

George's Year 1 class were getting changed in the classroom prior to going into the school hall for an indoor physical education session. George appeared very reluctant to get changed, making little effort. When approached by a familiar adult he started to cry and said that he didn't want to go into the hall in case the terrorists came and got him.

August 2009 – after the floods in Cockermouth, Cumbria

Bev noticed that her 5-year-old daughter became very agitated, nervous and stressed when it rained hard. When asked if she could explain why she was feeling like this, the girl said she was very worried that the rain would come into the house and wash everything away, like it had done on the television.

- 18–21 months – can be obstinate and unwilling to follow adult suggestions
- 8–11 years – intolerant of weak adults.

All of these aspects of development could lead to behaviours that may cause concern. In many ways there are no common causes of behaviour that raise concerns, as all children are unique. Children develop at different rates and respond to different situations or people in different ways. However, it is possible to group some possible behaviours/causes into four main groups as shown below.

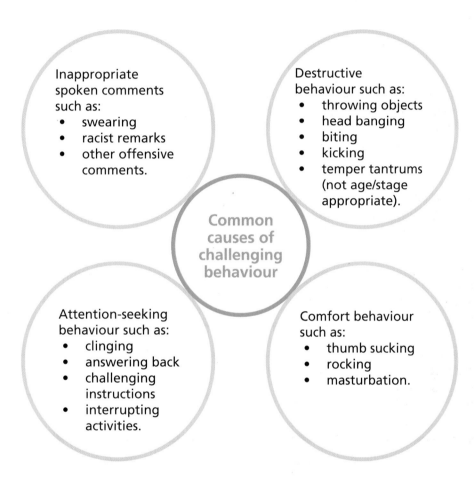

Inappropriate spoken comments such as:
- swearing
- racist remarks
- other offensive comments.

Destructive behaviour such as:
- throwing objects
- head banging
- biting
- kicking
- temper tantrums (not age/stage appropriate).

Common causes of challenging behaviour

Attention-seeking behaviour such as:
- clinging
- answering back
- challenging instructions
- interrupting activities.

Comfort behaviour such as:
- thumb sucking
- rocking
- masturbation.

Common causes of challenging behaviour. How would you tackle the different behaviours?

While the features on the spider diagram are common behaviours and causes, it is important that you also think about:

- the age and stage of development of the child
- the importance of positive role models
- the way a child feels about themselves (a poor self-image can result in challenging behaviour)
- peer group pressure, especially if children find themselves in conflict with their need to belong to a group and respecting the wishes of their parents or childcarer (this can be common in older school-aged children).

It is important to consider if some behaviours that cause concern in children may be linked to abuse.

Bullying can have a significant effect on a child's behaviour and the child may not be willing or able to talk about it. They may, therefore, become withdrawn, uncommunicative, angry, upset or aggressive.

- A child's behaviour may change if they are feeling unwell. Sometimes a child may **regress** in their behaviour, for example, a child that has been potty trained may start to have 'accidents' if they are not feeling well. They may also become more clingy or aggressive. Some children can also become withdrawn and unwilling to communicate or play, preferring to be left alone.

Key term

Regress – return to an earlier stage of development.

Think about it

Behaviourist theory explains why some children show behaviours which cause concern. Children receive attention from adults or other children when they behave in certain ways. From the child's point of view, negative attention is better than no attention at all, and in effect reinforces the behaviour that you are actually trying to stop. For example, a child may be playing cooperatively, but this does not attract your attention so the child hits another child. You have to respond to the first child regarding this behaviour, therefore they have gained your attention.

What would you do in this situation?

Case study: Adie looks for attention

Adie, aged 3 years, throws toys across the room, narrowly missing her baby brother. Jenna, her childminder, tells her to stop but Adie carries on throwing the toys. Jenna asks her to stop again. Jenna realises that Adie gets attention when she throws toys. Adie has learnt that behaving in this way will get Jenna to focus attention on her rather than on the baby. Jenna discusses this with the children's parents and they realise that they too give Jenna more attention when she does something that they consider unacceptable. Jenna and the parents agree that they will praise Adie and give her attention when she is playing well.

- Why do you think Adie needs to seek attention in this way?
- What would you do in this situation?

Link to assessment   AC 7.1

Describe typical behaviours exhibited by children linked to their stage of development and key events in their lives.

CACHE Task 9

You are asked to write a report in which you describe typical behaviours. Your description should be clear and detailed; you should be able to back up with reasons statements that you make. For example, if you write that temper tantrums are 'normal' behaviour for a 2-year-old, you should say why. You should also explain why certain events in a child's life could trigger different behaviours. Remember, however, that all children develop at different rates and you should avoid making broad sweeping general statements.

If you are not following CACHE tasks you may decide that this information could be presented in different ways, such as a chart or table; however, be careful that you do not generalise development and behaviour.

How to develop ground rules to promote positive behaviour

It is important to establish a framework or ground rules to promote positive behaviour in the home very early on in your career. You will probably base your house rules on things that are important and that matter to the children, their parents and to you. For example, most people believe that keeping children safe is very important, so your framework could focus on preventing children from hurting or injuring themselves.

Your ground rules could include the following.

- Children should treat toys and equipment with respect.
- Children are not allowed in the kitchen unless I am in there as well.
- Children are not allowed to open the gate.

You may not write these ground rules down, but they will become part of the everyday things that the children learn while in your care. You can discuss this with older children as well as their parents, talking about why these things are important and what may happen if they do not agree to the ground rules and your expectations.

Other things on which you could base your ground rules and expectations for behaviour are:

- preventing children from doing anything that is dangerous, offensive or hurtful to other adults and children
- doing things that will not make them welcome in other people's homes or things that other people would find unacceptable or offensive
- doing something that would cause damage to other people's possessions.

You could write down a few short, simple sentences about your ground rules and expectations for behaviour. This will be your behaviour policy, which you could give to parents and discuss with them at your first meeting. Developing and sharing your expectations and ground rules will help children feel secure; they are then more likely to conform once they understand what the house rules are and why they are there.

Children need to know and understand that your rules, expectations and boundaries will not keep changing. It is very important that you are consistent and firm in applying your boundaries for all children. If a child is not dealt with in a consistent way this could lead to difficulties in behaviour. Knowing what the rules are, and that boundaries are set, helps to develop a sense of security.

For childminders, it is inevitable that the expectations and rules you establish in your home may be different from the accepted rules in the child's own house. For example, you may not allow any child to go into the kitchen unless you are also in there; at home they may have no restrictions on going into the kitchen. It is therefore very important that you explain to children clearly and simply why you have that rule. For example, a registered childminder said:

> *I want to make sure that you, and all of the other children, are safe and not in any danger. There are things in the kitchen that could hurt you or other children, such as the electric kettle, the oven and the cupboard doors. I do not want any child to be hurt, so we all go into the kitchen together, then we can make sure that we are all safe.*
>
> *Trudy, registered childminder*

Case study: Mummy lets us do it

Jane, a registered childminder, has recently started to care for 3-year-old twin boys. They often jump on the chairs and sofa. Jane explains to the boys that they could fall and hurt themselves and that she does not let other children jump on the furniture. Jane explains to the boys why she does not want them to do this and that they can climb and jump outside in the garden. The boys tell Jane that their mummy lets them do it at home.
Jane arranges to talk to the mother and explains that she fears that the boys could fall and hurt themselves if they jump on the furniture. She also explains that she does not let other children behave in this way. Jane

reminds the mother about her behaviour policy that was discussed at their first meeting. The mother agrees with Jane that the boys should do as Jane asks when they are in Jane's home. She agrees to talk to the boys and explain that they must do what Jane asks them when she is caring for them.
- Do you agree with what Jane did? Give your reasons why or why not.
- Are there any other ways of handling this situation? If so, what are they?
- What would be your reaction if the boys' mother felt that Jane was making a fuss over nothing and that it didn't matter?

How would you deal with this situation?

However, a nanny may have exactly the same house rule — a child is not allowed to go into the kitchen without an adult; and the reasons for it are probably very similar to those of the childminder. When the child's parents are at home, the child may have no such limits. If explained simply and fairly to the child it will appear reasonable and not inconsistent.

Establishing your ground rules as early as possible is very important for you, the children, the parents and, if you are a childminder, other members of your family. It will mean that everyone knows what is expected of them and will lead to a consistent approach.

Your ground rules will consist of boundaries that set limits on behaviour and are simple rules that all children will learn must not be broken, for example, 'You must not open the stair gate.' When you start to establish your ground rules and expectations there are things that you can do.

- Help children to learn the rules by reminding them of these whenever appropriate; for example, when they come in from school ask them to put their bags and belongings in a safe place so others will not fall over them.

- Explain why you have rules; children are much more likely to remember your rules if they know why you have them.
- Use simple, clear language, for example, 'It's time to come in now.' Saying something like 'It is almost time for us to collect your sister from school, so we must start to put the toys away soon' is confusing. What is it you are asking the child to do? It may help to tell children in advance what's going to happen, for example, five minutes until it is time to come in, two minutes until it is time to come in.
- Explain in clear, simple language what will happen if your rules are broken. You could say, 'I will put that game away if you don't stop throwing the pieces at each other.'
- Some rules can be written down. This is especially appropriate for school-aged children, who often quite enjoy doing such an activity. You could get the children to produce a poster or chart of 'the rules of the house'.
- Always praise and encourage children when they do follow your rules and at times when they are playing well and happily.

ncma
says...

Why not produce a pictoral version of house rules for younger children as a reminder?

Strategies to promote positive behaviour

There are numerous strategies that can be employed to promote positive behaviour. Some strategies will be very effective for one child but completely ineffective for another, so it is important that strategies you use are appropriate for each child's individual needs. Remember every child is unique and therefore your strategy will depend on their age and stage of development.

Very often our response to a child's behaviour, whether causing concern or not, will send a message to the child. We should always aim to send positive messages to children at all times. It can be very difficult to be positive when working with children whose behaviour is challenging. However, it is good practice to try to turn around what you say into positive statements, for example, instead of saying 'Don't do that', try to say 'Let's do this.' Rather than saying 'Don't leave those toys there', try saying 'Let's put these toys in their box together, then we won't trip over them.'

There will be times when you will say 'Don't' or 'No' to protect a child from a potential hazard or danger. In such cases you want the child to respond immediately. But if you use words like 'don't' and 'no' frequently, there is the possibility that the child will not respond quickly or may well ignore you.

Strategies for responding to behaviour that causes concern

When you first meet a family and the children, you will need to ask about their views on behaviour. If you are a registered childminder you may well include aspects of your behaviour policy in your welcome pack or at your initial meeting to discuss the contract. There are several different family structures and traditions which may influence the way parents manage the behaviour of their children. It is important that you respect and understand these differences.

It is in the best interests of the child that home-based childcarers, whether nannies or childminders, and parents try to have a consistent approach to behaviour. When this does not happen, children will get very mixed messages and can become confused and bewildered. Parents should be seen as the main educators of their children; they know their children very well. Therefore home-based childcarers must work with parents to help children to manage their behaviour.

Many parents become stressed, distressed or even angry when they realise that their child's behaviour is causing concern. However, if they are working in an effective partnership with their child's carer these negative feelings can be less powerful, as they will feel more supported. If you have established good and effective relationships with the parents it will be easier for all concerned if you suspect that the child's behaviour might be related to something that is going on in the family.

It is very important that you discuss any concerns you have about a child's behaviour with the parents. You should tell the child that you and their parents are going to talk; maybe an older child will be included as well. This should not be regarded as an 'If you do not stop hitting I will talk to you parents' kind of threat, but should be seen by the child as a consistent approach. 'Let's all sit down and talk about what happens when you play with other children and how you feel' comes across as far more positive and respectful of the child's needs.

Sometimes concerns do not arise over one single aspect of behaviour; there may be several things that can cause concern. Decide what the most important thing to tackle first is, for example, you may be caring for a child who is biting other children, hitting and cannot share. It may be that they are too young to understand what 'sharing' means, but you can decide to try to stop the child biting and hurting others.

Keys to good practice

Dealing with challenging behaviour

- Use a positive approach to guide the child and distract them, thus avoiding situations where the chances of the behaviour that causes concern happening are increased.

- Be firm and consistent. If you say 'No', mean it, and make sure that your ground rules are firm and consistently applied for each child, dependent on their age and stage of development and needs.

- Avoid confrontation. Distract the child, or gently remove them from the situation. Offer an alternative play activity or toy, with a positive statement.

- Show your disapproval or displeasure that your ground rules have not been followed. Children naturally want to please adults, so showing your disapproval of their behaviour can be a powerful reason for some children not to behave in that way again. However, do not show your disapproval or displeasure by humiliating or embarrassing the child. Remember you are not showing disapproval of the child but disapproval of the child's actions.

- Explain why the behaviour is not consistent with your ground rules and if the child is old enough explain also the possible consequences of their behaviour.

- Be a positive role model; children learn by imitating and copying the actions of adults and others around them. If you use a loud voice and inappropriate language when you are angry, children will learn that it is acceptable to do this when they are cross.

- Try to create an environment where children have opportunities to be in control of situations. This is usually referred to as 'empowering' children. You could, for example, give children more choices about what they do, or different ways of doing certain activities. Children could be given special achievable responsibilities which are rewarded with lots of praise and thanks. This not only empowers the child but also helps to build their self-confidence and self-esteem.

Talk to the child about what they have done using developmentally appropriate language.

Think about it

Some childcarers use 'time-out' as an effective strategy to help manage challenging behaviour. However, the length of 'time-out' should depend on the age and stage of development of the individual child. Even though time-out should remove the child from adult attention, you should still supervise the child.

Sometimes when children are displaying behaviour that is causing considerable concern, it can be difficult to separate the child from the behaviour, for example, a child who hits could be told that he is a 'very naughty boy'. This is focusing on the child rather than on what they have done, and is one very good reason why you should avoid using the word 'naughty'. It is better to say to the child that hitting hurts and that they should not do it. This tells the child that what they have **done** is wrong and not, as in the first example, that **they** are wrong.

This approach does not damage your relationship with the child because you have responded to the actions of the child rather than the child as a person. You know that they can play cooperatively because you have seen them doing so, so tell them and praise them for doing it.

Case study: Managing Toby's anger

Toby, aged 4, has become defiant and will not do what his registered childminder, Angie, asks of him. He has become rude and angry towards Angie and the other children. Angie has cared for Toby since he was 9 months old and also his older sister comes to Angie after school, so she knows their mum very well. Angie telephones Mum one evening after work and they talk about Toby. Mum tearfully tells

Angie that their dad has left and Toby is very upset. If Angie had not established a good relationship with this mum she may not have been able to understand Toby's behaviour.

- What would you do to help Toby manage his anger?
- How would you manage Toby's defiant behaviour?

When there is an effective partnership with parents, children's behaviour is more likely to be dealt with in a consistent way. Partnerships take time and effort from both sides. It is not especially beneficial to the partnership if you only report to the parents negative aspects of what the child has done, and sometimes when a child is showing very challenging behaviour it can be difficult to be positive. While you must always be truthful in your dealings with parents, even the most challenging child will have done something positive, such as eating all of their lunch, or putting their coat in the right place, so make sure that you praise the child at that time and tell their parents.

Link to assessment — AC 7.2

Explain how ground rules for behaviour and expectations are developed and implemented.

CACHE Task 9
Your written explanation could be based around your policy and procedures for promoting positive behaviour. Include your policy and procedures and make reference to them in your work. Explain how you developed your ground rules, who was involved and how you ensure that you are fair and consistent while at the same time meeting the needs of all children in your care.

If you are not following the CACHE tasks you may find that you can evidence this criterion with a professional discussion with your assessor, using your policy and procedures for promoting positive behaviour as a starting point.

Common dietary habits

	Buddhist	Hindu	Jewish	Mormon	Muslim	Rastafarian	Roman Catholic	Seventh Day Adventist	Sikh
Alcohol	✗	✗	✓	✗	✗	✗	✓	✗	✓
Animal fats	✗	Some	Kosher only	✓	Some Halal	Some	✓	✗	Some
Beef	✗	✗	Kosher only	✓	Halal	Some	✓	Some	✗
Cheese	✓	Some	Not with meat	✓	Some	✓	✓	Most	Some
Chicken	✗	Some	Kosher only	✓	Halal	Some	✓	Some	Some
Eggs	Some	Some	No blood spots	✓	✓	✓	✓	Most	✓
Fish	Some	With fins and scales	With scales, fins and backbone	✓	Halal	✓	✓	Some	Some
Fruit	✓	✓	✓	✓	✓	✓	✓	✓	✓
Lamb/mutton	✗	Some	Kosher only	✓	Halal	Some	✓	Some	✓
Milk/yoghurt	✓	Not with rennet	Not with meat	✓	Not with rennet	✓	✓	Most	✓
Nuts	✓	✓	✓	✓	✓	✓	✓	✓	✓
Pork	✗	Rarely	✗	✓	✗	✗	✓	✗	Rarely
Pulses	✓	✓	✓	✓	✓	✓	✓	✓	✓
Shellfish	✗	Some	✗	✓	Halal	✗	✓	✗	Some
Tea/coffee/cocoa	✓ but no milk	✓	✓	✗	✓	✓	✓	✗	✓
Vegetables	✓	✓	✓	✓	✓	✓	✓	✓	✓

✓ will eat or drink   ✗ will not eat or drink

Fasting is often a matter of individual choice, however the following times are often observed:

• Jews will fast at Yom Kippur   • Muslims will fast at Ramadan   • Mormons will fast for 24 hours once a month
• Some Roman Catholics prefer not to eat meat on Fridays.

Useful resources

Every effort has been made to ensure that all details were up to date at the time of publication. Many of the details below are for each organisation's head office, which should be able to provide local contact numbers.

Organisations

Action for Leisure
c/o Warwickshire College
Moreton Morrell Centre
Moreton Morrell
Warkwickshire CV35 9BL
Tel: 01926 650195
www.actionforleisure.org.uk

ADD/ADHD Family Support Group
1a The High Street
Dilton Marsh
Nr Westbury
Wilts BA13 4DL

Alcoholics Anonymous
PO Box 1
Stonebow House
Stonebow
York YO1 7NJ
Tel: 01904 644026
www.alcoholics-anonymous.org.uk

Association of Spina Bifida and Hydrocephalus (ASBAH)
42 Park Road
Peterborough PE1 2UQ
Tel: 01733 555985
www.asbah.org

Asthma UK
Summit House
70 Wilson Street
London
EC2A 2DB
Tel: 0800 121 62 55
www.asthma.org.uk

British Allergy Foundation
Planwell House
LEFA Business Park
Edgington Way
Sidcup
Kent DA14 5BH
Tel: 020 8303 8525
www.allergyuk.org

Brake
PO Box 548
Huddersfield
West Yorkshire HD1 2XZ
Tel: 01484 559909
www.brake.org.uk

British Association for Counselling and Psychotherapy
15 St John's Business Park
Lutterworth
Leicestershire LE17 4HB
Tel: 01455 883300
www.bacp.co.uk

British Association for the Study and Prevention of Child Abuse and Neglect
17 Priory Street
York
North Yorkshire YO1 6ET
Tel: 01904 613605
www.baspcan.org.uk

United Kingdom Disabled People's Council (UKDPC)
27 Old Gloucester Street
London WC1N 3AX
Tel: 01244 346460
www.ukdpc.net

British Deaf Association

10th Floor, Coventry Point
Market Way
Coventry CV1 1EA
Text phone: 02476 550393
Videophone: 020 7496 9539
Voice phone: 02476 550936
www.bda.org.uk

British Dyslexia Association

Unit 8 Bracknell Beeches
Old Bracknell Lane
Bracknell RG12 7BW
National helpline: 0845 251 9002
www.bdadyslexia.org.uk

British Nutrition Foundation (BNF)

High Holborn House
52–54 High Holborn
London WC1V 6RQ
Tel: 020 7404 6504
www.nutrition.org.uk

British Red Cross (BRCS)

44 Moorfields
London EC2Y 9AL
Tel: 0844 871 11 11 (switchboard)
www.redcross.org.uk

Child Accident Prevention Trust (CAPT)

Canterbury Court
1–3 Brixton Road
London SW9 6DE
Tel: 020 7608 3828
www.capt.org.uk

Childline (NSPCC)

Weston House
42 Curtain Road
London EC2A 3NH
Helpline: 0800 1111
www.childline.org.uk

Compassionate Friends

53 North Street
Bristol BS3 1EN
Tel: 0845 120 3785
www.tcf.org.uk

Council for Awards in Children's Care and Education (CACHE)

Apex House
81 Camp Road
St Albans AL1 5GB
Tel: 0845 347 2123
www.cache.org.uk

CRUSE Bereavement Care

PO Box 800
Richmond
Surrey TW9 2RG
Helpline: 0844 477 9400
www.crusebereavementcare.org.uk

Diabetes UK

Macleod House
Parkway
London NW1 7AA
Tel: 020 7424 1000
www.diabetes.org.uk

Disabled Living Foundation

380–384 Harrow Road
London W9 2HU
Tel: 0845 130 9177
Text phone 0845 762 2644
www.dlf.org.uk

Disability Alliance Educational and Research Association

Universal House
88–94 Wentworth Street
London E1 7SA
Tel: 020 7247 8776
www.disabilityalliance.org.uk

Down's Syndrome Association

Langdon Down Centre
2a Langdon Park
Teddington TW11 9PS
Tel: 0845 230 0372
www.downs-syndrome.org.uk

Eating Disorders Association (Beat)

103 Prince of Wales Road
Norwich
Norfolk NR1 1DW
Tel: 0870 770 3256
Helpline: 01603 765050
www.b-eat.co.uk

Epilepsy Action

New Anstey House
Gate Way Drive
Yeadon
Leeds LS19 7XY
Helpline: 0808 800 5050
www.epilepsy.org.uk

EPOCH (End Physical Punishment of Children)

77 Holloway Road
London N7 9PF
Tel: 020 7700 0627
www.stophitting.com

Equality and Human Rights Commission (EHRC)

3 More London
Riverside Tooley Street
London SE1 2RG
Helpline (London): 0845 604 6610
www.equalityhumanrights.com

The Food Commission (Food Magazine)

94 White Lion Street
London N1 9PF
Tel: 020 7837 2250
www.foodmagazine.org.uk

The Foundation for the Study of Infant Deaths (FSID)

11 Belgrave Road
London
SW1V 1RB
Tel: 020 7802 3200
www.fsid.org.uk

Frank (drugs advice)

Helpline: 0800 776600
Text: 82111
www.talktofrank.com

Gingerbread (National Council for One Parent Families)

255 Kentish Town Road
London NW5 2LX
Tel: 020 7428 5400
www.gingerbread.org.uk

Hyperactive Children's Support Group

71 Whyke Lane
Chichester PO19 7PD
Tel: 01243 539966
www.hacsg.org.uk

Kidscape

2 Grosvenor Gardens
London SW1W 0DH
Tel: 020 7730 3300
www.kidscape.org.uk

Macmillan Cancer Support

89 Albert Embankment
London SE1 7UQ
Tel: 0808 808 00 00
www.macmillan.org.uk

The Meningitis Trust

Fern House
Bath Road
Stroud GL5 3TJ
Tel: 01453 768000
Helpline: 0800 028 18 28
www.meningitis-trust.org

MIND (National Association for Mental Health)

15–19 Broadway
London E15 4BQ
Tel: 020 8519 2122
www.mind.org.uk

MIND (Cymru)

3rd Floor Quebec House
Castlebridge
15–19 Cowbridge Road East
Cardiff CF11 9AB
Tel: 029 2039 5123
www.mind.org.uk

The Multiple Births Foundation

Queen Charlotte's and Chelsea Hospital
Du Cane Road
London W12 0HS
Tel: 020 3313 3519
www.multiplebirths.org.uk

Muscular Dystrophy Campaign

61 Southwark Street
London SE1 0HL
Tel: 020 7803 4800
www.muscular-dystrophy.org

National AIDS Trust

City Cloisters
196 Old Street
London EC1V 9FR
Tel: 020 7814 6767
www.nat.org.uk

National Association of Toy and Leisure Libraries

1a Harmood Street
London NW1 8DN
Tel: 020 7428 2288
www.natll.org.uk

National Childbirth Trust (NCT)

Alexandra House
Oldham Terrace
London W3 6NH
Enquiries: 0300 333 0770
www.nct.org.uk

National Childminding Association (NCMA)

Royal Court
81 Tweedy Road
Bromley
Kent BR1 1TG
Tel: 0845 880 0044
www.ncma.org.uk

National Children's Bureau (NCB)

8 Wakley Street
London EC1V 7QE
Tel: 020 7843 6000
www.ncb.org.uk

National Drugs Helpline (UK)

Helpline: 0800 776600
www.urban75.com

National Eczema Society (NES)

Hill House
Highgate Hill
London N19 5NA
Helpline: 0800 089 1122
www.eczema.org

National Extension College (NEC)

Michael Young Centre
Purbeck Road
Cambridge CB2 8HN
Tel: 01223 400 200
www.nec.ac.uk

National Institute for Health and Clinical Excellence (NICE)

MidCity Place
71 High Holborn
London WC1V 6NA
Tel: 0845 003 7780
www.nice.org.uk

National Lottery Funding

Tel: 0845 275 0000
www.lotteryfunding.org.uk

National Society for the Prevention of Cruelty to Children (NSPCC)

Weston House
42 Curtain Road
London EC2A 3NH
Helpline: 0808 800 5000
www.nspcc.org.uk

Parentline Plus

CAN Mezzanine
49–51 East Road
London E1 6AH
Tel: 020 7553 3080/0808 800 2222
www.parentlineplus.org.uk

Parents Advice Centre

(Head office) 2nd Floor Andras House
60 Great Victoria Street
Belfast BT2 7BB
Tel: 028 9031 0891
Helpline: 0808 8010 722
www.parentsadvicecentre.org

Parents Anonymous

6–9 Manor Gardens
London N7 6LA
Tel: 0171 2638918
www.parentsanonymous.org

Relate

Premier House
Carolina Court
Lakeside
Doncaster DN4 5RA
Tel: 0300 100 1234
www.relate.org.uk

Royal National Institute for the Blind (RNIB)

105 Judd Street
London WC1H 9NE
Tel: 020 7388 1266
Helpline: 0303 123 9999
www.rnib.org.uk

Royal Society for the Prevention of Accidents (RoSPA)

RoSPA House
Edgbaston Park
353 Bristol Road
Birmingham B5 7ST
Tel: 0121 248 2000
www.rospa.com

The Samaritans

The Upper Mill
Kingston Road
Ewell
Surrey KT17 2AF
Helpline: 0845 790 9090
www.samaritans.org

Save the Children

1 St John's Lane
London EC1M 4AR
Tel: 020 7012 6400
www.savethechildren.org.uk

Scope

6 Market Road
London N7 9PW
Tel: 0808 800 3333
www.scope.org.uk

Sense (for deafblind people)

101 Pentonville Road
London N1 9LG
Tel: 0845 127 0060
Textphone: 0845 127 0062
www.sense.org.uk

Sickle Cell Society

54 Station Road
London NW10 4UA
Tel: 020 8961 7795
www.sicklecellsociety.org

St John Ambulance

27 St John's Lane
London EC1M 4BU
Tel: 08700 104950
www.sja.org.uk

Stillbirth and Neonatal Death Society (SANDS)

28 Portland Place
London W1B 1LY
Tel: 020 7436 7940
Helpline: 020 7436 5881
www.uk-sands.org

Terrence Higgins Trust (THT)

314–320 Gray's Inn Road
London WC1X 8DP
Tel: 020 7812 1600
www.tht.org.uk

Twins and Multiple Births Association (TAMBA)

2 The Willows
Gardner Road
Guildford
Surrey GU1 4PG
Tel: 01483 304442
Twinline: 0800 138 0509
www.tamba.org.uk

Vegetarian Society of the United Kingdom

Parkdale
Dunham Road
Altrincham
Cheshire WA14 4QG
Tel: 0161 925 2000
www.vegsoc.org

World Health Organization (WHO)

Avenue Appia 20
1211 Geneva 27
Switzerland
Tel: (00 41 22) 791 21 11
www.who.int

Useful websites

BBC Children in Need

www.bbc.co.uk/pudsey

Children's rights

www.rights4me.org

Department for Education (DfE)

www.education.gov.uk

Department for Environment, Food and Rural Affairs (DEFRA)

www.defra.gov.uk

Every Child Matters

www.dcsf.gov.uk/everychildmatters

Families Need Fathers

www.fnf.org.uk

Food Standards Agency

www.food.gov.uk

Government publications

http://publications.education.gov.uk

Health and Safety Executive (HSE)
www.hse.gov.uk

HemiHelp
www.hemihelp.org.uk

International Child Abuse Network
www.yesican.org

National Association of Citizens Advice Bureaux (NACAB)
www.citizensadvice.co.uk

Royal Society for the Prevention of Cruelty to Animals (RSPCA)
www.rspca.org.uk

Further reading

N. Allen, et al. *We are all born free,* London, Frances Lincoln Children's Books, 2008.

N. Baldwin, *Protecting Children: Protecting Their Rights,* London, Whiting & Birch Ltd, 2000.

Helen Bee, *The Growing Child,* Harlow, Longman, 1998.

C. Meggit and G. Sunderland, *Child Development – An Illustrated Guide* (2nd Edition), Oxford, Heinemann, 2006.

S. Riddall-Leech, *Managing Children's Behaviour,* Oxford, Heinemann, 2003.

S. Riddall-Leech, *How to Observe Children* (2nd Edition), Oxford, Heinemann, 2008.

S. Riddall-Leech, *Heuristic Play,* London, Step Forward Publications, 2009.

M. Shah, *Working with Parents,* Oxford, Heinemann, 2001.

P. Tassoni and K. Hucker, *Planning Play in the Early Years* (2nd Edition), Oxford, Heinemann, 2005.

P. Tassoni, et al., *Level 3 Diploma for the Children and Young People's Workforce,* Oxford, Heinemann, 2010.

P. Tassoni, *Penny Tassoni's Practical EYFS Handbook,* Oxford, Heinemann, 2008.

P. Tassoni, *Penny Tassoni's Continued Success with the EYFS,* Oxford, Heinemann, 2010.

Glossary

Abuse — suffering or considerable harm from physical, emotional or sexual ill-treatment, neglect or bullying.

Accident — an unforeseen, unplanned mishap, calamity or mistake that may cause distress or injury to another individual.

Accredited — having produced a portfolio of evidence to show that you have met the NCMA's Quality Standards for Children Come First (CCF) Networks.

Allergy — adverse reaction or sensitivity to a substance, food product, animal or other environmental factor.

Assessment — an informed judgement about something or a measurement of, for example, the development of a specific skill.

Attachment — a unique emotional bond between a child and an adult.

Balance — a skill that requires co-ordination, but not necessarily from the eyes or ears. The ability to balance is developed by the body as the movements use information received from the central nervous system.

Behaviour — the way in which an individual acts or the actions they carry out.

Children's Centre — a one-stop establishment for children and parents where professionals from different agencies can offer support, for example, health visitors, Basic Skills tuition, Early Years education.

Cognitive development — another term for intellectual development, involving thought processes, memory, problem solving and so on.

Commitments — describe in detail how the principles and themes of the EYFS can be put into practice.

Communication — an exchange of ideas, contact between individuals, consultation and interaction.

Confidentiality — privacy, discretion, maintaining trust and keeping information secret.

Continuing professional development (CPD) — ongoing training and updating of relevant skills and knowledge.

Contract — a written agreement setting out the specific terms and conditions, for example, about the care of a child.

Coordination skills — control of hand, eye and foot and the ability to combine more than one skill or movement at the same time. In this aspect of development a child uses perhaps their eyes to guide their feet when going upstairs.

CSSIW — Care and Social Services Inspectorate Wales, the Welsh regulatory body.

Development — ways in which children grow and acquire skills and competences. Areas of development are sometimes categorised as physical, intellectual (or cognitive), language, social and emotional. All of these areas are interrelated and interdependent.

Developmental norms — quantitative measurements that provide typical values and variations in height, weight, skill acquisition; can also be referred to as milestones.

Disclosure — a child has told an adult or another child what has been happening to them. This can also include evidence of abuse or neglect.

Discrimination — treating someone differently and unfairly because of their race, gender, religion, disability and so on.

Empowered — having/being given the opportunity to be in control of situations.

Enhanced disclosure — a written document issued by the Criminal Records Bureau (CRB) which proves that the named person has no criminal convictions that would mean they were unsuitable to work with and care for children.

Environment — the surrounding, setting or situation in which you work and care for children.

Equipment — includes all toys, utensils, furniture, fittings and materials that may be used with or by children (or others).

Fine motor skills — small movements of the whole hand.

Gross motor skills — movements involving all of an arm or leg, such as throwing a ball.

Harassment — torment through constant bothering, interference, intimidation and so on.

Heuristic play — a form of play that encourages babies and young children to explore everyday natural objects through their senses; usually attributed to the educationalist Elinor Goldschmied (1910–2009).

Holistic — the co-dependency of one area of development on another.

Illness — a medical condition of sickness, poor health.

Incident — something that happens, an occurrence (minor or more serious).

Inclusion — the process of recognising, understanding and overcoming obstructions or barriers to participation.

Inclusive — all-encompassing, comprehensive, complete.

Independence — self-autonomy, freedom, self-reliance; therefore undertaking an activity or having an experience without intervention.

Infection — a disease, illness, virus or bug.

Infectious — a disease or illness that can spread through the environment, such as flu.

Intervention — action taken to prevent or change something, interference in another's actions.

Learning style — the way in which we process information. Most people will have a preferred learning style.

Legislation — laws, rules and regulations passed by Acts of Parliament.

Literacy — how we use words, either in writing or reading.

Long-term memory — allows us to process information that we may not need immediately and then retrieve it at a later date.

Medicine — a remedy, tablet, pill, lotion or liquid that can help alleviate a medical or health problem.

Milestones — quantitative measurements that provide typical values and variations in height, weight and skill acquisition. They are sometimes referred to as developmental norms.

Monitor — check or keep an eye on something.

Notifiable diseases — serious infectious conditions that must be reported to the public health authorities, for example, rubella, meningitis, measles.

Observation — watching, studying, examining or scrutinising the actions of others.

Ofsted — the Office for Standards in Education (England), the government department responsible for the inspection of childcare settings, schools and local education authorities.

Oracy — what is said and how it is said.

Physical development — how children get control of their bodies.

Policy — a written statement setting out a particular course of action in given situations or a set of guidelines.

Positive behaviour — ways an individual acts that are considered socially and morally acceptable.

Prejudice — narrow-mindedness, bigotry, unfairness, discrimination.

Prescribed drugs — licensed medicines and treatments authorised by medical practitioners, dentists, pharmacists and so on.

Procedure — the method or course of action required to carry out a policy.

Regress — return to an earlier stage of development.

Respect — (show) consideration for and recognise another individual's opinions, needs and values.

Rights — constitutional entitlements, privileges and/or civil liberties.

Risk assessment — a risk is a possible danger or threat to safety. To assess means to measure, evaluate or make a judgement. Risk assessment therefore is about careful consideration of possible dangers or threats to safety and taking appropriate action.

Routine — a custom, scheduled event or activity that is usually planned with regularity.

Safeguard — protect, look after and maintain the well-being of children.

Safeguarding — protecting, looking after and maintaining the well-being of children.

Short-term memory — used to process information quickly before discarding it.

Spontaneous play — when children play in their own way, and the adult needs to provide as much variety of equipment and resources as possible, with opportunities and time for exploration and experimenting.

Statutory — something that is legal, has been made law.

Stereotype — to label, put into artificial categories, to typecast.

Supervision — control, management or command of a situation or other individual(s).

Themes — the four guiding subjects or topics of the Early Years Foundation Stage (EYFS).

Theorist — an individual who has extensively researched a subject or topic and produced a unique and original view.

Theory — a well-researched and unique idea or perspective on a particular subject or topic.

Valued — given importance, appreciated.

Index